How to Promote Children's Social and Emotional Competence

Carolyn Webster-Stratton, a clinical psychologist and nurse, is a leading expert on parent training and promoting young children's social skills, problem-solving and reducing aggression. She is Director of the Parenting Clinic, and Professor at the University of Washington where she trains psychologists, nurses, social workers and teachers. She has been developing and evaluating training programmes for parents, teachers and children for more than 18 years with the goal of reducing children's misbehaviour and strengthening social competence. Her teacher, parent and child training programmes are being offered in many regions of the UK including schools and hospitals and NHS-funded programmes. Additionally recent evaluations in the UK attest to their effectiveness. She lives in Seattle with her husband and two children.

How to Promote Children's Social and Emotional Competence

Includes practical scripts, games, activities, pictures and circle time role plays and plans you can use with students (ages 4 to 8 years)

Based on the empirically validated Dinosaur Social Skills, Problem-solving and Anger Management Curriculum

Includes an emphasis on managing hyperactive, inattentive and aggressive students

Carolyn Webster-Stratton

P·C·P
Paul Chapman
Publishing Ltd

For my children
Seth and Anna
And all the children of the world –
that they may live in a nurturing and violence free world.

Paul Chapman Publishing Ltd
A SAGE Publications Company
6 Bonhill Street
London EC2A 4PU

SAGE Publications Inc
2455 Teller Road
Thousand Oaks, California 91320

SAGE Publications India Pvt Ltd
32, M-Block Market
Greater Kailash - I
New Delhi 110 048

British Library Cataloguing in Publication data

A catalogue record for this book is available from the British Library

ISBN 0-7619-6500-9
ISBN 0-7619-6501-7 (pbk)

Library of Congress catalog card number available

Typeset by Dorwyn Ltd, Rowlands Castle, Hants
Printed and bound by Athenaeum Press, Gateshead

Contents

Chapter Eleven: Helping Students Learn to Handle their Emotions   284

Preface

As an educational psychologist, I have worked extensively with teachers. Yet I am also a parent of two children, now aged 11 and 14 years, and sometimes it seems that these two roles have little overlap. Like all parents, I am concerned with supporting my children's optimal social and emotional development as well as their academic achievement. Naturally, this has involved many conversations over the years with their teachers – conversations which ideally should always be a two-way exchange. However, there have been times when my children's teachers responded to my attempts to talk with them in ways that discouraged collaboration and left me feeling reluctant to try again.

For example, a number of years ago, my daughter – a normally lively, self-confident girl – came home from school saying, 'I'm the dumbest in the class. Everyone but me can read!' I could see that her difficulty learning to read was affecting not only her enjoyment of school and her willingness to participate in class, but also her self-esteem. I felt it was important to talk with her teachers about this issue. But when I called to set up an appointment to meet, something about their response left me with the impression that scheduling a parent meeting was burdensome. Nevertheless, we did meet. My husband and I were told that our daughter was doing fine and that we should stop worrying about her reading. My concerns about the impact on her enthusiasm for school had not been allayed; yet I also began to feel guilty for having needlessly taken up their time even though as a professional I knew the importance of parent–teacher collaboration.

A year later our daughter was diagnosed as having a reading delay. I felt both angry with her teachers for having minimized my concern and incompetent as a parent for not being more effective in communicating my concern and advocating for her needs.

There is no doubt that this experience would have dampened my enthusiasm for collaborating with teachers, were it not for an experience I had the next year. One day I received a call from her teacher telling me about something wonderful our daughter had done in class to help some children problem-solve a tricky situation. My husband and I were beaming! A few weeks later her teacher came to watch her baseball game. (I later learned that her teacher attended special events for *all* the students in her classroom.) As a result my daughter was back to her bubbly self in school and we would have done anything for her teachers. My husband and I were so taken with these teachers that we would sing their praises to whomever would listen. With a few acts of kindness and a commitment to caring these teachers had bridged the home–school gap in a fundamental way.

Research Background

I have spent the past twenty years evaluating parenting programmes for parents of young children who are highly aggressive, impulsive and non-compliant and helping parents to understand the most effective ways to promote their children's social and academic competence and reduce behavior problems. My own research (Webster-Stratton, 1984, 1985, 1989, 1994, 1998a; Webster-Stratton, Hollinsworth and Kolpacoff, 1989; Webster-Stratton, Kolpacoff and Hollinsworth, 1988) as well as that of others has shown that when parents are trained to use effective child management skills their children become more pro-social, have higher self-esteem and fewer aggressive behavior problems. However, while parents have been successful in bringing about a more harmonious family life at home, there has not necessarily been a corresponding improvement in the children's relationships at school. Many of their teachers complained that the children were still defiant, inattentive and disruptive in class and had considerable peer relationship difficulties. Furthermore teachers reported feeling stressed by the time and energy it took to manage these difficult students in the context of a classroom of thirty or more students. They felt inadequately prepared for how to carry out the discipline required for these students or for providing the necessary social skills training.

In 1991 I developed a social skills, problem-solving and anger management curriculum for young children (called the Dinosaur curriculum). This programme was offered to children while their parents were participating in the parenting classes and to some children as an after-school programme each week. In a randomized controlled study evaluating the added effects of combining child training with parent training, I found that the children who had participated in Dinosaur School had significantly better problem-solving skills and pro-social behaviors when interacting with their peers compared with children who did not get this programme (Webster-Stratton and Hammond, 1997). This led me to believe that children who had difficulties with peers at school in addition to behavior problems at home could benefit from a curriculum designed to promote what some have called 'emotional literacy' (Goleman, 1995) or what I call 'social competence'.

Indeed it seemed to me that *all* children could benefit from an education that included an emphasis on effective social skills and problem-solving as well as academic achievement. Consequently I began a programme of research to evaluate the added effects of training teachers as well as parents[1]. This collaboration led to a fundamental change in parent–teacher relationships where each was supporting the other and planning together for the children's individual needs. Both teachers and parents felt less stressed, less adversarial and more supported in providing for the children's needs. While our data is still preliminary, the early results suggest that when teachers as well as parents are involved in the training programme, not only does the aggressive child's behavior improve, but the whole classroom becomes more co-operative and there is greater academic engagement (Webster-Stratton, 1998b).

Over the past seven years we have trained hundreds of Head Start preschool teachers as well as elementary school teachers of three to nine year olds. Some of these trainings have been targeted as special programmes to help aggressive students and others have been targeted as prevention programmes to improve the social competence of all the students. This book is the direct result of these trainings and the many ideas shared by the teachers who attended them. I am indebted to these teachers for teaching me and sharing with me their insights and strategies for promoting children's social competence. Without their input this book could not have been written.

Purpose of Book

This book is addressed to teachers of young children (ages 3 to 10 years) with several purposes in mind. The first is to suggest ways teachers can collaborate with parents in addressing their students' educational and emotional needs. Chapter 1 directly deals with this topic, but all the other chapters include material relevant to this

---

[1] *Incredible Years Training Series for Parents, Teachers and Children*, available from Seth Enterprises, 1411 8th Avenue West, Seattle, WA98119.

purpose. For instance, Chapters 2, 4 and 5 discuss how teachers can develop meaningful relationships with their students by involving parents in ongoing dialogues, home–school connected activities, classroom participation, and planning incentive programmes for helping children overcome difficult problems. Chapters 7 and 8 suggest ways parents can be included in discipline plans and assist teachers in understanding what works best with a particular child's unique temperament. Chapters 9, 10 and 11 address ways to include parents in a curriculum designed to promote social skills, anger management and problem-solving at school and at home.

The second purpose of this book is to present a variety of classroom management strategies which teachers can choose from to strengthen children's social and academic competence. The emotional literacy of children is considered as having equal importance to academic literacy. The teaching pyramid illustrates how each

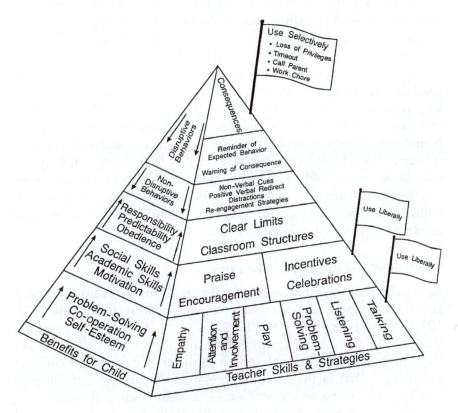

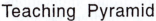

Teaching Pyramid

chapter builds on the previous one. The early chapters focus on ways to encourage student's positive behaviors and build their confidence, self-esteem, problem-solving and motivation for learning. This section provides the foundation for a successful teacher–student–family relationship. Chapters 3 and 6 focus on proactive, non-intrusive classroom strategies such as clear rules, predictable limits, re-engagement strategies and a discipline structure designed to minimize classroom disruption, avoid confrontation, and create a smoothly functioning classroom with students taking on increasing responsibility for their behavior. Chapters 7 and 8 focus on more intrusive discipline strategies such as Time Out and loss of privileges required when students are verbally and physically violent. Chapters 9, 10 and 11 present curriculum activities, games and scripts for teaching social skills, anger management and problem-solving.

The third purpose or theme of this book is to illustrate how teachers can set up individualized programmes which address the special social and emotional needs of high risk children. Children may be at higher risk for social and academic problems because of some biological factors or developmental delays such as learning disabilities, hyperactivity, impulsivity, attention deficit disorder, language and reading delays and highly aggressive behavior. Some children may be at higher risk for difficulties because of coming from home situations where the adults are unresponsive or abusive, or where the adults are so overwhelmed with stresses that they are unable to meet their children's needs. This book shows how teachers can integrate individualized interventions for high risk children in the mainstream classroom while at the same time enhancing the social competence of all their students.

The Importance of Early Intervention

Research points out that aggression in children is escalating – and it is evident among younger and younger children (Campbell, 1990, 1991; Webster-Stratton, 1991, 1998b). Recent studies have reported that 10 to 25 per cent of preschool or early school age children meet the criteria for oppositional defiant disorder or early onset conduct problems – that is they have aggressive, disruptive, oppositional and hyperactive behavior problems in a high or clinical range.

These trends have disturbing implications for all of us, not just for the families of these children, because 'early onset' conduct problems in young children have been shown to be predictive of subsequent drug abuse, depression, juvenile delinquency, antisocial behavior and violence in adolescence and adulthood (Kazdin, 1985; Kupersmidt and Coie, 1990; Loeber, 1990, 1991; Moffitt, 1993). Acts of murder, rape, robbery, arson, drunk driving, and abuse are carried out to a greater extent by persons with a history of chronic aggression stemming from childhood than by other persons (Kazdin, 1995). Thus the problem of escalating aggression in young children is a concern for society as a whole, and not only because of what it portends for the safety for ourselves and our children – regardless of our ethnicity, economic status or community. For conduct disorder is also one of the most costly of mental disorders to society (Robins, 1981). A large proportion of antisocial children remain involved with mental health agencies throughout their lives and/or become involved with criminal justice systems. In other words, everyone pays in the long run – personally, financially, or both – when these children are left uncared for and their behavior problems untreated.

Over the past twenty years a variety of family and school interventions have been developed to address child conduct problems (Estrada and Pinsof, 1995). In studies evaluating these interventions, results suggest that if intervention occurs early – when the child is still in preschool or early school age – rather than later, it is more effective and more likely to prevent a chronic pattern from developing. In fact, there is evidence that the younger the child at the time of intervention, the more positive the child's behavioral adjustment at home and at school (Strain et al., 1982). Therefore it is strategic to offer children interventions in the early years so as to prevent the development of conduct disorders and keep those children who show early signs of aggression off this track to delinquency.

The fourth purpose of this book is to lend support to the efforts of our schools to give more attention to developing the social competence and emotional well-being of children. Teachers understand that just as a child's cognitive competence affects his or her ability to learn, a child's social competence and emotional security affects his or her ability to learn. It is my hope that this book will be a useful tool to support this effort.

Stable and nurturing teachers who do this emotional teaching may be able to provide a buffer for some young children against the impact of parental psychopathology and family stress and may be able to provide support when parents are relatively unavailable to their children. When teachers and parents are able to work together in partnerships to promote social competence in children, we help not only the children who are at risk but all children and their families. Our shared goal is parents who are more involved in their children's schools, children who do better academically because their social and emotional needs are taken into account, and teachers who feel more satisfied because they have the support of paernts. To expand this vision, our goal is families with happier home lives, parents who use less harsh discipline, children who learn the relationship skills that will ultimately lead to happier marriages, less depression and less divorce. Ultimately I believe we all reap the benefits of helping to create a less violent and more caring society.

References

Campbell, S. B. (1990) *Behavior Problems in Preschool Children: Clinical and Developmental Issues*, New York: Guilford Press.

Campbell, S. B. (1991) Longitudinal studies of active and aggressive preschoolers: individual differences in early behavior and outcome. In D. Cicchetti and S. L. Toth (eds.) *Rochester Symposium on Developmental Psychopathology* (pp. 57–90), Hillsdale, NJ: Erlbaum.

Estrada, A. U. and Pinsof, W. M. (1995) The effectiveness of family therapies for selected behavioral disorders of childhood, *Journal of Marital and Family Therapy*, 21(4), 403–40.

Goleman, D. (1995) *Emotional Intelligence*, New York: Bantam.

Kazdin, A. (1985) *Treatment of Antisocial Behavior in Children and Adolescents*, Homewood, IL: Dorsey Press.

Kazdin, A. (1995) Child, parent and family dysfunction as predictors of outcome in cognitive-behavioral treatment of antisocial children, *Behavior Research and Therapy*, 3, 271–81.

Kupersmidt, J. B. and Coie, J. D. (1990) Preadolescent peer status, aggression, and school adjustment as predictors of externalizing problems in adolescence, *Child Development*, 61(5), 1350–62.

Loeber, R. (1990) Development and risk factors of juvenile antisocial behavior and delinquency, *Clinical Psychology Review*, 10, 1–41.

Loeber, R. (1991) Antisocial behavior: more enduring than changeable? *Journal of the American Academy of Child and Adolescent Psychiatry*, 30, 393–7.

Moffitt, T. E. (1993) Adolescence-limited and life-course-persistent antisocial behavior: a developmental taxonomy, *Psychological Review*, 100, 674–701.

Robins, L. N. (1981) Epidemiological approaches to natural history research: antisocial disorders in children, *Journal of the American Academy of Child Psychiatry*, 20, 566–80.

Strain, P. S., Steele, P., Ellis, T. and Timm, M. A. (1982) Long-term effects of oppositional child treatment with mothers as therapists and therapist trainers, *Journal of Applied Behavior Analysis*, 15, 1163–69.

Webster-Stratton, C. (1984) Randomized trial of two parent-training programs for families with conduct-disordered children, *Journal of Consulting and Clinical Psychology*, 52(4), 666–78.

Webster-Stratton, C. (1985) Predictors of treatment outcome in parent training for conduct disordered children, *Behavior Therapy*, 16, 223–43.

Webster-Stratton, C. (1989) Systematic comparison of consumer satisfaction of three cost-effective parent training programs for conduct problem children, *Behavior Therapy*, 20, 103–15.

Webster-Stratton, C. (1991) Annotation: strategies for working with families of conduct-disordered children, *British Journal of Child Psychiatry and Psychology*, 32(7), 1047–62.

Webster-Stratton, C. (1994) Advancing videotape parent training: a comparison study, *Journal of Consulting and Clinical Psychology*, 62(3), 583–93.

Webster-Stratton, C. (1998a) Parent training with low-income clients: promoting parental engagement through a collaborative approach. In J. R. Lutzker (ed.) *Handbook of Child Abuse Research and Treatment* (pp. 183–210), New York: Plenum Press.

Webster-Stratton, C. (1998b) Preventing conduct problems in Head Start children: strengthening parent competencies, *Journal of Consulting and Clinical Psychology*, 66, 715–30.

Webster-Stratton, C. and Hammond, M. (1997). Treating children with early-onset conduct problems: a comparison of child and parent training interventions, *Journal of Consulting and Clinical Psychology*, 65(1), 93–109.

Webster-Stratton, C., Hollinsworth, T. and Kolpacoff, M. (1989) The long-term effectiveness and clinical significance of three cost-effective training programs for families with conduct-problem children, *Journal of Consulting and Clinical Psychology*, 57(4), 550–3.

Webster-Stratton, C., Kolpacoff, M. and Hollinsworth, T. (1988) Self-administered videotape therapy for families with conduct-problem children: comparison with two cost-effective treatments and a control group, *Journal of Consulting and Clinical Psychology*, 56(4), 558–66.

Other Books and Material Available

The parent, child and teacher training materials with extensive manuals, books and videotapes may be obtained from:

Parents, Teachers and Children Training Series:
The Incredible Years
1411 8th Avenue West
Seattle, WA 98119
Fax: 206-285-7565
Website: www.incredibleyears.com
Email: incredibleyears@seanet.com

Acknowledgements

I would like to thank the many teachers and parents who I have worked with over the past 20 years who have taught me so much about their experiences raising temperamentally difficult children. It is their compassion, energy and commitment to help these children develop into socially competent individuals that has provided the fuel for this book. I would also like to thank the children who have attended Dinosaur School with me at the Parenting Clinic. They have helped me refine many of the ideas proposed in this book and have convinced me that aggression, bullying, peer rejection and ultimately violence can be prevented. Finally thanks to my family for their patience and support while I worked on this book during my sabbatical in Oxford.

Introduction: Managing Personal Stress

All teachers feel angry, depressed, frustrated and guilty when dealing with difficult students and difficult classes. Upsetting feelings are not only to be expected but are essential and beneficial. They signal the need for change and problem-solving, and provide motivation. Danger arises, however, when these feelings so overwhelm teachers that they're immobilized by depression or lose control of their anger. The issue, then, is not to avoid these feelings or to eliminate conflict, but learn to cope with emotional responses to conflict in a manner that provides more self-control.

Researchers (e.g. Seligman, 1990) have demonstrated a clear relationship between what we *think* about a situation, how we *feel* about it and how we *behave and relate to individuals in the situation*. To see how this works, let's consider the various ways a teacher might react to this situation. The classroom feels like it is in chaos – it is noisy, two children are shouting across the room, two others are chatting away privately while the teacher is trying to teach. Two more students wander in late – and then their classmates start up: 'Hey you are late!' Annoyed with the noise, the teacher might say to himself, 'This class is impossible, inconsiderate, irresponsible and lazy. It's a constant hassle to settle them down before I can teach.' As the teacher thinks these negative thoughts, his anger mounts and he begins criticizing the students and yelling at them. On the other hand, he might view the situation as hopeless or think that he is to blame – 'It's all my fault for being a poor teacher', 'There is nothing I can do'. In this case, he is more likely to feel depressed and tentative, and to avoid making a request or disciplining the students. If, however, he kept his thoughts focused on his ability to cope and to be calm, he might say to himself, 'I'm going to have to remind these students of the talking rule'. This would facilitate more rational and effective responses to the students' misbehaviors.

The truth is that we become angry not because of an event itself but because of the view we take of it. You may have already noticed that some days a noisy classroom is not bothersome to you and other days it is very irritating. The purpose of this chapter is to help teachers identify some of the negative self-statements they make

1

that increase their distress, and how to substitute coping responses during periods of conflict.

STEP 1: Be Aware of Your Negative and Positive Thoughts

Your thoughts are always with you, and they're under your control and no one else's. But since they're always with you, you take them for granted and pay little attention to them. Unless you learn to pay attention to your thoughts, you will not be able to change them. Imagine the following scene:

> You have a difficult class. It seems like you are putting out fires all day. The noise level feels like the playground. One boy constantly gets up and wanders around the classroom, stopping to interfere with a classmate's work. Other students giggle and chat privately rather than listen to your teaching. What are your thoughts now? They're probably negative.

STEP 2: Decrease your Negative Thoughts

After becoming aware of your negative thought patterns, the next step is to decrease them. There are four ways to do this.

1. *Use thought interruption*: As soon as you realize that you're having a negative thought, stop the thought. You might say to yourself, 'I am going to stop thinking about that now'. Some teachers wear a rubber band on their wrist and snap it every time they have a negative thought to remind them to stop it. 'Stop worrying. Worrying won't help anything.'

2. *Reschedule worrying or anger time*: Constantly going over in your mind all the ways a particular student or class of students make you angry or all your worries is very draining. Decide how long you need to spend on these thoughts and then schedule this time into your day. For instance, tell yourself that at 9.30 p.m. you will let yourself be as angry as you want. During the rest of the day don't allow these thoughts to interfere with your mood, work or play. The idea is not to stop thinking about unpleasant things altogether but to decide when is the best time to think about them. One half-hour each day should be enough.

3. *Objectify the situation*: The third approach to stopping negative self-talk is to ask yourself during moments of conflict whether what you're thinking or doing is helping you reach your goal:

(a) What is my goal? (for the noise level of the classroom to reduce and for my wandering student to spend more time in her seat)
(b) What am I doing now? (getting frustrated and angry)
(c) Is what I'm doing helping me reach my long term goal? No, we're arguing and I'm yelling.
(d) If it isn't, what do I need to do differently? Think more positively and come up with a plan.

This has been called the 'turtle technique', because you withdraw into a shell momentarily to assess your behavior. The ideal is to use this 'turtle' technique before you lose control, but in the beginning you may find yourself using this response mid-stream just before you yell at the class or just afterwards.

4. *Normalize the situation*: Another way to objectify a situation is to normalize it by remembering that all teachers have difficult and conflictual days with their students and all students have behavior problems. Moreover, all teachers and children have feelings of guilt, depression, anger and anxiety. Once you have normalized your thoughts, then it's important to stop the negative ones. You might say to yourself, 'I'm feeling uptight, but that's natural', or 'Lots of teachers feel discouraged at times. This feeling will pass.'

STEP 3: Increase your Positive Thoughts

Reducing the number of negative thoughts you have won't automatically increase positive ones. Here are six steps to help you increase your positive thoughts.

1. *Dispute negative self-talk*: Combat self-talk that contains *should*, *ought* and *must* statements or generalizations that include words such as *awful* or *terrible*. Instead of thinking 'I should be a better teacher', say to yourself, 'Why do I feel I have to be the perfect teacher?' Don't moan to yourself 'My students are animals!' say, 'My students aren't so bad'. The thoughts normalize and the misbehaviors are objectified. If you recall a situation when you overreacted, it's useful to go over it, identify the negative self-talk and think of ways to dispute it.

2. *Substitute calming or coping thoughts for negative ones*: Another approach is to replace upsetting thoughts and negative self-statements with alternative calming ones. If you find yourself thinking about a particular student in hostile terms ('He is misbehaving because he deliberately likes to get me upset'), then thought-stop and try to

substitute thoughts that emphasize your ability to cope ('I'm going to have to help him learn to control himself', 'It's up to me' or, 'He is misbehaving because his family have not taught him social skills, so I need to teach him those skills').

3. *Time projection*: The idea here is to think more positively by mentally travelling forward to the time when the stressful period will have ended. For instance, you say to yourself, 'I've had other students like this before and after several weeks on a consistent behavior plan they were much improved'. You acknowledge that the behavior problem and your feelings of depression or anger will go away eventually. If your student is misbehaving because you are ignoring him, it will probably take several minutes for the tantrum to stop. If a student is reacting to a stressful home situation, such as divorce or separation, it will be much longer before things get better. However, it is still important to acknowledge that the problems will lessen as a few months go by. Time projection recognizes stressful feelings, allows you see a more satisfying future and reminds you that psychological pain is not fatal.

You can even remind your students of the temporary nature of the problem. You could say to the 7-year-old who is frustrated because she cannot read, 'Next year at this time you will be reading. Won't that be great!' Or another example, 'This is a tough time now but it'll get better eventually'.

4. *Think and verbalize self-praise thoughts*: A fourth way to think more positively is to give yourself a pat on the back for your accomplishments. Many people don't give themselves credit for what they do, particularly for the difficult job of teaching, and then they belittle themselves when things don't work out right. Remember to look at what you have accomplished each and every day.

5. *Humour*: Humour helps to reduce anger and depression. Don't take yourself too seriously. You might say to yourself jokingly as you threaten to send your students to the moon for not listening, 'Oh yes, I'm perfect. I never lose my cool.' Laughing at yourself will probably help you to calm down and think about the situation more rationally. You might even keep a joke book on your desk to bring out at times when things feel particularly tense in the classroom.

6. *Model coping self-talk and self-praise*: As you learn to use coping and self-praise thoughts when confronted with a problem, try to state them out loud. Teachers are powerful models for their students. During the day there are countless opportunities for teachers to model out loud for their students how they thought about and

coped with a difficult situation. By observing these responses students will eventually learn to use them as well.

Examples of calming, coping and self-praise thoughts

- I don't like it when he acts like that, but I can handle that.
- My job is to stay calm and help him learn better ways to ask for what he wants.
- I can help her learn better ways to behave.
- She's just testing the limits, I can help her with that.
- This isn't the end of the world. He's a bright child and I'm a caring teacher. We will make it over this hump.
- He really doesn't do that much any more. This is a temporary setback.
- I shouldn't blame my impatience on him. I'll talk to him about it.
- I am doing the best I can to help her learn more positive behaviors.
- I can develop a plan to deal with it.
- I need to stick to the issue, and not take this personally!
- He doesn't really understand what those swearing words mean, I'm not going to let it upset me.
- Don't be so hard on yourself – don't expect perfection – take one step at a time.
- Look for positives, don't jump to conclusions.
- We're getting through this – each day gets better and better.
- I can cope.
- No one can make me mad; it's up to me.
- I can control my thinking and my anger.
- I'm a good teacher.
- I try hard.
- I need to stay focused on the primary issue and not the secondary annoying misbehaviors.

Of course, there will be times when you find it difficult to use self-control techniques. Don't worry – relapses and problems are to be expected. You'll become more proficient with practice. Think in terms of small gains and don't belittle gradual progress. Praise your *efforts*. Ask yourself, did you need to get angry in the first place? And don't forget to give yourself credit for trying.

Reference

Seligman, M. (1990) *Learned Optimism*, Sydney: Random House.

Chapter One

Working with Parents

Why Is It Important for Teachers to Collaborate with and Form Partnerships with Parents?

Widespread support for involving parents in their children's learning grows out of convincing evidence suggesting that family involvement has positive effects on children's academic achievement, social competence and school quality. The highly acclaimed book, *A New Generation of Evidence: The Family Is Critical to Student Achievement*, opens by saying, 'The evidence is now beyond dispute. When schools work together with families to support learning, children tend to succeed not just in school, but throughout life' (Henderson and Berla, 1994). Realizing that students' cultural backgrounds, economic conditions and home environments can profoundly affect their adjustment to and performance in school, schools are finding that they can best serve the needs of their students by becoming more family centred and more focused on students' emotional and social needs as well as their academic needs. Some innovative schools are providing non-academic services to children and their families, such as parent education classes and parent resource rooms, courses for parents to become classroom aides, General Education Diploma (GED) classes, employment training workshops and special courses to help children learn appropriate social skills, problem-solving and anger management strategies. Schools such as these demonstrate that the relationships between home and school are beginning to change in fundamental ways.

But despite the evidence of the positive effects of family involvement on a student's academic performance, its potential is still largely ignored in many schools. Many teachers do not systematically encourage family involvement and form partnerships with parents, and parents do not always participate even when they are encouraged to do so. Several major barriers to family involvement exist in schools. The first barrier is that teachers may discourage parent involvement because they feel they lack adequate time and are too stressed by classroom demands to be involved with parents. Large classes lead teachers to believe they have little time to spend with individual students, let alone with their parents. Furthermore, particularly in light of the pressing demands on teachers' time and energy, administrators may not support their involvement with family members.

A second barrier to parent involvement in children's schooling is the misunderstandings between teachers and parents. Teachers may believe that parents are neither interested nor qualified in participating in their children's education. Parents, in turn, can feel intimidated by teachers and school administrators, and feel they lack the knowledge to help educate their children. Parents may have had negative school experiences themselves leading them to have negative feelings about schools and a lack of trust in teachers. The change in demographic and employment patterns may further complicate the development of strong home–school partnerships. As the population becomes increasingly ethnically diverse, teachers and parents may come from different cultural and economic backgrounds, leading at times to contrasting values and beliefs. Disadvantaged and minority families may face language and literacy barriers, have no access to transportation to and from schools, have no experience asking teachers questions, and fear attending school functions at night if they live in certain neighbourhoods. Such families may feel so overwhelmed by the stress in their lives that they have little energy to be involved in their child's education. Moreover, the rise in the number of dual-worker families and single parent working families means there is less time for parents to spend on school involvement. Such barriers, be they lack of confidence, poverty, divorce, illness or job stress, contribute to parents' lack of involvement with teachers and unfortunately reinforces teachers' negative perceptions that parents are not interested in forming partnerships with them.

A third barrier is that some teachers lack the confidence or skills in how to work collaboratively with families (Epstein, 1992). The reason for this may be due to a lack of adequate teacher preparation in general family knowledge, ways to involve parents, how to conduct successful parent conferences and effective communication and negotiation strategies (Burton, 1992). Studies have shown that there is scant attention in teacher education programmes focused on how to build relationships and partnerships with parents (Chavkin, 1991). Teachers need concrete skills, knowledge and positive attitudes about family involvement in order to carry it out effectively. They need training in family involvement that emphasizes more than traditional parent-teacher conferences but rather recognizes the additional assistance (e.g. parent education classes and support services) and encouragement that families need in order to help their children in school. Evidence suggests that such assistance may be essential for many minority and economically disadvantaged parents, in particular, for whom school involvement is often an intimidating and difficult proposition.

In order for teachers to be successful at collaborating with parents they must recognize the intrinsic worth of families as contributors to children's learning, and be willing to reach out beyond the traditional roles of teachers. Successful partnerships between teachers and parents will result not only in the development of educational programmes for students that are based on understanding each student's individual emotional and academic needs, but also in teachers feeling less stressed as well as valued and supported by their students' families.

Ways to Promote Parent Involvement

Start before School Starts

Parent involvement efforts need to start even before school starts. You need to reach out right away to get to know families. You can do this by sending home a 'welcome' greeting to all parents and incoming students and asking families to complete interest surveys regarding their children's favourite activities and family interests. If you have been assigned a student who has a history of problems in school it will be important to call the parents before school starts to establish positive communication, reassure parents of your concern, and express your confidence in your ability to work with their child.

Before school starts you should also formulate your discipline plan and send all your parents a letter of introduction which includes:

- your philosophy of discipline (class rules, consequences, incentives)
- some information about you as teacher
- your commitment to parent involvement
- your homework policy
- how and when you can be reached
- invitation to first parent meeting at the school.

Send Notes Home and Make Positive Phone Calls

Start sending home good behavior messages about students at the beginning of the year and calling parents to tell them about something special their child has accomplished or to share how you feel about the student's positive behavior. Ask the parent to share the content of your call with their child. When you take the time to build up your positive bank account with parents, they come to realize how much you have invested in their child's learning. Once you have established a positive relationship with parents, they will be much more receptive if you have to call them to discuss a concern later in the year.

Most parents report they only hear from teachers when there is a problem or at the prescribed parent-teacher conference times. When communication is prescribed or negative, it's easy to see why partnerships with parents fail. Instead, take every opportunity to show families you care (e.g. send home birthday cards, special award notices, get-well cards, thank-you notes and good news phone calls). It is a good idea to keep track of these positive calls and notes so that you are sure to have communicated regularly with every parent in your classroom. Moreover, be certain to recognize through newsletters and personal notes those parents who are helping you by volunteering time in class, chaperoning on field trips, donating supplies and food and so forth.

Weekly Classroom Newsletter

The more you can tell parents about your curriculum and what is going on at school, the more collaboration you will eventually gain from parents. Send home a newsletter each week informing parents about what classroom activities occurred that week and as a reminder of the upcoming events. In these newsletters you can invite parents for lunches with you and suggest ways they might participate in the classroom that week. Be sure that these newsletters are translated for families who do not speak English.

Brown Bag Lunches – Have a Parent Involvement Plan

In addition to the 'back to school' nights at the beginning of the year and the regularly scheduled parent-teacher conferences to review a student's progress, it is also important to set up regular informal mechanisms for parents to communicate with teachers. Some teachers schedule brown bag lunches once or twice a month with parents. These are times when any parent can come with a packed lunch and join the teacher for an informal question and answer period.

Home Visits

A home visit is probably the most personal way for a teacher to show her concern and caring for a student. For the parent, it's an opportunity to meet the teacher in their familiar surroundings. For the student, it is a chance to see that their parent and teacher are working collaboratively. And for the teacher, it will give you a better perspective about the student's family life and contribute to a strong positive relationship.

Parent Education Groups

In some schools teachers are joining with school counsellors, school nurses and educational psychologists to offer parent education classes. These classes are an opportunity for you to develop joint plans with parents regarding your students' needs. They also help parents understand the ways they can support their children's education by working with their children at home. Parent groups are also a way for parents to get to know teachers, to let them know their concerns and what family situations may be influencing their children's emotional, social and academic learning. When parent groups involve teachers as co-leaders, long-lasting partnerships are developed which serve to empower each other as well as the children.

The Teacher–Parent Partnership Model

The ideal relationship between the teacher and parent is based on a collaborative partnership. This is in contrast to a hierarchical relationship whereby the teacher by virtue of knowledge is assumed to be the expert who dispenses advice or commands to parents. Meaning 'to labour together', collaboration implies a reciprocal relationship that uses the teacher's and parents' knowledge, strengths and perspectives equally, and considers them of equal importance. The teacher is more knowledgeable about teaching principles, curriculum and the child's learning needs while the parent is more knowledgeable about the child's temperament, likes and dislikes and emotional needs. Accepting the notion of complementary expertise creates a relationship between parents and teachers which is mutually respectful and supportive. In this non-blaming and non-hierarchical model, the teacher promotes collaboration through reflection, summary of suggestions made by parents, reinforcement, support and acceptance, humour and optimism, encouragement of parent participation and sharing of her own ideas and key learning concepts.

Sample Teacher–Parent 'Get Acquainted Meeting' in September

Teacher: Hello, Ms Jones, I'm Ms Parks, thanks for taking the time to come in and get acquainted. I've enjoyed working with Takisha these first two weeks of school. (*Recognize parents' efforts to meet with you*)

Parent: It's nice to meet you early in the year. Takisha's been telling me about how much she likes circle time. She's so excited about circle time that I don't hear about the rest of the day. I'd love to know what else is on the schedule so I can ask her questions about the rest of her day.

Teacher: Well, circle time is the way we start the day. It's a good opportunity for kids to talk about themselves. We also do calendar and talk about the weather and Friday is Takisha's show and share day. (*Explains daily schedule*)

Parent: Oh, that's good to know. I didn't know she could bring things in to share.

Teacher: Yes, I really like the children to bring in something inexpensive, like a book they've been reading, or a small toy, or a memento from somewhere they've been. And you are welcome to come as well. (*Welcome parents to classroom*)

Parent: Oh, she has some little stones she picked up on the beach. I'm sure she'll want to bring those.

Teacher: That sounds good. After circle time the kids get to choose their first centre. All of the centres have pre-reading or pre-maths activities.

Parent: I'm wondering, what centre does Takisha usually choose? She doesn't really know any maths nor can she read.

Teacher: Oh, I've noticed she loves the manipulatives table. That's a centre where there are boxes of coins or stones or blocks and the children can make patterns or count or sort the pieces. It looks like they're just playing, but actually what they're doing is getting comfortable with the concept of numbers. After their first centre activity, they all switch, and the children have a chance to work at one of the other centres. Then we have a snack and a 20 minute outdoor recess.

Parent: You know, sometimes Takisha is shy with other kids in the neighbourhood. Is she making friends here during free play and recess?

Teacher: I haven't noticed any problems but thanks for alerting me. I'll keep an eye out for how things are going for her. If she has any trouble I'll let you know and we can talk about how to help her. For now she seems to be joining in well with the others. (*Acknowledges parent's concerns and lets her know she will work with her concerning this possible problem*)

Parent: What can I do to help Takisha do well this year?

Teacher: Next week I'll be sending home a list of books for parents to read with their kids. It would be great if you and Takisha could read together for 10 minutes every night. I have the books in the classroom if you'd like to borrow them, or I know most of them are available at the library. By reading together I mean you reading to her or just looking at pictures together and talking about what might be going on in the pictures. You don't have to get her to sound out the words. Just let it be a fun, enjoyable time for you both. (*Shares something the parent can do at home to support her child's learning*)

Parent: That will be easy, she loves looking at picture books. Thanks for taking the time to meet with me. If there's anything I can do to help or if there's anything I should know about Takisha's progress, please call me.

Teacher: It was great meeting you. I know you work full time, but if there's ever a day that you'd like to come and observe or help out in the class, I'd love to have you. I think Takisha's going to have a good kindergarten year.

Effective Communication with Parents: Tips for Setting Up Successful Meetings

The key to successful collaboration with parents is the teacher's use of effective communication and problem-solving or negotiation skills. The following discussion includes some of the blocks to effective communication between teachers and parents and some ways to overcome them.

Involving Parents from the Start – Speaking Up

It doesn't matter if it is the first week of school, or even the first day of school, teachers need to contact parents as soon as they become aware of a child's academic or behavioral problem. This is at the core of successful collaboration with families. Sometimes teachers try to avoid conflict, disagreement or disapproval from parents by not talking with them about their children's behavior or learning problems. They may avoid setting up parent meetings and asking for help with the child with the hope that the child will eventually improve or outgrow the problem. However, if the child continues to misbehave, teachers may begin to store up grievances and even though they haven't called the parents for help, they may even begin to blame them for the child's misbehaviors. The teacher in the following example clearly has been storing up a lot of resentment.

Teacher: I've had it! I've tried for three months with this child. Nothing seems to help. I can't do this with a large class. I don't get any support from the parents. I never see his parents at the school and I don't think they care. If they don't care, why should I care?

There are several reasons why teachers need to speak up and contact parents at the first sign there is a problem. First, if you don't involve parents in planning in regard to a student's behavior problems you may come to feel resentful of the parents for their lack of recognition of your efforts. (Of course, they can't support you if they don't know what you have been doing.) Secondly, by involving parents early in the planning you may discover there are other family factors that have a bearing on the child's misbehaviors such as a divorce, death in the family or some other family crises. Understanding a particular child's family circumstances will help you put his behavior (and his family's) into perspective so that you can focus on ways to increase his feelings of security given what may be an unpredictable situation at home. Thirdly, if you wait too long before talking with parents, you may find that when you finally do meet with them you are angry at them, and they are angry at you for keeping them uninformed about the problem for so long. This can damage future collaborative efforts. Indeed, one of the most common complaints among parents is that teachers wait too long before contacting them about a school problem.

Sometimes a teacher does not speak up with parents because he or she fears being punished or criticized by the parents for not being a competent teacher. These individuals may think it is a sign of inadequacy to ask for help or to admit to a parent that they need their help in managing a child's problems. They may believe in the 'good teacher' myth, that is, that good teachers should handle all of their students' problems on their own without the help of parents. Rather, just the reverse is true. It is the most competent teachers who will involve parents from the outset in collaborative planning regarding a student's difficulties.

Call parents and offer flexible time choices
The first thing a teacher must do when there is a problem is to call the parents and arrange a meeting with them. Make every effort to contact the parents (both mothers and fathers) and don't give up after one or two tries. If you can't reach them at home, try sending them a letter (or registered letter) asking them to contact you. If you can't reach them by phone or note, then try them at work. Make that phone call with the knowledge that it is your professional duty to do so. (Would a doctor hesitate to call a parent about a medical problem?)

Once you reach the parent, express a positive, caring attitude and explain that you are calling because of your concern for their child. Briefly state why you would like to meet. For example, 'I am calling because I am concerned about how Jessie gets along with the other students'. Tell the parents that you have already taken some action to help Jessie but that you would like to have their input in regard to anything else that might help her. Express your confidence in being able to work the problem out together. Offer the parents a range of times (daytime and evening) when you are available to meet with them. For some highly stressed families it may be advantageous to have the meetings at their home.

Welcome parents
Your initial welcoming when you first greet the parents can be key to the success of your meeting. Start your meetings on time, and

begin by thanking them for taking the time to meet with you. Check with them as to the time you have set aside for your meeting together. For example, 'I am so pleased you could manage to meet with me. I have an hour scheduled for us, can you still manage this much time?'

Use 'I' messages instead of 'You' messages
'I' messages communicate what the teacher wants or feels. They're a way to be clear about an issue without having a destructive effect. 'You' messages tend to blame, criticize or pass judgement, and they often generate anger or humiliation. If you think about what your reactions would be if you were on the receiving end of the following remarks, you will see why 'I' messages are more effective in eliciting co-operation.

Teacher to Parent: Your child is always late for school and he has missed a lot of days? What is going on? Why can't you get him to school in the mornings? (*'You' message focuses on blaming parent*)
Alternative: I am concerned that Carla is arriving late in the mornings and missing so much school. I wonder if there is a way we can work together to help motivate her get to school on time. (*'I' message focuses on teacher's feelings and desire for change*)

Teacher to Parent: Dan is a real problem in this class. He is hitting other kids and other parents are complaining. He is wild and disruptive and irresponsible. I can't get any teaching done. What is going on at home with Dan? (*'I' message focuses on criticizing child*)
Alternative: I'm concerned about Dan's hitting in class. I would like to work with you to develop a plan to help him learn to be more co-operative. (*'I' message focuses on concern and what teacher wants*)

Teacher to Parent: I'm not at all pleased with Sally's progress in reading.
Alternative: I am concerned about how Sally's reading is progressing.

Begin with a statement of concern
Start your meetings by letting the parents know that you care about their child and that it is his or her welfare that is of primary concern to you. Your introductory statement expressing concern will set the tone for the entire conversation.

Be brief, clear and specific

In order to be able to speak up, you must think about exactly what you *want* rather than focusing on the negative, or what you don't want. Once you have a clear idea of what you want, state it positively and briefly. It is not necessary to recount episode after episode of a child's problems to prove your point about how messy or irresponsible a student has been. Instead, describe the problem or behavior clearly and briefly and focus on the positive outcome that is desired. See the 'I' messages in the above examples to see how this is done. Avoid describing the child's problems with vague statements such as 'She's not behaving', or 'Her attitude isn't good', and avoid judgemental comments such as 'Your child is mean' or 'Your child is lazy'. These give no useful information and will alienate the parent.

Ask for feedback

Sometimes you may not be sure if the parent has understood your point of view. If this happens, you should ask, 'Am I making sense?' This is much more effective than rambling on and on, and it assures the parent that his or her comprehension of the situation is important.

Avoid too much speaking up; be selective

Speaking up does not mean you should be insensitive about where, when, or how you express your feelings. First of all, it is important to ask yourself: 'Do I have a legitimate bone to pick or am I in a bad mood?' 'Am I overreacting?' 'Am I really interested in solving anything?'

Describe steps taken to solve problem

It is important for parents to recognize that you have already thought about the problem and have taken appropriate action to deal with the situation – that you're not calling them in lieu of solving the problem yourself. For example, the teacher might say, 'I had a meeting with your son about his yelling out and swearing in class. We reviewed the rules of the classroom discipline plan. In addition, I am giving him extra attention and praise for polite talk. But I would also like your input and to co-ordinate a plan with you at home if that is possible?'

Active Listening – Obtaining Parental Input

Another of the most frequently voiced complaints by parents about teachers is that they don't feel listened to and respected by teachers. Unfortunately, instead of listening and allowing parents to say what they want to say about their child's problem, teachers sometimes respond to parents' concerns with interruptions, questions, arguments, criticisms and advice. Some parents report they feel confronted with a 'know it all attitude' when teachers lecture to them about what to do or how to feel. In fact, few people really know how to listen or understand its potential power. Moreover, whenever a person doesn't feel listened to, it is likely that he or she will either restate the problem again and again or withdraw totally from the relationship. For instance in the following examples the teachers deny the problem or provide instant advice:

Parent to Teacher

Parent: I am having a frustrating time reading with Billy. He gets mad when I correct him and doesn't seem to want me to read with him.

Teacher: Well, maybe you shouldn't correct him so much. (*Provides instant solution*)

or

Parent: Billy doesn't seem to have any friends. He never gets invited to any birthday parties.

Teacher: Don't worry about it. It happens to all children sometime. (*Deny problem*)

or

Parent: You need to understand I am a single mother. I work. I don't have time to deal with this.

Teacher: Don't you care about your child? (*Blaming*)

Listening attentively is one of the most powerful ways you can support a parent. However, due to teachers' busy schedules it is rarely done, and time spent by teachers talking to parents is often undervalued. Listening means giving the parent 'the floor', allowing him or her to state feelings or ideas without interruptions. However, good listeners are not passive, merely nodding their head with a blank expression or listening while continuing to mark student papers. Instead, teachers listen by watching parents closely, using appropriate facial expressions, asking open-ended questions in an effort to understand the situation and reflecting on their thoughts and feelings. Here are some tips to become an effective listener.

- Maintain eye contact. (Stop whatever work you are doing.)
- Make sure there are no physical barriers between you and the parent. It's best to sit next to each other or in a circle. Don't sit at your desk with the parent on the other side.

- Give the parent a chance to finish speaking before responding.
- Listen to both the content *and* feeling of what the parent is saying. (Every message has both a content component, which is the actual information that is conveyed, and a feeling component, which is the non-verbal message.)
- Express interest by asking open ended questions about the situation. Ask what the parent thinks is causing the problems.
- Feedback: summarize and then paraphrase in your own words the content of the message and the feelings expressed by the parents. When you do this you are not making a judgement about what the parent has said and you are not agreeing or disagreeing. You are simply letting the parent know you understand.
- Validate: try to see the problem from the parent's point of view. Let the parent know that you see his or her point of view as a valid one. Validation can help reduce the gap that may exist between teacher and parent. It is important to admit that there are views that differ from your own and that, given a different position, the perspectives might alter.
- Encourage the parent to continue.

Note: Of course it is also important for the teacher to give some thought about *when* he or she is available to communicate with parents. If the teacher is walking out to the car park, is in the middle of setting up for a class event, or is in a rush to get home it will be difficult to communicate effectively. Instead, teachers should let parents know a good time for communicating with them about their children's needs.

In the next examples the teacher shows how he or she is listening carefully to what the parents are saying.

Parent: I am having a frustrating time reading with Billy. He gets mad when I correct him and doesn't seem to want me to read with him.

Teacher: I'm glad you came to talk to me about that, it must be frustrating for you especially as I know you are eager for him to do well in school. Tell me more about what happens when you read together. (*Validating feelings and asking questions to understand problem*)
         or

Parent: Billy doesn't seem to have any friends. He never gets invited to any birthday parties.

Teacher: I'm glad to know about that. Billy must be feeling very lonely. What does he say about friends at school? (*Reflecting child's feelings and gathering further information*)
           or
Parent: You need to understand I am a single mother. I work. I don't have time to deal with this.
Teacher: I understand how overwhelmed you must feel. (*Validating feelings*)

In these instances, the parent's feelings were validated as the teacher tried to see the problem from the parent's point of view.

Some teachers mind-read, believing they know the parent's motives or opinions without first checking them out. If you find yourself making assumptions about what a quiet family member is thinking or feeling during a meeting, encourage him or her to talk. You can often do this by discussing things that are of interest to him or her, or by sharing your own experiences. You might tell a parent about some aspect of coping with your own children if it is relevant to the situation. As you try to get a reluctant family member to communicate, it's important to put yourself in that person's shoes. Think about how the parent might see an issue, then validate this feeling. You might say, 'I can see how that must have hurt your feelings' or 'That would have made me cross too' or 'Yes, I feel frustrated when my son does the same thing' or 'The change in culture must be very confusing to him and to you'.

Be Polite and Positive and Edit your Complaints

As you listen you may feel some frustration with a parent's seeming lack of involvement with or interest in their child or you may disagree with their style of parenting, or be angry about the fact they are criticizing you. Even so, it is essential to remain positive and avoid criticisms of the parent. Put-downs will evoke anger, resentment, defensiveness and guilt, or depression in the parent, and undermine effective communication and problem-solving. Here are some examples of teacher put-downs.

Teacher to Parent: You are too harsh in your discipline.
                     or
                     If you spent more time with your child he wouldn't misbehave so much.

A professional attitude is extremely important in the effective resolution of a situation, and you can make a conscious decision that you will be polite no matter how anyone else is acting. The fact that someone else is rude and angry does not make it acceptable for the teacher to behave that way. You won't always feel polite, however, so you will have to learn to do a bit of editing before you speak. Here are some tips to help become a good editor.

Say what you can do and what you want to do
Edit out statements referring to what you can't do.

Parent to Teacher
Parent: Why can't you do more individual work with my son?
Teacher: I can't. I've got 32 kids and other kids that are worse than your son! I've got a million things to do and can't take the time for one student. (*Focus is on what she cannot do, which creates opposition*)
Alternative: I would like to give him more attention. Perhaps on Fridays at lunch I can meet with him individually for 20 minutes until we can see about a tutor possibility. (*Focuses on what she can do*)

Focus on the positive
Edit out complaints about parents. Imagine a situation where you set up a behavior plan at school and sent home daily behavior report cards to the parents. The parents had agreed at your meeting to set up a star chart at home and to give the child a special reward for getting ten positive notes home from the teacher. After a while you find out that the parents didn't manage to set up the star chart. You are furious because you have put so much energy into the classroom programme and feel it is being sabotaged by the parents. You no longer feel like continuing the positive calls home or sending home notes until the parents have completed their part of the bargain.

However, this kind of thinking on the part of the teacher creates a stand off and it is the child who will lose out in the end. Thus it is important that teachers do not take personally parents' failures to follow through. It is also important that teachers take responsibility for continuing the behavior plan and for sending positive messages home as well as for seeing that the child can be successful in the classroom – regardless of whether the parents are able to follow through at home. You may not feel that your efforts are being recognized at first but over time you may find that parents become more involved as they begin to trust that you really do go the extra mile for their child. Students' learning should not be jeopardized because their parents are not able to be involved in their education.

Think about the child's needs and point of view

If you find that you are thinking only of yourself, then edit those thoughts. Instead, think about what your student needs or what might be going on for his family. For example you might think, 'I wonder if the parents are nervous about meeting me in a school, perhaps they would prefer a home visit?' or 'Johnny's mother is so stressed out because of her poverty and being a single mother of four children that I bet she doesn't have the energy to do a star chart or even to get the stickers. I wonder if I set it up for her if that would help?'

Focus on Fixing the Problem

Sometimes effective communication is hindered by blaming. This occurs when people place the responsibility for a problem with someone else. They may directly accuse others of creating the problem or they may do this more subtly. Here are some common examples of blaming as reported by parents.

Teacher: Your daughter gets her own way and you never discipline her. That's why she's such a behavior problem. You're not tough enough.

or

Teacher: I think you spank her too much. That's why she's so aggressive.

or

Teacher: You are not attached to your child, if you were she would not have these problems.

or

Teacher: Your child is the most aggressive child I have ever seen. He is really crazy and I've handled tough kids before – but not like your child.

Blaming sets people against each other in battle rather than uniting them to solve a problem. When teachers talk to parents, it is important to focus on fixing the problem not the blame. Following teachers meetings, parents often report that they felt blamed by the teacher for their children's behavior problems at school. However, once parents realize that you are primarily interested in working together with them to solve their child's problems (and not to blame them) they will soon become your partners. For instance, the teacher says to a parent, 'The problem seems to be that Gillian is overly aggressive. Let's decide how we both want to handle these problems in the future so that we can be consistent with each other. I know if we work together we can help her be more co-operative.' This approach emphasizes collaboration and consistency is more likely to lead to a successful outcome.

A Problem Is Always Legitimate

A parent may bring up an issue with the teacher, only to have it dismissed by the teacher as not being a serious problem. For instance, parents may be concerned that their child is acting aggressively at home or is overly anxious about school work. However, the teacher doesn't believe there is a problem in the classroom and therefore doesn't see the value of discussing it. Here are some examples of denying or discounting a problem.

Teacher:　Don't worry about it, his behavior at school is fine. There are a lot worse kids than him.
　　　　　or
Teacher:　That is normal behavior for his age. It's not a problem. You expect too much of him for his age.

Although you may not see an issue as a problem for the child at school, the parent does. Therefore, in the interest of good collaboration with parents, you need to address the situation and co-operate to help resolve it. Active listening and validation will help you if you are tempted to discount the problem and will allow you to better understand the parent's point of view.

Focus on Realistic Changes

Statements such as, 'Nothing works with this child', 'He's just like his brother who was always in trouble', 'He'll never change', 'I'll try but it won't do any good', communicate a hopeless message that all efforts towards change are futile. It can also be communicated by subtle cues, such as one- or two-word replies. 'I don't know', 'I guess' or 'Whatever', spoken in a passive, depressed voice, indicate lack of hope as well as implying a lack of interest. Hopelessness can even be indicated non-verbally by deep sighs or eye-rolling.

If you or the parents feel a sense of hopelessness when tackling a problem, you need to focus on what changes you can realistically make. Although no major problem can be resolved in one discussion, each one does have a workable solution. This is an important attitude to convey. For instance, you might communicate an attitude of hope by saying: 'Okay, we are going to have to be patient with him as it takes time to change. He's been through a lot. First let us talk about how we will manage the hitting behavior and then we will talk about what social skills we want to teach him. We want to develop a short term and a long term plan.'

Stop Action, Refocus and Stay Calm

Occasionally when teachers or parents are trying to discuss a problem, they end up 'unloading', that is dragging in all sorts of gripes about the child. They may even go on to list every misbehavior the child has done over the past two months. Pretty soon both parties feel overwhelmed and angry.

Teacher:　He's irresponsible. He hits other kids, he doesn't listen, he runs around and won't stay in his seat. He so disruptive that I can't teach the other kids. He's always interrupting me in class and then doesn't do what I ask him to do. He's driving me wild!

Call a stop action, or truce, and halt all discussion when you realize unloading is occurring. To facilitate calling a truce, you should decide in advance exactly how you will signal that a discussion needs to be stopped. You might simply say, 'I need to stop talking about this right now' or 'I think we should think on this awhile and set up another meeting to continue our planning'. (Note the use of 'I' messages.). It is important if you postpone a meeting or cut it short that you set another time for continuing it. And the sooner you can discuss the problem the better.

Get Feedback

People become defensive when they feel they are being blamed, whether or not they actually are being accused, and whether or not they really are to blame. They may react by becoming angry or argumentative, making excuses, becoming distraught and crying, or withdrawing and refusing to participate in further discussion.

Mother:　You seem to have a lot of aggression in your classroom. My son has told me several times about being hit by several boys.

Teacher:　*(He thinks she is saying he can't control the classroom and reacts defensively.)* You don't have thirty kids all day without any help. There is bound to be some hitting – all young kids do that.

Studies have shown that there are two filters whenever two people are talking. One affects how a person communicates and the other affects how the message is received. It is important to try to become aware of these filters and how they may alter how you talk to parents and the way they hear what you say to them. For instance, if you feel you are being blamed or criticized, it is a good idea to stop the discussion and get feedback about what the parent meant. For instance, the teacher in the above example could attempt to clarify what the parent meant by asking a question.

Teacher: Are you concerned that I am not managing the aggression? (*Asks for feedback*)

Dealing with Parental Resistance and Complaints

Teachers sometimes find themselves suggesting possible solutions to parents only to be met with 'yes-buts' from them. Yes-butting occurs when every attempt to make a suggestion or state a point of view is discounted because something is wrong with it. You may get the feeling, 'I'm wrong again. Nothing I say is acceptable to this parent.' This results in, 'What's the use of trying to help? This parent doesn't care about her child, why should I care?' The parent who yes-buts is often unaware of rejecting the teacher's views.

Teacher: I think we should get a tutor for Andrea to help her with her reading.

Mother: Yes, that's a good idea, but it would never work. You know she wouldn't do the extra reading at home and it would be a waste of money.

Teacher: Well, maybe you could do the individual tutoring with her yourself?

Mother: I don't have time to do extra home work with her. Isn't that the teacher's job? (*Defensive*)

Teacher: Don't you care about your daughter's success in school? (*Critical*)

As we have said it is important that you remain positive and confident rather than become critical with the parent as we have seen in this example. Sometimes parents react defensively to a teacher's advice because they feel the teacher doesn't really understand their situation or when their own ideas have been discounted. Therefore, before coming up with a final plan, it is always important to be sure that the teacher has listened carefully, validated the parent's point of view and has invited the parent's solutions to the situation.

Another distressing situation for a teacher is to be on the receiving end of complaints or criticisms by a parent. This is usually unantici-pated and almost always hurtful. Consider your responses to the following parental comments:

Parent: Why am I hearing about this problem now? You should have been helping her sooner in the year.
or
If you knew how to teach, my son wouldn't be having these problems.
or
Your homework is so uninteresting, no wonder she doesn't want to do it.
or
My son has never had difficulties before in class, it must be something you are doing wrong. He says you don't do anything to stop the kids from picking on him.

Remember to maintain a professional and respectful attitude and don't react defensively or angrily, otherwise the cycle of criticisms will continue. Recognize that you're dealing with a parent who is highly distraught about their child. You can diffuse a parent's anger using one of the following strategies: admit your mistake if there is one; listen attentively to the parent without defending yourself; show concern by getting more information about the complaint; and refocus the nega-tive complaint into a positive recommendation for dealing with the situation. For instance, instead of saying 'Don't you care about your daughter's success?', the teacher could say, 'Yes I will give her extra attention at school but I think she could do with help outside of school. I know you want her to be successful. Since I know how busy you are at work, I wonder if there is another way we can provide her with some extra tutoring?' The following are some other examples of ways you can respond to the parental criticisms presented above:

Teacher: You have reason to be angry about that. I was not aware she was struggling with her reading and I should have been.
or
Yes I should have contacted you sooner. You have reason to be upset. (*Admit mistake*)
or
That really concerns me, can you explain more what you mean? (*Show concern*)
or

I hear what you're saying, how can we make the homework more interesting for her? (*Refocus on positive*)
or
Can you tell me more about how the kids are picking on him? Are there other times where he felt I did nothing to help him? (*Get more information*)

Agree on Mutual Goals and Brainstorm Solutions

Once the issue or problem has been discussed and both the parent and teacher feel they have expressed their views and been listened to, the next step is for them to agree upon their common goals and to share possible solutions. The teacher can ask the parents if they have any suggestions for how to solve the problem. The teacher also shares her ideas for what she has already tried and what she thinks will be helpful to the child given the new information from the parents. Then the teacher and parents should work out a plan of exactly what the teacher will do at school and how the parents will be involved. For example, the teacher might say, 'Here's what I will do at school, I will set up a reward programme to help him remember to listen and not blurt out in class. Then I will send home a note each day to let you know how many stickers he has earned that day. You can record these on your sticker chart at home and when he gets twenty-five of them perhaps plan a surprise.'

Express Confidence

Whenever there is a problem with a child, parents are probably anxious. They need to know they are dealing with a confident teacher who has the ability to handle the situation and to work with their child to teach him or her alternative pro-social behaviors. Let the parents know you are confident and that with the extra support at school and at home you believe the problem will be resolved.

Plan Follow-Up

It is important to plan a follow-up meeting or phone call to review the success of the planned intervention. The follow-up plan is vital if parents are going to believe in your commitment to their child. For example the teacher might end the meeting by saying, 'I've had a lot of experience with children like Robbie. I know that by working together we can get results. I will contact you in two days to let you know how things are progressing. Let me know if anything else comes up that I should know about Robbie.'

Sample Meeting with the Parent to Discuss a Problem

Teacher: It's good to see you again Ms Parks. You said you wanted to talk about a problem. (*Welcome parent*)

Parent: Yes, I'm concerned because Takisha is refusing to sit down for our reading time at home. She's always seemed to like reading with me in the past. Now she just says, 'I don't want to do it. I hate reading.' Last week she even threw her book across the room. I'm not sure if I should force her to sit down and listen or if I should just let it go.

Teacher: How long has this been happening? (*Listen and get information about problem*)

Parent: It's just been in the last two weeks. Did anything happen at school?

Teacher: You know, about three weeks ago a new girl joined our class. She's a little older than the other kids and she's just begun reading some single words. She's been struggling with reading, and I've been praising her a lot each time she reads a new word. Perhaps I haven't been noticing Takisha's progress as much as I was. (*Suggests an idea*)

Parent: Well Takisha is really fond of you. If this new girl is getting a lot of attention from you, Takisha may be feeling left out. At home when her cousin is over, Takisha sometimes sulks if her cousin gets more attention than she does.

Teacher: I wonder if some other children are also feeling a little left out. Maybe I went a little overboard in making the new girl feel welcome. I guess I need to make an effort to praise each child's special abilities more often.

Parent: That's a good idea. I think that would help Takisha at school. What do you think I should do about her reluctance to read with me at home?

Teacher: Maybe you could do reading in a little different way for a while. I have some audio cassettes of some children's books that you could listen to. I know that in the past Takisha has liked dinosaur books. I have some great tapes of some of those. Also, if you have a VCR, I do have movies of some of the other books that we have in the classroom. You could listen or watch the story and then go to the book to see the pictures. This might help Takisha feel less pressure to read. And perhaps you could just read to her and not ask her to read for a while so it is a fun time for you both. Also anytime you want to come in to class and read to the children you are welcome. We have reading times twice a day. (*Offer something she can do to help and invite her participation*)

Parent: Well, I don't have any way to play audio tapes, but I do have a VCR. Maybe we'll start with that. Now that I know how she might be feeling, I'll praise her more for listening and coming up with ideas.

Teacher: Oh that's a great idea. Also, it might be good not to give her tantrums and resistant behavior too much attention. Why don't we talk this coming Monday about how Takisha's doing. I'm glad you brought this to my attention so quickly. Takisha asks such great questions during circle time. I really love having her in the classroom. (*Be positive about solving the problem and support parent*)

Parent: Thank you very much for taking the time to meet with me. I feel better now that I know what's going on. Shall I call you on Monday or do you want to call me?

Teacher: Could I call you in the evening, because it's hard for me to call during the school day? (*Plan time to talk again*)

Parent: Yes, any time after 6.30 would be fine.

Conclusion

Involving parents in your students' education requires a commitment to families, a proactive plan for involving parents which is carefully crafted prior to school starting, and teacher time set aside for communicating and collaborating with parents. It is a process which is demanding and time-consuming, sometimes frustrating and often rewarding. For the already overworked teacher it can seem difficult to know where to carve out any extra time for this collaboration work during the day. However, the value of this approach for children's social and academic growth cannot be underestimated. In the long run this commitment to work with parents may actually save you time for it can lead to more positive relationships with students, less stressful classrooms and more support for yourself and the family. For the child it will make all the difference.

To Sum Up

- Make a plan for parent involvement before school starts.
- Send home positive notes and make positive phone calls.
- Set up informal and formal mechanisms for parents to communicate with teachers.
- Don't store up grievances; call a meeting with a parent when a child's misbehavior first occurs.
- Express your concern for the child.
- Be brief, clear and concise when describing a behavior problem.
- Ask for parent feedback and suggestions for solutions.
- Don't interrupt, argue or give advice; listen attentively and validate parents' concerns.
- Stick to the point and avoid unloading multiple gripes.
- Edit; be polite and positive.
- Focus on fixing the problem and avoid blaming.
- Recognize the parent's point of view.
- Take one step at a time.
- Get and give feedback.
- Don't attack angrily; stay calm.
- Stop and call a time out if anger mounts.
- Make positive recommendations.
- Plan a follow-up with parents.
- Encourage ongoing conversation.

References

Burton, C. B. (1992) Defining family-centered early education: beliefs of public school, child care, and Head Start teachers, *Early Education and Development*, 3(1), 45–59.

Chavkin, N. F. (1991) Uniting families and schools: social workers helping teachers through inservice training, *School Social Work Journal*, 15, 1–10.

Epstein, A. (1992) School and family partnerships. In M. Alkin (ed.) *Encyclopedia of Educational Research* (pp. 1139–51), New York: Macmillan.

Henderson, A. and Berla, N. (1994) *A New Generation of Evidence: The Family is Critical to Student Achievement*, Columbia, MD: National Committee for Citizens in Education.

Chapter Two

Building Positive Relationships with Students

Getting to Know Students and their Families

Building positive relationships with your students is essential. Perhaps the most obvious reason for teachers to develop meaningful relationships with students is because a positive teacher–student relationship built on trust, understanding and caring will foster students' co-operation and motivation and increase their learning and achievement at school. Moreover, for those students who come from abusive or neglectful homes, there is research indicating that when there has been a teacher, counsellor or relative in the student's life who has established a close relationship with that student, the long-term outcome for that student has been much better than for those who lack a close relationship with an adult during the early years. Consequently, teachers can make a big difference to a child's future when they spend the extra effort developing positive relationships with students.

Certainly teachers strive for positive relationships with all their students – but as you know it is more difficult to build positive relationships with some children than with others. Why? We have all had experience with difficult children who demand more attention than others, children who are disruptive or unmotivated or defiant, and children who are frequently off-task. For teachers these children are particularly frustrating. It takes only one of these difficult children to bring an entire class to a halt. These are the children who can make us feel bad about ourselves as teachers, causing us to get angry, yell, give excessive punishment, make harsh criticisms or, worse, actively avoid them. Although these responses to their behavior are natural, expressing them doesn't help promote good relationships in the classroom. How can we break the cycle of negative feelings towards some students and work productively with all our students, including the more difficult ones?

Let's think about why some children might be more difficult to manage in the first place. There are many possible reasons. Perhaps they don't perceive teachers in a positive light, and as a result they do not care what you say. They may distrust teachers because of past negative experiences with teachers or other adults. Perhaps they have come from home situations where the adults are unresponsive or even abusive, or too overwhelmed by their own stresses to meet their children's needs. Children from homes like these do not perceive adults as caring; to them, adults are not a source of support and help. Their reaction to this situation may have made them distrustful of adults in general as well as defiant and non-compliant. Or, perhaps they are more difficult because of developmental, neurological or biological problems such as attention problems, hyperactivity, impulsivity, lack of language skills, and so forth. Thus they may be more easily distracted and find it difficult to listen and follow directions. Or perhaps as a result of their background they have low self-esteem and are unmotivated because they lack belief in their own capacity for achievement. Perhaps they're distracted and off-task because they're hungry or tired. Or perhaps they are starved for affection and act up because of the attention that comes their way when they misbehave.

Whatever the underlying reason for the misbehavior, it is important for teachers not to take children's misbehavior or negative attitudes personally or to blame the child for not trying or not caring. Instead, the teacher must look past the disruptive behaviors and reach out to the child. Developing positive relationships with these children is far from simple. As you know, it takes a commitment that must be renewed frequently. It takes consistent effort. It requires that we take a proactive stance, for if we simply react we will usually respond out of frustration. This is easier said than done, but this chapter will show you some concrete ways to build positive relationships with all your students.

Get to Know your Student as an Individual

The first step in building positive relationships is, of course, getting to know your students as individuals and showing an interest in what they are interested in. You can convey your interest in individual students by sending out interest surveys to parents at the beginning of the year, asking for some personal information such as the child's special interests and hobbies, the nature of his or her temperament and personality, what helps the child calm down, what the parents see as the child's strengths and talents, and any particular concerns the parents have regarding their child.

Sample Interest Survey Letter
Regarding Child's Interests

Dear Parents,

Welcome to Year 1! I am excited to get to know your child and looking forward to working with you over the next year to support your child's education. In order to get a 'jump start' in developing a relationship with your child you can help me by filling out the following information and returning it to me as soon as possible. Knowing what activities and interests your child has helps me to develop a curriculum that is exciting and meaningful for your child. Knowing areas you perceive as more difficult for your child helps me to stretch and encourage your child in new areas or places s/he might be tempted to avoid. Thanks for your help. Parents are the most important people in a child's life, and we need to work together for the benefit of your child. With home and school working together I know that each and every student can have the most successful year yet.

Child's Name:

Areas I see as strengths for my child: (academic or social)

Areas I see as more difficult for my child: (academic or social)

What I hope my child will learn this year:

My child's interests are: (include favourite magazines, toys, activities, outings, play-acting, maths, art, computer time, sports, etc.)

Things my child perceives as especially rewarding: (e.g., special privileges, leadership roles, special food, stickers, football cards, films, etc.)

Things about my child that are special: (include pets, siblings, clubs, grandparents or other people involved closely with your child)

Looking forward to a great year!

Of course one sure way of developing a meaningful relationship with a child involves getting to know the child's family and understanding any special circumstances. For example, it is important to know whether there has been a recent divorce, illness or death in the family, what the current living arrangements are, what forms of discipline the parents use, what language is spoken in the home, and what the parents' cultural values and expectations are regarding school. This information can help you better understand the child's perspective and temperament so that you can tailor some of the classroom activities and discussions to include the child's special interests, personality, family situation and culture.

Make Home Visits

Home visits at the beginning of the year (even prior to school starting) are a powerful way to get to know your students and their families and to gain a wealth of information about the child and family in a short period of time. While it may not be feasible to do home visits for all the students in your classroom, it could be invaluable for students who have some special social and/or academic problems. These visits can be initiated with a letter sent to the families (perhaps in the summer so that you can know ahead of time which students will need extra planning) explaining the purpose of the home visit and asking the child to be the host or hostess for the visit. The child then has the task of deciding what to share with the teacher when he or she visits and showing the teacher through the home.

Wouldn't a home visit from a teacher feel intrusive to parents? How do teachers initiate these visits?
When planning a home visit you need to explain to parents why home visits are beneficial (i.e. to get to know the child by seeing their bedroom, favourite animals, etc.). State that home visits help their child feel more comfortable with you when school starts. It is important to reassure parents that is not necessary for them to clean their house for a home visit, and to reassure them that the main reason for doing the home visit is to get to know the child and the family. A survey form sent out in the summer prior to school starting can ask parents to indicate whether they would be agreeable to having a teacher home visit before school starts. By offering a home visit the teacher is extending herself to build a bridge in an effort to promote stronger home–school bonds. This can be particularly

important in the case of parents who may be reluctant to initiate communication with teachers either because of prior negative experiences with schools or teachers or because of cultural or language differences.

Some teachers find that home visits are more comfortable if they are structured. Having a form to fill out with parents can help 'break the ice'. This form can include questions about the child's interests, temperament, special learning needs, and so forth. Some teachers find it fun to take with them on home visits a special cloth bag filled with different items from around the classroom (e.g. doll dress, marking pen, block, Lego, glue stick), from which the child can pick out one thing to keep until the first day of school. When they arrive at school on the first day, the student's first task is to find out where this item belongs.

Make Positive Phone Calls and Send Notes Home

Other strategies that foster supportive and collaborative relationships with students and their parents include making positive phone calls to parents or sending notes home to tell them about something special the child has accomplished that day. For example, you might call parents to tell them about their child sharing something interesting or funny in class or their child's willingness to try something new or their success at a particularly difficult task. In addition you may call the student to give him or her a compliment about some aspect of their school behavior or work.

Invite Parents to Participate

You can also show your commitment to developing positive relationships with your students and their families by issuing invitations to parents to attend informal brown bag lunches or evening potlucks with you at school. These informal gatherings can be used as opportunities for teachers to share their classroom philosophy and discipline plan, to talk about the details of the curriculum, and to discuss ways the parents can support classroom learning through home activities. Parents can be encouraged to ask questions at these gatherings and invited to participate in the classroom by sharing something about themselves and their family (e.g. an interesting trip or special occupation or some aspect of their culture). They also can be invited to assist you by reading to students in class or helping with some classroom activity, or going on a field

Parent-to-Teacher Communication Form

To:

Comments:

From: Date:

Teacher-to-Parent Reply

To:

Comments:

From: Date:

trip and so forth. Parents who cannot get away from work to attend such meetings should not be left out but rather encouraged to participate in other ways such as recommending a special story they would like read in class or sending the teacher notes with any concerns or questions.

Showing You Care

Another way you can get to know your students outside of the classroom is to attend an event in which they are participating – football games, dance or music recitals. Other options include the teacher spending individual time with some students in the lunch room or joining them on the playground during break.

However, when children are at break or lunch, most teachers naturally seize the opportunity as a much needed relaxation time and a chance to refuel after a busy morning. Or they may use this time as an opportunity to catch up on paperwork or to return phone calls from parents. And the teacher's planning time after school is already filled with preparations for the next day's lessons. So you ask, 'Are these home visits and playground or lunch room visits really necessary?' 'Don't I have a right to a personal life?'

While we would not expect teachers to give up all their lunches or after-school time to be with students, finding some time to be with individual students during the year is as essential to teaching as marking papers, preparing curriculum and attending school administrative meetings. And this is especially true in the case of the difficult child or the child who is experiencing social or academic difficulties. Making this extra effort demonstrates your caring and commitment to developing relationships with your students. It contributes to a classroom that will be more co-operative and caring with fewer behavior problems. Such efforts on the part of the teacher create a bank of positive feelings and experiences between the teacher, student and the family that can be drawn upon in times of conflict. In fact, research has shown that students, especially young children, will work for attention from teachers and if you give them positive attention and build a positive relationship with them they will have less need to devise inappropriate ways of forcing you to respond to them (Brophy, 1981, 1996). Teachers have told us that when they devoted extra time at the beginning of the year in building these relationships with children and with their families, they found that later in the year they had more personal time because their classrooms were less stressful and because they were not spending so much time managing behavior problems.

Use Dialogue Journals and Daily Greetings

Another, less time-consuming way of fostering closer relationships with your students and their parents is to use 'dialogue journals'.

When the children first come into the classroom in the morning they are asked to spend 10 minutes writing anything they want in their 'dialogue journals'. Students are encouraged to share this writing with the teacher by putting their diaries in his or her 'in box' or agreed upon place when they are ready for the teacher to read them. The students are given the choice of when or whether they want the teacher to read their dialogues. These diaries are referred to as 'dialogue' journals because the students often will ask the teacher questions to which she or he can respond with comments, questions, stickers, special notes or private chats. The dialogue journal approach allows you to have more personal discussions with each individual student as well as allowing for privacy. (Other children are not allowed to read dialogue journals without the owner's permission.)

While this dialogue journal approach requires that the student be able to read and write, it can be adapted for use with children who do not write or read. This could be accomplished by having the teacher write in the child's journal describing something that happened that day at school, which the parent can then read to the child when he or she picks up the child at the end of the day. The parents may be encouraged to write a response of their own in the journal or to write a response that the child dictates. This approach fosters close communication between parent, teacher and child on a daily basis.

Another way you can promote positive relationships with your students is to greet each of them individually by name when they arrive at school. A high five, handshake or friendly personal word to each student as they arrive in the classroom is an easy and effective way to start the day with a positive contact.

Give Out 'Happy Grams'

Giving out 'happy grams' is another way to build positive relationships with your students. A 'happy gram' is a brief written statement given by the teachers to the child announcing his success or accomplishment or something the teacher has enjoyed about the student's participation in class. Students can be given a box on their desk for their happy grams, and each day you can read them with the students and send them home to their parents. These happy grams may say things like, 'Today I enjoyed hearing about Anna's pet rabbits at home, she is good at sharing with others in class' or, 'Patrick was very friendly today, I noticed when he helped Robby

after he fell down on the pavement' or, 'Gregory controlled his anger and was able to talk about his feelings – he is building good self-control skills'.

Listen to your Students

Finding the time in a hectic day to listen to your students' understandings, perspectives and feelings about their learning is probably one of the most powerful ways you can foster a positive relationship with your students. Carl Rogers originally developed the concept of 'student centred' learning, which is based on the belief that both emotional and cognitive domains of our personalities need to be developed if effective learning is to take place (Rogers, 1983). He offered a daring challenge to teachers to teach less and listen more. Given the demands for meeting particular curriculum goals, it is unlikely all learning will be handed over to students. However, if there is not some attempt on the part of teachers to listen to students' feelings and perceptions and concerns, then there may be a fundamental mismatch between the teacher's goals and the students' motivation to accomplish them. A child may feel significantly relieved and unburdened just by being able to talk to someone about their experiences and worries. Moreover, children's self-esteem and self-confidence can be raised by a teacher who takes an interest and respects them for their expertise and interests. Being listened to by teachers enables children to feel valued and special and fosters a supportive and trusting relationship out of which will flourish academic performance.

Set Up Circle Times to Promote Relationships

Providing regularly scheduled Circle Times (at least once a week) lasting 15 to 30 minutes (length of time depends on the age of the students) is an ideal way of assuring that time is committed to  listening to your students and to giving them opportunities to get to know each other. The 'Listening Bear' game discussed below can be used during Circle Time in the beginning of the year as one way of getting to know more about students' interests and feelings. Sometimes for young children it is helpful if the person speaking or sharing an idea holds a special hand-held object (e.g. stuffed animal or toy microphone) and then everyone in the group knows who is speaking and who is listening. When finished sharing ideas, the speaker passes the microphone to the next child to speak. Regularly scheduled Circle Times that are non-competitive, honest and openly sharing indicate your commitment to developing a classroom family atmosphere consisting of caring and meaningful interpersonal relationships. (See Chapter 9 for more information on how to use Circle Time to help students solve problems and Chapter 10 for information about compliment Circle Time.)

Circle Time Games for Getting to Know each Other

Use a 'Listening Bear': One fun strategy for getting to know your students is a 'Listening Bear'. 'Listening Bear' (an actual teddy bear) goes home each day with a student who has demonstrated exceptional listening in class that day. When Listening Bear is at a student's home he is listening, watching and participating in all that goes on in the family (he may go to restaurants, football games, etc.). The family members are asked to write in the journal about the bear's visit to the family – that is, what the bear saw and did while he was there. If the child cannot write, she or he may dictate to the parents. The next day the student brings Listening Bear back to school with his or her journal that is read aloud to the class. This is a very effective way to get to know students and their families, and it reduces some of the pressure on the child because the story is told from Listening Bear's perspective. It also fosters a home

---

experience between the parents and child which can be shared at school. While it is fun, it also reminds everyone of the importance of listening. (Teachers should be sure that all the students get to take Listening Bear home at some point.) This idea can be modified to address children's specific needs (e.g. using a 'Sharing Bear' for a shy child).

Peaches and Ice-Creams: To make sure students sit beside different students at circle time, alternatively label them a 'peach' or 'ice-cream'. Then the teacher or a chosen child calls out one of the categories (e.g. peaches) and they change seats with someone else.

Finding out similarities: Start the circle time discussion by asking about why it is important to learn more about others. Then pair up each of the students (peaches with ice-creams) and give them 2 minutes to find out two things they both enjoy doing outside school. They both must agree to the activities. Now send around the toy microphone and each child has to say, 'we both like . . . '. If other children agree with this they may say, 'yes', to the activity. This same game can be played by asking children to find out their favourite food, sport, TV programme or colour.

The same game can be played by asking students to find out two ways they might be different – for example, hobbies, food preferences and interests. This game reminds children that everyone is different from each other.

I know your name: Ask the students to stand up in their circle. Ask a child to call out the name of another student (not a best friend) and throw a beanbag to that person. The person who catches the beanbag must call out another child's name and throw it to them. The game continues until all the children have been named.

Who has gone? The children sit in the circle wearing blindfolds. A chosen child who is not wearing a blindfold touches someone from the circle. The other children have to ask the chooser questions to try to guess the identity of the child touched. Each child is allowed one question and one guess. The child who makes the correct identification then becomes the next chooser.

Birthday game: The children are all sitting inward-facing. The teacher calls out any month of the year and all the students who have birthdays that month run round the outside of the circle until they reach their spots and sit down again. The game continues until all the months have been called.

Show Students You Trust Them

Any positive relationships must be built on a foundation of trust. Trust is established gradually, as children discover that you are there for them and will do everything in your power to help them. Difficult children will need massive amounts of support, attention and caring before they will fully trust you – for difficult children have probably received considerable negative feedback in the past as a result of their behavior. Difficult children are accustomed to teachers giving up on them, expressed in behavior such as criticism, put-downs, ridicule, and even ignoring them. To build a positive relationship with difficult students, teachers need to take every opportunity to demonstrate they have confidence in these students' abilities and that they have high expectations for them. For example, you can show your confidence in a difficult child by giving him or her special responsibilities such as passing out the assignments or snacks, or taking attendance, or helping you organize some materials and so forth. Usually the well-behaved students are chosen for these responsibilities leaving the more difficult child with the impression that he is not capable, thus compounding the problem.

Another way to help students feel trusted is to encourage them to help each other. Teachers can channel children's natural preoccupation with each other into positive interactions by giving them opportunities to collaborate together on assignments working in pairs or in small groups. While you can simply allow students to ask for help from another student when they feel a need, this will often leave out the less popular students. The teacher may be wise to pair up students strategically. For example, the child who is somewhat behaviorally difficult may be particularly good in an area such as reading, maths or sports. This child should be encouraged to help a child who is less skilled in this area. When students help each other, their self-esteem rises, and they feel valued and trusted by you.

Allow Students to Make Choices

Another way to promote meaningful relationships with students is to allow them to make choices. So often in the classroom children do not have a choice; their only option is to comply or not comply. But if we can give them more substantial choices as often as possible, we increase the likelihood that they will feel responsible and committed to what goes on in the classroom. Giving them choices also gives them the freedom to say no in appropriate ways and shows them we respect their right to say no. This respect is essential to developing a trusting relationship. Choices can be given to children about such things as what book they would like to read, what activity they choose for free play, and what work chore they do.

Promote Positive Self-Talk in Students Who Lack Confidence in their Ability to Establish Relationships

Some children lack confidence in their ability to establish meaningful relationships. They often have considerable negative self-talk based on their prior school experiences and on how others have responded to them. When faced with a teacher who is sincerely trying to get to know them, they repeatedly think, 'She doesn't really like me, I'm a troublemaker' or 'Teachers don't care about me, it's just a job'. These self-statements decrease their motivation to learn and to develop trusting relationships. It is important for teachers to identify this self-talk, not to take it personally, and to help such children replace these self-defeating statements with more positive self-talk. Teachers can give them statements to repeat to themselves such as, 'I can ask for help, my teacher wants to help me', 'My teacher says I'm good at maths, I'll keep trying', 'I can do it', 'If I think I can, I can', 'With some work I can do it'. Have a rule that for every negative statement children make about themselves, they must counter with two positive statements. This practice helps them develop a more positive self-image.

Students who lack confidence in themselves will be more difficult to get to know because they may be defensive, unresponsive, and will probably reject the efforts you make to reach out to them. This is to be anticipated and expected when working with a student who has experienced parental rejection, abuse and deprivation. These are the students who need a teacher who refuses to be rejected by them and who consistently, patiently and repeatedly offers caring, encouragement and hope. These are the students whose teacher can make the most difference to their future.

Share Something Personal about Yourself

One teacher shared with us an experience she had with several students who were reluctant to volunteer any personal information about themselves either individually or in class. The teacher approached the problem by sharing with them some personal information about herself and telling them some funny experiences that happened to her when she was growing up. She said the children became engaged in asking her questions about these events, which eventually led to their disclosing more about themselves. In this teacher's example, she is modelling self-disclosure and a willingness to be known to her students. The result can be a child's greater feeling of comfort with the teacher as well as greater intimacy among classmates.

The Importance of Play with your Students

One of the most powerful ways for promoting positive relationships is through teacher play times with students. Why? When teachers are playful with students and engage in play activities with them, the relationship between teachers and students is temporarily made more equal. That is, instead of the usual hierarchical relationship where the teacher dominates or is in charge of what the child must do in the classroom, in the play situation the teacher and student are having fun together as equals – in fact, the teacher may be following the students' directions. This opportunity for reciprocity in any relationship serves to build intimacy and trust. It also can promote co-operation, for the teacher can model compliance to the students' suggestions. Not only does teacher play with students foster positive feelings towards the teacher and contribute to a student's motivation to learn and please his or her teacher, but teachers, too, will find that it makes their job more fun.

It is important to remember that children learn through play. Play is a time when children can try out ideas, take risks, try on different roles, share feelings and thoughts, be intimate. It provides a safe context for children to learn.

Is there such a thing as too much play in the classroom?
Some teachers have expressed fear that if they are playful in the classroom they will lose control of their students – that is, the students will become too silly and wild. While being playful can be a very effective way of promoting close relationships with students, it is still important for the teacher to be able to set limits and provide structure. Even if play does get a little out of hand in a classroom and a teacher needs to rein it in, this, in itself, is a helpful learning process for students. Since young children are emotionally labile and can have difficulty regulating their emotions, it is helpful for them to learn how to make the transition from silly fun time to

calmer activities. The teacher models this regulatory process for them, and students learn by being led through it.

Another fear is that students will not respect a teacher who is playful. Some teachers are reluctant to sing or 'be silly' because they feel embarrassed and worry that their students will laugh at them. For these teachers, frequent practice at being playful with students will soon dispel the embarrassment and replace the fear of being laughed at with the students' delight. Certainly being playful does not mean allowing disrespect in interactions. The paradox is that we often find that the playful teachers actually have created an environment where there is more respect in the classroom because teachers show students the respect of giving them opportunities to take the lead. Moreover when these playful teachers need to be assertive and impose consequences for some infraction, the contrast in their demeanour from the playful teacher to the serious teacher gets the students' immediate attention and compliance.

A related concern for some teachers is that their colleagues or the students' parents will perceive their playfulness as unprofessional – not taking their job or the school work seriously. This fear of disapproval from others can dampen a teacher's efforts to be creative and experiment with playful approaches to teaching. We urge teachers to remember it is this very creativity and willingness to take risks and to approach students at their developmental level that is the 'art of teaching'.

Finally, some teachers argue that there is so much curriculum and 'work' to cover that there is no time for play. This reflects the widespread belief in our society that the time adults and children spend together is frivolous and unproductive. Being playful with children should not be perceived as separate from curriculum; it is, rather an integral part of curriculum – a process that enhances a child's learning or work. Remember if teachers are serious all of the time, if school is no fun, students will come to dislike school. The ultimate goal of schooling in the first years is to help students perceive school as enjoyable, a place where students and teachers value and trust each other, a place where individual differences and learning styles are appreciated and respected, a place of sharing and growth.

Sometimes it is difficult for teachers to be playful with certain students – particularly those who are impulsive, non-compliant, aggressive or disrespectful with teachers. It can be difficult to let go the negative feelings about these problem children and be playful with them. These are the very students who probably have had very few play opportunities or other positive experiences in their lives either with peers or with adults; they are the ones who need it most. While it may seem counter-intuitive, investing time in play with these children (and building a relationship) will lead eventually to increased respect and co-operation.

Making Play More Effective

Be playful yourself
One idea to foster playfulness is for teachers to keep a special box that contains items such as a wig, glasses with springing eyeballs, a microphone, funny T-shirts and so forth. The teacher can surprise students when they arrive by wearing something from this box, or can turn to it when students' attention is wavering. For example, the teacher might put on the wig and pull out the microphone to announce a special instruction or transition to a new activity. This playfulness serves to keep children engaged so that they can be learning.

Follow your students' lead in play
Some teachers try to structure play by giving lessons on what to do – how to build the castle the right way, to make the perfect valentine, or complete the puzzle correctly. Possibly they believe that in this way they are making the play a worthwhile activity. Unfortunately, the result of this undue emphasis on the product of play is a string of commands and corrections that usually make the experience unrewarding for both students and teachers.

The first step for these free play times with students is to follow their lead, ideas and imagination, rather than imposing your own. Don't structure or organize activities for them by giving commands or instructions. Don't try to teach them anything. Instead, imitate their actions and do what they ask you to do. You'll soon discover that when you sit back and give students a chance to exercise their imagination, they become more involved and interested in playing, as well as more creative. This approach fosters students' ability to play and think independently. Moreover, when teachers follow students' lead, they show respect for their ideas and demonstrate compliance with their requests. This modelling of compliance to appropriate requests from students helps students become more compliant with teachers' requests in other situations. Moreover, it contributes to reciprocity in the relationship – a power balance, so to speak. Such reciprocity leads to closer and more meaningful relationships.

Be an appreciative audience

It is important to be a good audience when you play with your students. Some teachers become so involved in playing themselves that they ignore the child or take over what he or she is doing. It is important when playing with students to focus on them instead of getting involved in what you are doing. These play times may be one of the few times in their interactions with you where they can be in control. It is also one of the few times whey they can have you applaud what they are doing without a lot of rules and restrictions getting in the way. Try to think of yourself as an appreciative audience. Sit back and watch whatever your students create and praise their efforts with enthusiasm.

Use descriptive commenting

Teachers have a tendency to ask a string of questions while playing: 'What colour is that?' 'What shape is that?' 'Where does it go?' 'What are you making?' These questions are usually intended to help their students learn more. All too often it has the reverse effect, causing them to become defensive, silent and reluctant to talk freely. In fact, question-asking, especially when the teacher knows the answer, is really a type of command since it requires the student to perform. Queries that ask students to define what they are making often occur before they have even thought about the final product or had a chance to explore their ideas. The emphasis ends up being on the product rather than the process of play.

Teachers can show interest in students' play by simply describing and providing supportive comments about what they are doing. This approach actively encourages language development. For instance, you might say, 'You're painting that a bright, beautiful purple. Now you're thinking patiently about what colour to use next. You look very pleased with your picture', and so forth. Soon you will find that your students spontaneously imitate your commenting. You can then offer further encouragement and they will feel excited about their accomplishments. Descriptive commenting is a running commentary on your students' activities and often sounds like a sports announcer's play-by-play description of a game. Did you notice also in this example that the teacher commented on the child's feelings and patience as well as the actual art work? This approach helps students to develop a rich array of emotional language which assists children in regulating their emotions and learning how to express their feelings in appropriate ways. Labelling students when they are playing in ways that are peaceful, calm, thoughtful, happy or helpful will be especially important for the child who is by temperament impulsive, angry and hyperactive. Usually such children are noticed and commented upon by adults mostly when they are angry or out of control. These children may even fail to recognize that there are times when they are capable of calm and happy play.

Because descriptive commenting is a novel way of communicating, you may feel uncomfortable when you first try to speak this way. The discomfort will diminish as you practise in a variety of situations. If you are persistent, you will find that your students come to love this kind of attention and that this communication style enhances their emotion vocabulary as well as their attention span for an activity.

If you do ask questions, be sure to limit the number and to complete the teaching loop. This means that when you ask a question, you follow with positive and non-critical feedback and encouragement. Children should be praised for independent actions and given a chance to respond without interference.

Conclusion

Teachers can make a big difference to a child's future when they spend the extra effort and time developing positive relationships with all their students. This is not an easy task and requires a teacher's consistent commitment to this process and a willingness to become intimate with students and their families. However when a teacher does this, she becomes a powerful model, because by demonstrating her caring she not only is modelling important social relationships skills for her students to learn, but she is contributing to their self-esteem and emotional development. This emotional security in young children's relationships with their teachers is necessary for them to be able to feel confident to try out their imaginations, test new ideas, make mistakes, solve problems, communicate their hopes as well as their frustrations, and gradually gain academic skills.

To Sum Up

Show students you care by:

- giving them a personal greeting each day when they arrive
- asking about their feelings, e.g. dialogue journals

- asking about their life outside of school, e.g. Listening Bear
- listening to them
- eating in the cafeteria occasionally with students
- recognizing birthdays in some way
- sending cards and positive messages home, e.g. happy grams
- finding out about their hobbies and special talents, e.g. interest surveys
- making home visits
- sharing something personal about yourself
- spending time playing with them – at break or during free classroom time
- establishing positive relationships with every child regardless of their academic or social abilities
- getting to know their parents through home visits and classroom meetings
- calling parents periodically to report their child's success or accomplishments.

Show students you believe in them by:

- identifying negative self-talk
- promoting positive self-talk
- communicating your belief they can succeed
- making 'I can' cans out of empty juice cans and drop strips of paper in them on which students have written skills they have learned – e.g. maths facts, spelling words, sharing with others, helping. (This is also useful to show parents the child's progress.)
- making phone calls to students to applaud their special efforts or accomplishments
- helping every child in the classroom to appreciate others' special talents and needs
- following their lead, listening carefully to their ideas and being an 'appreciative audience' at times.

Show students you trust them by:

- inviting students to help with daily tasks and classroom responsibilities
- offering curriculum choices
- encouraging collaboration among students
- encouraging students to help each other
- sharing your thoughts and feelings with them.

References

Brophy, J. E. (1981) On praising effectively, *The Elementary School Journal*, 81, 269–75.

Brophy, J. E. (1996) *Teaching Problem Students*, New York: Guilford.

Rogers, C. (1983) *Freedom to Learn for the 80's*, Columbus, OH: Merrill.

Chapter Three

The Proactive Teacher

When students are disruptive or behave in ways that are counterproductive to learning, it's all too easy for teachers to automatically react emotionally. The understandable impatience and frustration we feel towards negative behavior in the classroom undermines our ability to think strategically about how best to respond in order to modify the child's behavior. Rather than reacting to problem behaviors when they arise, teachers can anticipate the kinds of classroom conditions that are likely to produce disruptive or disengaged behaviors and take *proactive* steps to prevent them. Research has shown that proactive teachers structure the classroom environment and the school day in ways that make problem behaviors less likely to occur (Doyle, 1990; Gettinger, 1988; Good and Brophy, 1994). They establish schedules, routines, consistent limit setting and norms of behavior that help students feel calm and safe and likely to succeed. Indeed, classrooms that have few clearly communicated standards or rules are more likely to have children who misbehave. In this chapter, you will find some of the proactive strategies used by teachers to help create a safe and predictable environment for their students to learn and a place where problem behaviors are less likely to occur.

Provide a Predictable and Safe Learning Environment

Classroom structure provides the basic framework which supports the child's ability to learn. A proactive approach includes predictable classroom routines and schedules, how transitions are handled, as well as clear guidelines for the expected behaviors.

Classroom Rules Should Be Stated in Terms of Observable Behaviors

Classroom rules and expectations should be clearly spelled out, posted in the classroom, and reinforced when students follow them. There should be no more than five to seven rules that are stated in positive terms. For example, a rule such as 'Stay in your seat' is clear, whereas 'no fooling around' is vague and focuses on something negative. The rules should be stated in terms of observable behaviors, that is behaviors you can see. For example, 'Keep your hands to yourself' is preferable to 'Show respect' or 'Be nice' because a child will have a clear mental image of what specific behavior is expected. Similarly, 'Complete all homework and put it on my desk the next morning' is preferable to 'Be responsible about your homework' because the required behavior is clear and unambiguous. Rules such as 'Be a good citizen' or 'Be responsible' are ineffective because they are ambiguous, and it is unclear what behaviors are being asked for.

Involve Students in Discussion about Rules

Teachers can involve students, even those as young as age 4, in developing the classroom rules and discussing why they are important. For example, the first day of class the teacher should have a discussion with her students to derive the important classroom rules. The teacher can start by asking, 'What do you think our classroom rules should be?' As the students generate ideas for the rules, the teacher can ask them why the rule is particularly important. For example, you could explain, 'Rules help students feel safe and protect your rights to be treated with respect'. Then help them describe the rule in terms of the positive expected behaviors. By collaborating with students about the rules, they will feel more ownership in them and be more committed to adhering to them. Usually students will generate all the important rules, but if they don't, you can always add the missing ones and then lead a discussion about why they are important.

In addition to establishing rules it is essential to discuss the consequences for breaking the rules. Students need to know exactly what behaviors will result in a loss of privilege, Time Out or cool-off time away from the class. It can be explained that the behavior they use involves them making a choice about whether to follow the rules or not and that this choice can result in a consequence. (See Chapters 7 and 8 for consequences for breaking rules.)

Teach and Role Play the Rules One at a Time

Once the rules have been discussed on the first day of class, then the teacher can take one rule each week to carefully review it for the class. Some of the most common rules for young children are as follows:

- Keep your hands and feet to yourself (manners rule).
- Enter the classroom quietly, hang up your coat, and sit at your desk.
- Put up a quiet hand to ask a question (talking rule).
- Arguments and problems should be talked about (problem-solving rule).
- Speak quietly and politely to each other.
- Hands washed before lunch.

Let us say the first rule the teacher focuses on is entering the classroom quietly. The teacher asks one of the students to give a demonstration of how to enter the classroom quietly in the morning. Once the student has demonstrated this, several other students may also take a turn, each receiving teacher praise and approval for doing it correctly. The role plays and practice ensure that the students understand exactly what behaviors are required in order to follow the rule.

For young children, the rules will initially need to be stated and described very specifically. For older children they may eventually be categorized into general rules. For example, keeping hands to self, entering the classroom quietly, staying in seat and walking in the hallway may be called the 'movement rule'. Or, speaking politely, sharing and washing hands might be called the 'manners rule'.

Planning Positive Consequences for Following Rules

When a rule is first being taught, the teacher needs to respond with praise and encouragement every time s/he notices the students following the rule. The teacher may even set up an incentive programme (e.g. tickets, stickers) to help students who have particular difficulties remembering the talking rule or the movement rule and so forth. 'That is fantastic, you remembered the rule about entering the room quietly and sitting on the carpet area facing the board. Thanks. You get a bonus sticker for that!'

Carefully Consider Physical Placement of Particular Students

Another important aspect of classroom structure is consideration of where each student is sitting in relationship to the teacher. All children need to be close to the teacher, but this is especially true for inattentive, disruptive children who are easily distracted. Sitting them close to you makes it easier to signal or redirect them to a task without disrupting the rest of the group.

Establish Predictable Routines and Planning for Transitions

Making a transition from an interesting activity to another activity (perhaps one that is less interesting) can be difficult for all young children, but especially for children who are inattentive, impulsive and distractible. Teachers can help make a smoother transition by preparing children ahead of time for the upcoming transition, and by having predictable routines surrounding the transitions.

Uncertainty about routines leads to behavior problems, while predictable routines help avert problems.

One way to make the routine predictable and clear is for teachers to post the daily classroom schedule on the wall so that children know that Circle Time is followed by small group activities that are followed by recess and snack. For young children it is important to include visual pictures of each activity so that non-readers can understand the agenda. For some anxious or inattentive students we have found it helpful to post the daily schedule on the student's desk with a place for them to check when moving from one activity to the next.

One way to help with transitions between activities is to prepare students for the end of an activity by saying, 'In 5 minutes we will be finished with art time and will go to recess' or, 'When the bell goes off in 3 minutes we will need to put away our books', and so forth. For young children who don't have a concept of time, music, switching the lights off and on or a standard clapping rhythm also help signal the change from one activity to another. If there is a change in schedule on a particular day, the teacher can help the child who has difficulties with transitions by asking him or her to physically change the order or placement of the events on the daily schedule posted. For example, the student could replace the agenda item that depicts small group activity with the new activity, such as a field trip.

In addition to having a familiar, predictable routine for transitions, it is also helpful initially for the students to practise and rehearse exactly what will happen during these transitions. You can say, 'Before we go to music, what is the first thing we are going to do?' or 'After we get into the cafeteria, what will you do?' or 'Before you go in, remember to hang your coats, hats and lunch boxes in your cubicles'. You might want to take preschool children back out into the corridor for a second practice if you think they haven't understood the steps. Positive practice helps these routines to become automatic.

Greetings and Farewells

Beginning and ending the day are important transitions that also should have predictable routines. It is important to give a welcoming greeting each day as well as a positive farewell. Learning and using the students' names as quickly as possible is very important at every age. You might want to use name tags, put their names on their work tables or play name games.

Give Hyperactive and Inattentive Students Opportunities to Move in Appropriate Ways

All children who have been sitting for a long time, and adults too for that matter, need some time for movement. This is especially true for the hyperactive and impulsive or inattentive student. We suggest that such a student will need a 'wiggle space' in the classroom – a place to go if s/he needs to move around quietly for a few minutes. This place may be a quiet area of the room or a particular place marked with adhesive tape on the floor. Children can decide if they need to go into this space and can go without interrupting the class activities. Thus they are taking responsibility for going to the wiggle space and returning.

Sometimes teachers worry that everyone in the class will want to go to the wiggle space or that if they permitted such a procedure it would cause a great deal of disruption to the entire classroom. However, the teacher must establish clear rules about the use of the wiggle space – for instance, only one child allowed in the wiggle space at a time! – and then hold students responsible for following the rules. It is important that the teacher be clear about the rules – for example, defining clearly who can use the space and how many times a day one person can use it. The teacher may even decide to reserve the wiggle space for only one or two children who have particular difficulty staying seated. These students may be given a certain number of wiggle space tickets each day so that they can choose when they want to trade in a ticket for a chance to go to the wiggle space.

Use Creative Ways of Getting and Holding Children's Attention

Most young children have trouble listening to teachers, especially if they are absorbed in an activity. Consequently, it is important for teachers to use innovative strategies to catch and hold their students' attention. If a child's attention is wandering, he or she will not hear the instructions and consequently will be further removed from the task at hand. For example, praising the students who are following the teacher's directions can signal the other children to do the same in order to get the same attention.

Teachers need multiple ways of engaging children and ensuring they are listening to the instructions. Strategies such using jokes, varying their tone of voice (e.g. whispering often gets children's attention), doing something funny such as wearing weird goggles or a hat to give a particular instruction, or asking their students to read the teacher's mind, or making a game out of it by playing Simon Says or asking the children to mimic their clap all serve to get the students' attention. For example, a teacher asking the students who are wearing green or who have curly hair to answer the next question is a simple yet effective way of getting students involved in the discussion.

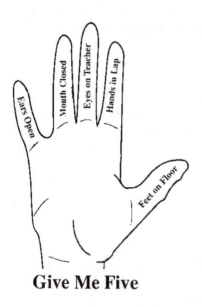

Give Me Five

Another strategy to get students' immediate attention is to use the 'give me five' freeze signal. This signal, which is taught to students, uses each finger on the hand to represent a behavior – hands in lap, feet on floor, eyes on teacher, mouth closed and ears listening. In the beginning when young children are learning what 'give me five' means, they may have a picture of a hand placed on their desk. A sticker is placed on each finger concept that they remember (e.g. listening, feet on floor etc.). Indeed, this is the challenge of teaching young children – coming up with new and interesting ways of engaging children in the learning process.

Working the Room – Monitoring and Scanning

Research has shown that the more time a teacher spends behind her desk, the more the students will be disruptive and off-task in the classroom. Walking around the classroom and providing vigilant monitoring and visual and auditory scanning is key to effective classroom management. Several things happen when the teacher walks around. First, the teacher can praise the group and individual children as s/he sees their work in progress. Second, the teacher can catch problems early and can stop and help students as necessary. This leads to less frustration on the part of students and more support for their learning efforts.

Walking around the room also permits the teacher to monitor noise levels and off-task behaviors. The teacher can point to the visual cues of quiet hand up, working hard or the noise meter to unobtrusively signal children they need to quiet down or attend to their work. Actually, simply walking over to the area of the room where the noise is occurring (usually the back left corner) will often stop the noise without any verbal or non-verbal reminder.

Remember it is also important that the teacher has arranged her classroom furniture and desks in such a way that she can scan the room at any time and have every child in her view. (See also Chapter 6.)

Effective Limit Setting and Redirecting

When you do not get the compliance you expect from your students remember that all students will test their teachers' rules and commands. This is especially true if teachers have been inconsistent in the past and not enforced their rules. Be prepared for such testing, as it is only by breaking a rule that children come to learn that it is really in effect. Consistent consequences for misbehavior will teach students that good behavior is expected. Research shows that normal children fail to comply with their teachers' requests about one-third of the time and difficult children non-comply at even higher rates (Forehand and McMahon, 1981). Young children may argue, scream or throw temper tantrums when a desired activity is prohibited. School-age children, too, may argue, swear or protest when an activity or object is denied. This is normal behavior, and a healthy expression of a child's need for independence and autonomy. When such protests happen, don't take them as a personal attack. Remember, your students are simply testing your rules to see if you are going to be consistent. If you are inconsistent, they are probably going to test even harder the next time. Try to think about your students' protests as learning experiences, ways that they can explore the limits of their environment and learn what behaviors are appropriate and inappropriate.

However, it is also possible that part of the reason for non-compliance may lie in the way the rules or instructions are phrased. Instructions that are vague, such as, 'Settle down' or, 'Show me you're ready' are difficult for a child to follow, for they don't tell the child what behavior is expected. Commands that are expressed as criticisms, such as '7-year-olds don't do that!' or 'Why can't you follow the directions?' or 'You never listen', are more likely to lead to resentment and opposition than to desired behavior. Negative commands that say what behavior you want stopped but not what behavior you want to see, for example, 'Cut that out' or 'Stop running', leave it up to the child to decide what to do instead. And commands expressed as questions, such as 'Do you want to put your name on your paper?', confuse children, because they can't tell whether they are being given a command or a choice. Teachers should strive for clear, specific commands and instructions expressed in positive terms. Here are some ways which research has shown will maximize the effectiveness of your limit setting (e.g. Van Houten *et al.*, 1982).

Settle your Class First – Use Descriptive Comments

Before you can give your class instructions about a transition, teach a new idea, or give a reminder of a rule, it is necessary for your class to be quietly settled. All too often teachers yell out instructions to students when the classroom is noisy and unsettled. Thus not only will many students not hear the instructions, but your students will learn that this noise level is the expected classroom behavior. It is essential that teachers pause and wait for the class to quiet or remind them that you are waiting for all eyes on you before you will proceed. For example, the teacher might say, 'There are several people in the back talking, I will wait until they stop so everyone can hear.' This type of descriptive comment is not intrusive and often makes it unnecessary to give a direct command or positive correction regarding the noisy students.

Reduce the Number of Commands

Few teachers are aware of the actual number of direct commands they give their students. Would it surprise you to hear that our research indicates that the average teacher gives approximately thirty-five commands in half an hour? In classrooms where children have more behavior problems, the number rises to more than sixty commands in half an hour. Moreover, research has shown that as the number of teacher commands, particularly critical or negative commands, increase in a classroom so do the number of behavior problems (Brophy, 1996). Frequent commands, then, do not improve a child's behavior. Therefore, it is essential for you to evaluate both the number and type of commands that you give your students and only use those that are necessary and that you are prepared to follow through on.

Child in a command storm

Often when a few students misbehave and refuse to follow directions, teachers respond by repeating and escalating direct commands, even when some students are already doing as requested. For example, the teacher says, 'Please put away your reading books now' and some students begin to put away their books while others continue reading. The teacher, focusing on those who are not following the instructions, becomes irritated and repeats the command a second and third time. She says, 'I said put those books away now! Haven't you put those books away yet? Can't you hear?' However, if the teacher had praised the students who were following her directions, the second command might not have been necessary. Certainly her escalating negativism and confrontational manner is not likely to induce co-operation in difficult children.

Sometimes teachers give commands about issues that are not important. They might say, 'Colour that frog green, not yellow', 'Stop wiggling', or 'Stop fiddling with your hair'. These orders are unnecessary. Students should be allowed to decide such matters for themselves rather than become involved in a battle of will with teachers. It's important to remember that if teachers are constantly giving commands, it is impossible to follow through on all of them. The result is that confusing messages are given to students about the importance of commands. Moreover, difficult students respond least well to excessively authoritarian approaches that can contribute to their 'digging in their heels' in defiance.

Before giving a command, think about whether or not this is an important issue, and whether you are willing to follow through with the consequences if the student doesn't comply. One exercise that can be helpful is to write down the important rules for your classroom. You will probably find that you have five or ten that are 'unbreakable'. These are the ones you have posted where the entire classroom can see them. In this way, everyone, including temporary teachers and aides, will know what the rules are. Such a list might include:

- Helmets must be worn when riding tricycles on the playground.
- Hitting is not allowed. Be gentle with friends (no hitting).
- Talk with an inside polite voice in class.
- Walk in the classroom.

Once you have clarified the important rules, you will find not only that you are more precise when you state them but also that you are able to reduce other, unnecessary commands. The result is that your students will learn that your commands are important and compliance is expected.

One Command at a Time

Sometimes teachers string commands together in a chain, without giving the student time to comply with the first command before going on to several more. For young children, this can result in information overload. For example, the teacher says to her preschool classroom, 'It's time for recess. I want you to put your markers away, pick up your papers, go in the hall and get your coats on, and wear your boots because it's raining.' A series of commands such as this is difficult for youngsters to remember. Most can retain only one or two things at a time. Another problem with rapid commands is that the teacher is not able to praise the students for complying with any of the individual commands. This string of commands usually results in non-compliance partly because the student simply can't comply with everything, partly because there is no reinforcement for compliance.

Another type of chain command involves the teacher saying the same thing over and over again as if the child has not heard it. Many teachers repeat the same instruction four or five times, and their students quickly learn that there is no real need to comply until the fifth time. Moreover, chain commands reinforce noncompliant behavior by the amount of attention constant repetition provides.

Instead of repeating commands as if you expect your students to ignore them, state your command once. Say it slowly and clearly and then wait to see whether or not the students will comply. If it helps you to wait, you might want to count silently as you watch to see how your students will respond. This will help you resist nagging.

Give Realistic Commands

Occasionally teachers give commands that are unrealistic or not appropriate for the age of their students. For instance, a preschool teacher asks Lisa, a 4-year-old girl, to share her favourite stuffed animal with another child in the classroom or, a teacher of 7- to 8-year-olds expects Carl, an inattentive, impulsive and uncoordinated child, to do a sewing activity which involves threading a needle. These requests will fail because they're not realistic for Lisa's age or Carl's developmental ability. Other examples of unrealistic or inappropriate commands include expecting a 4-year-old to keep the play kitchen area clean, a 3-year-old to be quiet while adults have a long discussion, or children of any age to eat everything on their plate all the time.

Give commands that you believe your students are capable of carrying out successfully. Don't set up students for failure and yourself for frustration. And if you have a student who is inattentive, hyperactive and impulsive, it is especially important to give instructions that are realistic. You shouldn't expect such a child to do a particularly frustrating activity without help, or to stay still for a long while. A more realistic expectation would be staying at the table for 5 or 10 minutes.

Give Clear Commands

While some teachers have too many rules and commands, others dislike establishing any rules are vague and indirect about rules, disguising their commands. Some examples of common vague or nonspecific commands are 'Watch out', 'Be careful', 'Be nice', 'Be good', 'Knock it off', 'Settle down', or 'Show me you are ready'. These statements are confusing because they do not tell the student what behavior is expected.

Another type of unclear command is that which is stated as a descriptive comment. For instance, the teacher says to a student at lunch time, 'Oh Denise, you're spilling your milk. You'd better watch out!' Or another teacher looks out the window and says, 'Billy, your bike is still not put away!' In addition to lacking clarity, these statements contain an implied criticism. Not only is it difficult to get a child to comply with this type of statement, but the critical aspect of such an approach is likely to breed resentment. Direct commands ('Hold the milk glass with both hands', 'Put your bike away') are clear and positive messages to your students.

Another type of unclear direction is the 'Let's' command: 'Let's finish drawing', 'Let's clean up the art table'. This can be confusing for young children especially if the teachers have no intention of becoming involved. For instance, a teacher who has been doing a play dough sculpture project with the students now wants them to put away the clay. She says, 'Let's put the play dough away'. If she isn't willing to help them, they probably won't do as requested, and she will become cross with them for not complying with her unclear command.

Be specific about the behavior you want from the student when you give a command. If Jenny puts up her hand with a question, instead of saying 'Just a minute', you might say 'Wait until I finish reading this page with Nick, then I'll come over and answer your question'. Don't tell Robbie to 'Be careful', when he is spilling juice say, 'Use both hands to pour the juice into your glass'. Instead of 'Let's put the toys away' say, 'Please put the toys away'.

Examples of Effective Commands and Rule Reminders

'Walk slowly thanks'

'Keep your hands to yourself'   'Face the front and listen, please'

'Talk softly'   'Keep the paint on the paper'
'Play quietly'
'Mouths quiet'   'Wash your hands'
                                   'Sharing, thanks'
                                   'Helping, thanks'
'Remember to put your chairs   'Waiting, thanks'
under your desks'
'Remember our class rule for
quiet hands up'
'Please put the toys away'
'Talk with your inside voice'
'Cross your legs and face this
way'

'No you can't work on the
computer, you haven't
finished your maths'
'Put it either in your
backpack or on my desk'
'I'll listen when you're using
quiet voices'

Examples of Unclear, Vague or Critical Commands

'Let's put away the toys'
'Don't yell'
'Stop running'
'Why don't you put your
name on your paper?'
'Stop whining'
'Didn't I tell you to pick that
up?'
'Can't you stay in your seat?
I've told you before'
'You made a mess! Can't you
be careful? Go wash up, you
are not doing that now'
'Are you supposed to be
doing that?'
'You, I mean you, get over
here – now! Listen I don't
care how you speak to him
but in my class . . . '
'Do you want to run the
lesson, eh?'
'I've shown you how to do
that a hundred times, here I'll
show you again'
'I'm fed up, get over here,
don't argue with me, go'
'Why haven't you started to
work?'
'Why can't you . . . '
'How many times do I have
to tell you to . . . '
'You never . . . '

'Why don't we . . . ?'
'You over there, shut up'
'Let's don't do that anymore'
'Be nice, be good, be careful'
'Watch it'

Give 'Do' Commands – Avoid Question Commands

Question commands can be particularly confusing for children. For example, the teacher who says to a student who is wandering around the room, 'Are you supposed to be over there? I didn't think so' or, 'Are you supposed to be sharpening your pencil now, where are you supposed to be?' At issue here is the subtle distinction between a request and command. A request implies that the student has the option of choosing whether or not to do what is requested. If you expect your students to comply but phrase your command as a question, you are providing a confusing message. Another problem with question commands is that you may find yourself backed into a corner. If you say, 'Would you like to put the books away now?' or 'Do you want to put your name on your paper?' and your student says 'No', you are stuck. The student can't tell whether he or she is being given a command or a choice. You asked a question, received an answer you didn't want, and now must decide how to convince your student to put the book away or put his name on his paper.

Teachers should strive for clear, specific, direct commands expressed in positive terms rather than as questions. Give 'do' commands, with the verb at the beginning of the sentence: 'Please come and sit in your seat', 'Write your name on the top of your papers', 'Put the books away under your desk', 'Walk slowly', 'Speak with your inside voice', 'Face this way'. Here the action verb is the first word in the command and, therefore, your students cannot miss it.

Give Polite and Positive Commands, Avoid Criticisms and Negative Labels

If teachers are too angry when they give a command, they may inadvertently encourage non-compliance by yelling or including a criticism with their command. For example, a teacher might say, 'Billy, why don't you sit still for once in your life!' Or he might tell Billy to sit still in a sarcastic tone of voice. Or he might say, '7-year-olds don't do that!' Or 'Why can't you follow directions? When will you ever learn? How many times do I have to tell you?' Sometimes a frustrated teacher might use a negative global label about an entire class such as, 'These kids are idiots', or 'These kids always . . . ' or 'These kids never . . . '. Labelling and put-downs are included with a command as a way of venting frustration because a student or a classroom has not done something that the teacher has asked them to do many times before. However, the feeling that is expressed behind the teacher's command is just as important as the actual words that are used. The student who senses the teacher's frustration and discouragement may choose not to comply as a way of retaliating for the criticism.

Maintaining a positive or encouraging tone is especially important in the case of students with behavior problems. All of us either 'shut down' or become upset and defensive when we hear negative comments or a negative tone, but these students are usually hypersensitive to negativity from adults. When they hear negative comments or a negative tone of voice from an adult, they may dysregulate emotionally, i.e. become disengaged, anxious, frustrated and disorganized. As a result they will not be able to process the learning or hear instructions.

Avoid criticizing, yelling, or confronting your students when you give a command. Negative commands and ridicule cause them to feel incompetent, defensive and less inclined to comply. Students' feeling about themselves as worthwhile people should be considered at least as important as obedience. Commands should be stated positively, politely, quietly and with respect. If you find yourself becoming negative with a particular student or with the class as a whole, sometimes this is a good time to do the unexpected or to use humour – for this can break the negative cycle. Developing a positive and respectful verbal style is something to be worked at – it doesn't always come naturally. Another advantage to using respectful language with students is that you are treating them as if they are able to make good choices and with a positive expectation.

Use Student's Name

Always use the student's name when giving directions. This will capture the student's attention and will assure that he knew the direction was being given specifically to him.

Move in Close to Student – Gain Eye Contact

The average teacher gives a command from 20 feet away, 'you there, you there, . . . ' and this causes problems because the child may not realize the command was directed at her and the teacher is so far away that she cannot easily ensure follow through with the command. Therefore it is recommended that commands be given when the teacher is about 3 feet from the student. For example, 'I need your attention' with a hand on the student's shoulder is more likely to achieve student compliance than a command yelled from 20 feet away. Research has shown that just gaining eye contact with the student will improve compliance significantly.

However, forcing eye contact with statements such as 'Look at me when I'm talking to you' is unhelpful. It is better to ask for eye contact, and if it isn't given, to speak to the ears. Extended eye contact can be confrontational. Moreover, in some cultures, eye contact with a person of authority is considered disrespectful.

Use Start Commands

A stop command is also a type of negative statement because it tells a student what not to do. 'Stop shouting', 'Don't do that', 'Stop it', 'Shut up', 'Cut it out', 'Enough of that', 'No you can't because you've left a mess' are all stop commands. Not only are these critical of the student, but they focus on the misbehavior instead of telling the child how to behave correctly.

Sports psychologists have found that if the coach tells the bowler 'Don't throw a fast ball', a fast ball is just what the bowler is likeliest to throw; not out of spite but simply because that is what the coach's words have made him visualize. It's worth making every effort, therefore, to give positive and 'do' commands that detail the behavior you want from your child, rather than 'don't' commands. Instead of saying 'Don't call out when I'm teaching' or 'Stop wandering around' or 'Don't yell out' say 'Please speak quietly', or 'Stay in your seat please' or 'Quiet hands up please' or 'Face this way and listen please'. Whenever a student does something you don't like, think of what alternative behavior you want and then phrase your command to focus on that positive behavior.

Allow Time to Comply

'No-opportunity' commands do not allow students a chance to comply with requests. For instance, Ninya's teacher says 'Put away the books', and then he starts putting them away himself before she complies. Or Rino's teacher says 'Get down from that swing' and removes him from the swing before waiting to see if he will comply. While immediate compliance is sometimes necessary, especially around safety issues, for the most part children deserve an opportunity to succeed at complying.

After giving a command, pause. If it helps you wait patiently, you might want to count silently and slowly to five. If the student has still not complied, then you can consider this non-compliance. However, when you give students time to comply, you will often find that they do. Waiting after you give a command also forces you to pay attention to whether the student has complied or not. Then, you can reward compliance or follow through with consequences for noncompliance.

Allow for Lead Time

Some teachers give commands abruptly, without any warning. Picture the scene: Jenny is totally absorbed at the art easel painting. Suddenly the teacher walks into the room and tells her to put away her paints. What happens next? Probably much unhappiness, protesting and resistance from Jenny.

A proactive teacher gives warnings and reminders regarding upcoming transitions or when students are starting to diverge from expected behavior, as well as reinforcement for successful self-management. Whenever feasible, it is helpful for a teacher to give a warning prior to a command. This can be an effective way of preparing children to make transitions. If Jenny's teacher had noticed that she was engrossed in painting and said 'In two more minutes, it will be time to put your paints away', Jenny would probably not have made a fuss. There are many ways to give warnings. For young children who don't understand the concept of time, a timer or bell or flicked lights, or a familiar clapping rhythm can be helpful. Then you can say, 'When the timer goes off, it will be time to put these paints away'. For older children, you can refer to a clock.

Students' requests and preferences should be considered, as well. For instance, if your students are busy reading books, you might say, 'When you finish the page you are now reading, I want you to put your books away'. If you are responsive to your students' wishes and give them some lead time, you are more likely to obtain compliance than if you expect immediate obedience.

'When–Then' Commands

Occasionally teachers give commands that sound like threats: 'You keep getting out of that seat and you're asking for trouble!' or 'You're going to be sorry that you did that'. While the intention may be to warn or signal children that they are getting in trouble, these kinds of threats and their vaguely implied consequences tend to cause children to be defiant and negative rather than compliant.

Use 'when–then' commands that tell your students in advance the exact consequences of their actions. In the examples above, you should say, 'When you're sitting down, then I'll help you with your maths problem' or 'When you finish putting your paints away, then you can go outside to recess'. First you get the appropriate behavior that you want and then you provide some positive consequence. This type of command gives your students the choice to comply or not to comply, and knowledge of the consequences of each choice. However, it is important in giving a 'when–then' command to ignore all protests and arguments, and to follow through with the consequences. Obviously, this kind of command should only be used if you can allow your students to decide whether or not to comply. If you need compliance to your command, then give a direct positive command.

Give Students Options and Choices

Most of the time, teachers give commands that students are expected to follow – for example, putting up a quiet hand, waiting one's turn, doing the maths lesson. But there are other times when a teacher gives a student a choice about whether or not to comply, times when a student may legitimately refuse a teacher's request. Such moments of real choice create a temporary shift in the balance of power between teachers and students. In order to develop a trusting relationship with a student, it also means that the teacher must respect a child's decision not to share some aspect of their lives. Teachers must become conscious of when a situation requires compliance and when a 'no' response from a student is acceptable. Moreover, if students can see their teachers respecting their decision at these times, they are more likely to comply with the teacher's commands at other times.

There are also times when teachers need to prohibit their students from doing something they really want to do. In such instances teachers may tell their students what they cannot do but may forget to tell them what they can do instead. For example, the teacher marches over to a student who is playing on the computer and says, 'Turn that off, right now!' Or, a child is supposed to be working but is playing surreptitiously with a toy he brought from home and the teacher noticing this says, 'Give that to me'. When children feel rigidly restricted and prohibited from fun activities, they are more likely to react with protests and non-compliance.

Commands that prohibit a student from doing something should include suggestions for what to do instead or alternative choice. You might say, 'You may not play on the computer now, but you can use it after school if you like' or 'Nice toy, you can put it in your locker or on my desk' or 'You can't play with the pet rabbit now, but you can get the books out for reading time' or 'You can do your maths now or give up recess to finish it'. Such an approach can help reduce power struggles because, instead of fighting about what your student cannot do, you're giving the child another positive option.

Give Short Commands and Instructions

Smothered commands are shrouded in explanations, questions or a flurry of words. For instance, the teacher says to the students, 'Put away these toys', followed by many questions about why all the toys and paints are out and what they are drawing. The result is that the original command is forgotten. A related problem is that teachers sometimes give too many explanations with a command. They probably believe that giving a long explanation will increase the likelihood that their students will co-operate, but this approach usually has the opposite affect. Most children will argue with the rationale and try to distract their teachers from the original command.

Keep your commands clear, short and to the point. If you give some rationale for the command, it should be brief and either precede the command or follow your child's compliance. Suppose you ask your students to tidy up the classroom. As they proceed you might add, 'Thanks, you're doing a great job. I really needed this room cleaned up because we're having a parent meeting here tonight.' Remember to ignore arguments and protests about your commands as giving attention to them will actually reinforce noncompliance.

Follow Through with Praise or Consequences

Sometimes teachers do not notice whether or not their students comply with their commands. If there is no follow-through and students are neither reinforced for their compliance nor held accountable for their non-compliance, then teachers must expect that their commands will be ignored.

Praising compliance encourages your students to be more co-operative and to value your requests. If your students don't do as they're told, then you must give a warning statement. This should be an 'if–then' statement: 'If you don't put your books away Kevin, then you'll lose a minute of break'. You should wait five seconds to see whether or not the child does as requested. If the child complies, he should be praised and if he still doesn't comply, he should have a minute of break removed. (See Chapters 5 and 6 for more information.)

Conclusion

Having a clear classroom structure and rules, a predictable schedule and giving specific commands does not require you to be authoritarian and rigid or to expect 100 per cent compliance from your students. Rather, the emphasis is on being proactive (not reactive) and thinking carefully before you give a command to be sure that it's really necessary and that you're prepared to follow through with the consequences if necessary. It's important to strike a balance between a student's choices and adult rules.

Effective limit setting is harder than you might first expect. In some situations, teacher commands should be given clearly as absolutes. In situations involving seat belts, hitting, not running into the street and limitations on computer use, for instance, you need to have control over your students and must state your rules and commands in a positive, polite, respectful and firm manner. There are other situations where direct commands are not needed and it is preferable to use physical redirection, reminders, non-verbal cues, proximity praise or humour to engage the distracted child. There are other situations where you can give up control and avoid unnecessary commands or unrealistic expectations and give your students choices. Why not allow students to have control over decisions such as what activity to choose at free time, whether or not to eat all the food on their plates, what stories to read and what colours to use on their pictures? Under yet other circumstances you and your students can problem-solve and learn to share control. Introducing negotiation and discussion with children as young as 4 or 5 can provide excellent early training for learning conflict management skills. What is key to effective limit setting on the part of teachers is striving for *balance* in your use of control with students, that is balancing your use of direct and indirect control approaches as well as offering students legitimate opportunities for problem-solving and sharing control. And as always it is important to strive for a higher ratio of positive to negative methods.

To Sum Up

- Develop clear classroom rules and discuss them with children ahead of time.

- Have predictable schedules and routines for handling transitions.
- Be sure to get children's attention before giving instructions.
- Place inattentive or easily distractible children close to the teacher's desk or near the teacher.
- Strive for clear, specific commands expressed in positive terms.
- Redirect disengaged children by calling out their name in a question, standing next to them, making up interesting games and using non-verbal signals.
- Use positive warning reminders about the behavior expected rather than negative statements when children are exceeding the limits.
- Give frequent teacher attention, praise and encouragement to children who are engaged and following directions.
- Be creative in your use of redirecting strategies – avoid repeated commands. Instead, use non-verbal cues and engaging activities.

References

Brophy, J. E. (1996) *Teaching Problem Students*, New York: Guilford Press.

Doyle, W. (1990). Classroom management techniques. In O. C. Moles (ed.) *Student Discipline Strategies: Research and Practice*, Albany, NY: State University of New York Press.

Forehand, R. L. and McMahon, R. J. (1981) *Helping the Noncompliant Child: A Clinician's Guide to Parent Training*, New York: Guilford Press.

Gettinger, M. (1988) Methods of proactive classroom management, *School Psychology Review*, 17, 227–42.

Good, T. L. and Brophy, J. E. (1994) *Looking in Classrooms*, New York: HarperCollins.

Van Houten, R., Nau, P. A., Mackenzie-Keating, S. E., Sameoto, D. and Colavecchia, B. (1982) An analysis of some variables influencing the effectiveness of reprimands, *Journal of Applied Behavior Analysis*, 15, 65–83.

Chapter Four

Promoting Positive Behavior: Attention, Encouragement and Praise

Children who need love the most, ask for it in the most unloving ways; the same can be said of children most in need of positive attention, praise, and encouragement.

The Importance of Teacher Attention, Encouragement and Praise

When we look at the classroom environment to see what factors help students become motivated and successful learners, the quality of the teacher's attention emerges as one of the most important. Consistent and meaningful encouragement and praise from a teacher build children's self-esteem and contribute to trusting and supportive relationships. These forms of attention to positive behavior reinforce and nurture children's growing academic and social competence.

Yet, our own research as well as that of others has shown that teachers give three to fifteen times as much attention to student misbehavior (e.g. talking, fiddling, out of seat behavior) than to positive behavior in their classrooms (Martens and Meller, 1990; Wyatt and Hawkins, 1987). Not surprisingly, this attention reinforces the misbehavior, leading to increased classroom behavior problems, particularly in the child who is starved for adult attention. When teachers recognize the power of their attention as a reinforcer of students' behavior and begin to simultaneously decrease their attention to inappropriate behaviors and increase their use of attention, praise and encouragement for positive behaviors, it has a dramatic impact not only on the individual child but on the whole classroom. For in observing what a teacher attends to, students are learning what behaviors are valued by their teacher. In this chapter we will look at what research has indicated are effective ways of teachers giving attention,

72

praise and encouragement (Brophy, 1981; Cameron and Pierce, 1994; Walker, Colvin and Ramsey, 1995). First, we would like to address some of the questions and concerns that teachers have about praise.

Questions Teachers Ask

Won't Teacher Praise Given to Some Children Create Insecurity in Others Who Don't Get Praised?

Doesn't praise given to one child make the other children who didn't get praised feel bad?

Sometimes teachers are reluctant to praise or to give positive attention to children with behavior problems because of their fears that there will be possible negative ramifications for other children. For example, some teachers worry that if they praise one child, the children seated nearby will feel inadequate because they were not praised. And they may be concerned that it is *not fair* to praise some children more than others. As long as the teacher gives consistent, positive attention to *every* child at some time or other, children will not feel they are being treated unfairly. Over time, with periodic doses of positive attention from their teacher on a regular basis, children will feel secure enough in their relationship with their teacher to avoid jealousy when others receive praise – in fact, with time they will even learn to celebrate each others' successes.

In the long run, giving more praise and positive attention to the problem child for his or her progress (e.g. 'you did a great job sharing the art supplies' or 'you are really focused on your work') can be beneficial for all the students in the classroom because these labelled descriptions of the expected academic and social behaviors act as a reminder for everyone. In reality, 'difficult' children typically have received very little praise and excessive amounts of criticism and disapproval in the classroom in comparison with their peers. They (and their peers) have learned to expect this, and will behave in ways that fulfil this expectation. Teachers of such children will need to work extra hard to reverse this pattern. It has been said that the children who need the love the most will ask for it in the most unloving ways; the same can be said for the children most in need of positive attention.

Isn't It More Important for Children to Judge their Own Work for Themselves than to Depend on Teachers' Praise?

How early can you encourage children to judge their work for themselves?

Indeed it is also important for children to learn to self-evaluate – that is, to pass judgement on their own work and feel pride in their accomplishments without relying on external sources of approval. This is an important long-term goal, yet the teacher needs to be aware of the particular world view of each individual child. For example, children who come from a family environment charac- terized by positive feedback, a commitment of support and a relationship with parents that centres on building the child's self- esteem, may have the self-confidence to begin to evaluate their own work. Even so, it is unrealistic to expect young children who are still developing emotionally and socially not to need some external val- idation for their learning efforts. In fact, adults need this too, regard- less of their age or how self-confident they may be.

Unfortunately, some children do not come from supportive fam- ily circumstances. Some children have experienced a great deal of negative feedback and even abuse from their parents for mis- behaviors. Other children have parents who are so overwhelmed with their own problems that they have been unable to focus on their children's needs or interests, and consequently these children may feel their parents don't care about them. Still other children may have been expelled from previous schools and experienced rejection from teachers and peers. In any case, children come to the teacher with very different experiences of what relationships with adults are all about and varying degrees of self-confidence. The child with behavior problems is likely to have a very negative view of what it means to have relationships with adults. Likewise, such a child may have a negative self-evaluation and low self-worth. If such a child is left to do his own evaluation of his work he will likely pronounce it worthless.

For these children, teachers will need to supply extra amounts of positive and consistent *external scaffolding* that the child has not experienced in the crucial early years. Teachers can think of this added support as providing a kind of 'environmental prosthesis' for the child – necessary for his academic and social success. This positive teacher encouragement may be necessary for several years before the messages internalize and the child develops a positive self-image and is capable of beginning to self-evaluate in a realistic way.

Biologic factors also play a role in a child's ability to self-evaluate. A child who is inattentive, impulsive and/or hyperactive will be delayed in learning to self-evaluate, as this requires the ability to reflect on one's actions and anticipate outcomes. Hyperactive and inattentive young children live 'in the moment' and do not easily learn from past experiences or anticipate future events. These children need much more external positive scaffolding from the teachers than children who are by temperament reflective.

Doesn't Teacher Praise Lead to Student Reliance on External Approval?

Doesn't praise create a student who will only be motivated by external approval rather than internal motivation?

Sometimes teachers worry that too much praise may be bad for children. Perhaps they feel that students who are praised too often may become conceited or overly confident in their abilities. Perhaps they fear that children may become dependent on praise – a form of external reinforcement. Research indicates that children who are praised by parents and teachers internalize the positive approval and develop positive self-esteem. They typically feel competent and seem to need less praise in the long run because they have developed confidence in their own unique abilities. This effect is especially likely if children are praised for their efforts and their abilities, rather than for what they achieve.

This question concerning internal motivation is somewhat related to the question about self-evaluation noted above – the concern on the part of some teachers that praise (or positive attention, or any social reward) from adults will create a child who is dependent upon external adult approval and who will not develop an internal sense of worth. Sometimes teachers fear that over time, children will need greater and greater amounts of praise in order to achieve the same effect – and fail to develop intrinsic motivation to learn. A research article reviewing ninety-six experimental studies comparing rewarded students with non-rewarded students did not support this theory but rather just the opposite – children who received lots of positive feedback from parents and teachers had an increase in intrinsic motivation (Cameron and Pierce, 1994). Children who are praised are self-confident, have high self-esteem, and seem to internalize these early messages so as not to need them in the future. This effect is especially likely if children are praised for their efforts and their abilities, rather than for what they achieve. Moreover, children who have received a lot of praise are popular with other children and give other children and adults positive feedback; that is, they have modelled this behavior and use it in their interaction with others. On the other hand, the children who demand praise and are dependent on others' evaluations are those insecure children who have received very little positive feedback and have low-esteem. Unfortunately, the children who most need the positive attention and praise rarely get it. The reality of most classrooms is that the problem children receive far more criticisms and negative attention than praise statements or positive attention.

Can Teacher Praise to One Student Stifle Creativity in Others?

If you praise a student's answer, isn't there a danger that all the other students will copy that answer or tell you their answer is the same? Might they be afraid to give a different answer for fear the teacher's response won't be as enthusiastic?

Some teachers worry that if they respond to one student's answer with labelled praise (such as praising a child's choice of a particular subject to discuss), every other student will imitate that student, so that suddenly that student's answer becomes the 'correct' answer. It is true that children will watch to see what behaviors teachers give attention to and then will repeat those behaviors in order to get the attention as well. This is an expected part of the learning process; and using one child's answer as a model to motivate other children is a good teaching strategy. Once teachers have children working for their positive attention (and not the negative attention), the next step is for teachers to use this technique to broaden the range of students' responses – that is, to reinforce diverse, creative and unique ideas. So the teacher might say to the students, 'That was an interesting and thoughtful answer. Does anyone else have a different experience they would like to share?' As students realize they will not receive the same kind of positive attention for repeating another student's answer, eventually they will become less likely to copy someone else's responses to get attention and more motivated to generate their own ideas.

How Often Should You Praise a Child?

If a child is spelling a word, should you praise each letter or wait until the spelling of the word is completed?

Whether the praise is given for each correctly spelled letter or saved until the spelling of the word is correctly accomplished will depend on the child's particular abilities and motivation. For children who are reluctant to take risks, frustrated with their spelling ability, or insecure about their relationship with the teacher or peers, praising frequently during the process (after each letter) will be important, for it will give the child confidence to keep trying. The principle here is shaping the desired behavior – that is, breaking the behavior down into small components and praising each small component. For the child who is a good speller and confident in the classroom, praising the end result may be sufficient.

It is also important for children to learn that it is okay for them to make mistakes. If they feel that positive attention will be withdrawn if they make a mistake with a teacher, then they will be unwilling to take the risk in the first place. Thus, if a child gets one or two letters wrong, the teacher should praise the child's efforts and focus on the five letters that were correct rather than focusing on the mistakes. For example, 'That was a very good effort and you thought about the spelling carefully, you got all but one letter absolutely correct!'

In general teachers should make sure they have at least four positives for every criticism or corrective statement they make to a child.

Some Children Don't Seem to Respond to Praise – Why?

Some children (usually those who have experienced excessive criticism and other negative feedback) are uncomfortable with praise and may show no response or even reject teachers' efforts to praise. Such children are well defended – in psychological armour. They act as if they don't care about praise. Another reason for a lack of response may be that they don't have the social skills – they don't know how to respond to teachers when they get positive feedback, so they shut down instead. When faced with these responses, it is easy to think the praise is not working or the child is unmotivated or doesn't care. Teachers must work extra hard to continue giving positive attention, praise and encouragement to these children who are not reinforcing them for their efforts.

Children who are inattentive, impulsive and distracted will miss praise that is vague or delivered in a neutral tone of voice. Such children will have trouble interpreting a neutral facial expression and may even interpret it as negative when teachers mean to be positive. For these children the praise needs to be underscored by means of an enthusiastic tone of voice, clear descriptions ('labelling') of the positive behaviors and clearly positive facial expressions. Think of this as a need to use a *megaphone* when praising this type of child.

Developmental age can also influence children's responses to praise. While younger children usually respond best to praise given in front of the whole classroom and overheard by others, sometimes with older children it is more effective to make the praise more private and personal and less obvious.

How Can You Praise a Child for Work that Doesn't Meet your Expectations?

How can you use praise when the child's work is not adequate and you want to direct the child towards something better?

Perhaps the teacher's goal is to encourage the students to use more colour in their drawings, but one child has submitted a completed drawing in black and white. Wouldn't it be counterproductive to praise this student's drawing? Actually it would be better to praise what the child has done well in that particular picture and avoid being critical of its lack of colour – for praise and positive attention will add to the child's pleasure in drawing and that pleasure will lead to her wanting to continue to draw. Then the teacher might turn to another child's drawing and talk about its use of colour, thus conveying to the first child how she might add colour. Later, when the children are working independently, the teacher could talk privately with this particular child and encourage her to use some different colours.

Doesn't It Set Up Competition and Resentment for Teachers to Compare Children with Other Children?

Illustrating a few children's work as excellent models used to stimulate other children's work can be effective as long as the teacher demonstrates examples from all the children from time to time and illustrates a variety of creative ways to approach the work. Since in these early years there is such variability in children's developmental abilities, it is important to recognize and communicate the value of each child's work. For example, the teacher might highlight a child's work because of the unique aspects of the art work (even though that child couldn't write) or because of the hard work a particular child had made in completing a project. Or the teacher might have made a single comment about each child's particular work or perhaps highlighting several one day and others on a subsequent day. Recognizing children's work in front of other students can be carried out in a way to encourage valuing of differences as well as to praise individuals – and to discourage comparison of students with each other.

Why Should Difficult Students Get More Praise than Other Students? It's Not Fair to the Other Students!

Difficult students, in particular, need massive amounts of positive attention and praise for appropriate behaviors. The reason for this is that typically they have been the brunt of adult criticism and peer ridicule, and as a result their self-esteem is low. Such children want attention so badly that they would rather have negative attention for misbehavior than no attention at all. Consequently, teachers need to develop skills that prompt them to notice the positive behaviors in difficult children – to 'catch them being good'. This cannot be left to chance; it must be planned, for there may be relatively few episodes of good behavior. In the case of difficult children, it can be hard to remember to praise and give positive recognition. But there are strategies to help yourself remember to do so. For instance, the teacher can put a red sticker on the classroom clock or his or her watch as a reminder to praise a particular student. Or he or she can put coins in one pocket that have to be transferred to the other pocket for each praise statement made to the child during the day. Teachers need a concrete plan for what particular behaviors they want to promote in individual children with problems and how they will reinforce those behaviors.

The question of teacher fairness in the classroom is an interesting one to ponder. Most teachers probably wouldn't argue that the child who has a language or reading delay is entitled to extra tutoring, or the child with a physical handicap will need physical therapy, or the child with pneumonia needs an antibiotic. It would seem then that the same rights hold for the child with attention difficulties, social and peer relationship problems, and environmental disadvantages. Moreover, this extra attention to the problem child in the form of labelled praise, encouragement and incentives for improvements will in the long run be beneficial for all the students in the classroom because these labelled descriptions of the expected academic and social behaviors act as a reminder for everyone. Not only that but the teacher is modelling empathy and acceptance of individual differences in children's abilities to learn social and academic skills.

One final point in regard to the issue of fairness. It isn't fair that some children come from homes where they are loved and provided with predictability whereas others do not, but that is the reality. It is therefore even more important that we set up classroom interventions that adjust for these individual differences in relationship abilities.

Making Praise and Encouragement More Effective

Be Specific

Vague praise is often given quickly in a chain, with one comment following another. For example, the teacher might say, 'Good job . . . good . . . fine . . . '. Unfortunately while these statements do convey some degree of positive attention, they are non-specific and unlabelled. It is unclear what aspect of the student's behavior that the teacher is praising with these words.

It is more effective to give praises that are labelled. Labelled praise describes the particular behavior that you like. Instead of saying 'Good job', you would say, 'You have worked so hard and have figured out that entire puzzle all by yourself' or 'Wow, what a wonderful job you've done of picking up all those blocks when I asked'. By pinpointing exactly what you like about a child's behavior (independent work, compliance to teacher's request), the praise statement conveys much more to the student and informs him what specifically was praiseworthy about his behavior so that he can do it again. It provides a stronger motivator of future behavior.

A few examples of ways to praise

- 'You do a super job of . . . '
- 'Good idea for . . . '
- 'What a wonderful job you've done of . . . '
- 'That's correct, that's a cool way to . . . '
- 'You are a real problem-solver for . . . '
- 'Great thinking . . . '
- 'My! That . . . was great teamwork.'
- 'You are being a good friend by . . . '

- 'Pat yourself on the back for . . . '
- 'Give me five for . . . '
- 'Thanks for being so patient and waiting while I was . . . '
- 'I like the way you remembered to walk quietly to your desk.'
- 'I knew you'd remember to . . . get ready for the next activity without any reminders.'
- 'Keep at it, you are working really hard and getting it!'
- 'Thank you ————, for making a quiet choice during work time. Your neighbours appreciate your thoughtfulness.'

Show Enthusiasm

Some praise is ineffective because it is boring, offered in dull tones, with no smiles or eye contact. The same words may be repeated over and over again in a flat, unenthusiastic voice. Such praise is not reinforcing to children.

The impact of a praise statement can be increased by using non-verbal methods of conveying enthusiasm. Smile at the child, greeting her with warmth in your eyes or giving him a pat on the back. The praise should be stated with energy, variety, care and sincerity. Words thrown over the shoulder in a careless fashion will be lost on the child.

Remember children who are inattentive, impulsive, and distracted will be the most likely students to miss praise that is delivered in a neutral tone of voice or is vague. These children, in particular, need praise that is underscored by means of an enthusiastic tone of voice, clear descriptions ('labelling') of the positive behaviors, clearly positive facial expressions and positive touch.

Praise and Encourage the Child's Efforts and Progress

In addition to praising specific observable behaviors such as sharing, helping or correct answers to questions and so forth, it is important to praise a child's efforts and improvement. For example, to the child who has had a difficult time reading the teacher could say, 'You have really worked hard at learning how to read, see how many pages you have finished all by yourself! Look at the progress you have made!' or 'See how you have improved in your reading, you recognize most of the words now'. This approach places the emphasis on the child's effort, feelings of success and progress rather than the teacher's evaluation of the child's reading ability *per se* or the teacher's feelings of pleasure. When you give children social rewards for improvement, you are measuring them against themselves, not against others in the classroom or against some other external standard. You could do this by showing their earlier work in the year and noting how it has changed.

Another way to encourage students is to use a strategy we call, 'tailgating'. This is when you repeat something the child has said and then build on it with a comment which expands the idea. For example, a student says, 'I am drawing a rocket to fly in the air' and the teacher replies, 'Yes you are drawing a rocket and you've drawn some powerful engines to propel it very far, that is cool!' This tailgating serves to encourage the child because it validates the child's ideas letting the child know the teacher understands and then by the teacher's further comments praises the child's detail in his drawing.

Focusing on the process of learning, rather than the product, strengthens students' self-esteem because it helps their students remain invested in their work and their learning, instead of measuring themselves by the outcome of their efforts. If the outcome is less than perfect, they can still take pride in their work because their teacher has rewarded it with her attention.

A few more examples of phrases

- 'You must feel proud of yourself for . . . '
- 'See how you have improved in . . . '
- 'You have worked so hard . . . '
- 'That's a creative way of . . . '
- 'You are a real problem-solver for . . . '
- 'Hey, you are really thinking, you . . . '
- 'Wow, you have learned how to . . . '
- 'It helps us when you . . . '
- 'You put a lot of thought into that . . . '
- 'You took the time to clean up the art materials, that's very thoughtful.'
- 'You really know how to tidy up, you put all the lids on the felt pens!'
- 'It's a pleasure to have a class like this because . . . '
- 'You went out of your way to help . . . this morning.'
- 'You are making a good choice.'
- 'You figured it out . . . way to go!'
- 'I'd love to call on you now but I need to give someone else a chance.'
- 'What a good way to be a friend by helping him with that.'

Promote Child Self-Praise

In addition to praising effort and progress, teachers can help the child learn how to recognize his or her own feelings of accomplishment by the way they phrase the praise. For example, a statement such as 'you must feel proud of yourself for reading that entire chapter all by yourself' focuses on the child's own positive recognition of his work.

Teaching children to recognize their own achievements is vital. Otherwise they may wait for others to notice, which we all know can be an endless wait. We want them eventually to be able to look inside themselves for self-approval. For example, sometimes when a teacher addresses a question to the class a lot of hands go up to answer the question, and the children who don't get called on feel left out or devalued. One way to prevent this from happening is to say, 'All those who had the same answer, pat yourself on the back for your answer'. Thus each child gets to reinforce herself with a pat on the back and be noticed for her ideas, rather than feeling disappointed because she didn't get called on.

Avoid Combining Praise with Put-Downs

Sometimes, teachers give praise and, without realizing it, they contradict it by being sarcastic or combining it with a punisher. This is one of the most disruptive things a teacher can do in the reinforcement process. In particular, seeing a student doing something they haven't done before seems to tempt teachers to make a critical remark about the new behavior. For example, the teacher says to a student, 'You finally finished your homework, but why couldn't you complete it on time?' or 'You picked up the toys like I asked. That's great. But next time how about doing it before I have to ask?' or 'You didn't hit today'. The criticism or correction on the part of the teacher negates the effect of the praise; children, particularly the insecure children, are more likely to remember the negative comment than the positive praise. Praises mixed with criticisms are very confusing for young children to interpret.

Consequently try to keep your praise 'pure', uncontaminated by qualifiers. If you want your students to learn something else such as completing homework on time, then set this up as a specific goal to be discussed on a separate occasion.

Praise and Encourage Social and Academic Behaviors

All too often teachers find when they keep track of the kinds of praise they give, that they are most likely to notice and praise a particular type of behavior. For example, some teachers find they praise academic excellence and cognitive competence but rarely praise social competence or vice versa. Some teachers find they praise only outstanding work relative to the whole class, rather than accomplishments relative to the individual child's growing abilities. It is important for teachers to be aware of these predispositions and try to praise a variety of cognitive, behavioral and social behaviors. In fact, for young children we would expect that social skills such as listening, co-operation, sharing, paying attention and appropriate question-asking would be praised liberally, for these are the foundation for developing academic skills. Even for older school-age children, teachers should use a balance of praise and encouragement directed at both academic and social behaviors. In order to get a perspective on what aspects of students' behaviors you praise, you might ask a colleague to spend an hour in your classroom recording what behavior and how often you praise.

In addition to praising how students behave and perform socially and academically, teachers should encourage other aspects of the child's unique personality, such as a child's patience, thoughtfulness towards others, creativity, enthusiasm, friendliness and willingness to try something new. Even a student's grooming, haircut or clothing may be commented on by teachers, for this teaches students that these are important social aspects to be aware of when developing friendships.

Praise Difficult Students More Often

As we noted earlier, children who most need our praise and other social rewards are the most difficult to praise and reward with our attention – because of their inattentiveness, disengagement and non-compliance, they are not reinforcing to teachers and do not elicit the teacher's desire to praise them (rather their desire to criticize them). How can you avoid this trap? By understanding that these difficult children can extinguish our efforts, teachers can make conscientious efforts to be sure they extend extra encouragement and praise to these children. All children will eventually respond to the same behavioral principles – but children with developmental delays, attention or behavioral problems will need the praise or attention more often. They require more learning trials, with behaviors broken down into small component parts followed by repeated praise and encouragement from teachers, before they will learn the new behavior.

Consequently, teachers need to develop skills that prompt them to notice the positive behaviors in difficult children – to 'catch them being good'. This cannot be left to chance; it must be planned, for there may be relatively few episodes of good behavior. In the case of difficult children, it can be hard to remember to praise and give positive recognition. Teachers need a concrete plan for what particular behaviors they want to promote in individual children and how they will reinforce those behaviors.

Remember the Shy Student

Just as you must work hard at finding behaviors to praise in the obstreperous child with behavior problems, so must you remember to praise the non-demanding, shy student who is normally co-operative. Such children are sometimes invisible in the classroom and need to be noticed for their kindness, generosity and helpful participation.

Target Specific Behaviors to Encourage According to Individual Students' Needs

It can be very effective for a teacher to target the particular behaviors she wants to strengthen in each individual student. For example, s/he may plan to praise the quiet, withdrawn student every time he ventures an answer or participates in a discussion. On the other hand, s/he may plan to praise the overbearing, controlling child for being able to wait his turn, or for letting someone else go first to answer a question. The same approach goes for strengthening academic skills. For the child who has difficulty writing and spelling, the teacher can plan to praise the child's efforts in order to keep up the child's interest in writing. Or, for the child who writes well, the teacher might focus on his expansion of ideas or organizational skills.

For the oppositional and highly distractible child, the single most important behavior to target for praise is the child's compliance to teacher directions. This is key because a teacher must have student compliance in order to be able to socialize or teach anything. Thus for these students, the teacher's first efforts must be to notice any time they follow the teacher's directions and listen carefully to their instructions.

A few examples of behaviors to encourage and praise

- Sharing.
- Talking politely.
- Quiet hand up
- Helping a classmate.
- Giving a compliment to another classmate.
- Complying to teacher requests, listening and following directions.
- Solving a difficult problem.
- Achieving something that was hard for a particular student.
- Co-operating on the playground.
- Persisting with a difficult academic task (working hard).
- Thinking before answering.
- Putting classroom materials away.
- Completing homework assignments on time.
- Being thoughtful.
- Being patient.
- Staying calm and cool and in control in a conflict situation.
- Walking in the hallway.
- Trying something difficult for the first time.
- Following one of the classroom rules.

In order to plan systematically for strengthening certain behaviors you can complete a written behavior plan. By identifying the student's negative or inappropriate behaviors you would like to see less of and when they are most likely to occur, you can then identify the appropriate pro-social behavior you would like to replace them with. This will help you be more specific with your praising and more consistent in paying attention to the behaviors when they do occur. This plan can also be shared with co-teachers or playground supervisors as necessary. Start this process by picking one behavior to work on at a time.

The other advantage to teachers identifying which target behaviors they want to reinforce ahead of time is that they can double the impact when they tell other teacher aides or parent volunteers in the classroom to praise them as well.

Use Proximity Praise

Instead of focusing on the student who is disengaged and daydreaming, the teacher praises other students who are attending to the task and completing their work. This use of proximity praise serves as a means of reminding and redirecting the disengaged

Behavior plan: Jenny

Negative Classroom Behaviors to Reduce	Occasion	Desired Behaviors to Increase	Specific Praise
Poking, touching other students	In line	Keep hands to own body	Responds well to praise 'You are doing a good job keeping your hands to yourself'
Speaks without raising hand	Small group discussion	Raise a quiet hand	Does not like to be hugged 'Wow you remembered to raise a quiet hand'
Talks while directions are given	Large classroom	Listen quietly when directions given	Give attention to and praise listening behavior 'You are listening carefully and doing just what I asked you to do'

student as to what behavior is expected without drawing attention to him or her. For example, the teacher says, 'I like the way Frederick is getting his books put away so we can go to break' or 'I will ask Anna to answer since she has a quiet hand up'.

Use Non-contingent Praise

In addition to contingent praise (praise given contingent on a particular positive behavior occurring) it is also important for teachers to give non-contingent praise. Non-contingent praise is general praise which is contingent on nothing that the child has to do to earn the approval. Examples of this include, 'It is nice to see you this morning' or 'It is fun working with you'. These encouraging words build a climate of unconditional positive regard of the teacher for the students.

Have Positive Expectation for All Students

Positive expectations are a powerful motivator. If you believe a child can learn and you communicate that belief – verbally or non-verbally – he or she is likely to keep trying. On the other hand, if you are convinced that a child is likely to have trouble, you will probably communicate that message, and the child probably won't keep trying. You can show your faith in students by making encouraging comments such as 'See you are able to do this, I knew you could' or 'I know this is hard, but with practice I know you will learn to do it'.

Use General Praise to Groups of Students

So far, we have been looking at the use of teacher praise and encouragement used with individual children. Praise can also be an effective tool used with a group of children because of the potential power of peer pressure to motivate students. For example you may divide your classroom into teams which may be given names. When you notice a team following your directions or a class rule you might say, 'I am very pleased with Team 6 because Team 6's listening has improved immensely today' or 'I see everybody at the Dinosaur table is ready for break with their books away, and their chairs put in quietly, that is fantastic'. You may also combine this verbal praise for teams with a point system which can be collected and turned in for a prize. This is described in more detail in Chapter 3.

Acknowledge the Difficulties of Learning Something New

The teacher says to the students after teaching them subtraction for the first time, 'I know this is hard stuff to learn and it was a lot of concentrated work today. But each day it will get a little bit easier and by the end of the year you will be very good at this.' The recognition that something is hard from the point of view of the teacher reduces distance between teachers and students. Having a closer relationship with the teacher (while maintaining appropriate boundaries) heightens the 'reward' value of the teacher's attention. This closer relationship will contribute to a child sharing more of his or her accomplishments as well as being more open about his or her areas of difficulty.

Encouragement is also needed when students make mistakes or feel they have failed. The teacher might say, 'Okay, you made a mistake. That's okay. It is easy to make mistakes, we all do. What can you learn from that mistake? What will you do differently next time?' Here the teacher acknowledges that making mistakes is part of the learning process and then encourages the student to think about what was learned from the experience. It also helps for teachers to model this themselves. For example, the teacher says, 'Oops I made a mistake. It's messed up. What do I need to do to fix it?'

Encourage Children to Praise Themselves and Others

Giving children positive recognition in the form of praise and encouragement has another value as well. Ultimately we want children to learn to praise others, for this is a skill that will help them build positive relationships with other children. We also want them to learn to praise themselves, for this will help them attempt and stay with difficult tasks. As we said, the use of effective teacher praise will lead to increases in the use of praise by students with each other and increased positive self-talk. Teachers can also strengthen this process through the use of compliment circles where children are actively encouraged to give each other compliments and notice special achievements. Or a teacher can stop a whole class to notice a group of children are doing something special together with a particular project.

A teacher can also watch for students who praise another student's work and praise them for this friendly behavior. When children share in the teacher's role of identifying other children who are engaged in positive behaviors, such as sitting quietly or co-operating, it also serves to reinforce the desired behavior for themselves. It is very reinforcing for children to be identified by their peers as behaving well – for some children this form of social reward is even more reinforcing than a teacher's attention.

Non-verbal Encouragement

Non-verbal signals of encouragement are very helpful so teachers can give students recognition without disrupting the entire class. For example, the teacher can use signals such as a thumbs up sign, a 'high five' or positive wink to acknowledge a child who deserves to be specially noticed for some achievement.

Another way to increase the impact of positive approval is to combine it with non-verbal support in the form of a hug, or a pat on the shoulder. Don't be hesitant to show your affection. Just think how much more powerful a hug coupled with lots of verbal praise must be.

Behavior Doesn't Have to Be Perfect to Deserve Recognition

Behavior doesn't have to be perfect to deserve your praise or positive attention. In fact, when children are first attempting a new behavior, they need to be reinforced for each small step toward the goal. Otherwise, if they have to wait for reinforcement until they have mastered the new behavior, they will have to wait too long, and may give up altogether. Praising a child at every step along the way reinforces the child for her efforts and learning. This process, known as 'shaping', sets the child up for success.

Working the Room

One of the ways to increase your use of positive recognition is to 'work the room' looking for positive behaviors – that is, while the students are working independently, circulate throughout the room and respond with attention and praise whenever you see the desired behavior occurring. Use independent work time as an opportunity for actively reinforcing individual behavior. Circulating around the room also makes you more accessible to students who want to ask for help.

When you are working with a small group of students or an individual, look up every 3 or 4 minutes and monitor the students who are working independently. Take a moment to notice and reinforce their positive behavior.

Use Classroom Compliment Circle Times to Promote Peer Praise

Classroom Circle Times can be used as compliment Circle Times in order to teach students how to give and receive positive feedback or compliments from each other. It is important that students do not always look to adults to receive positive feedback; they need to receive it from their peers as well. During Circle Time each student is encouraged to say one nice thing they liked or appreciated about what one of their classmates did that day or week. For example, 'Lisa was helpful when she helped me with my maths'. During these circle meetings the teacher can also model how to give positive feedback to the students. For example, 'I noticed Seth and Anna sharing and taking turns with the Lego; that was very friendly'. The teacher can end the circle session with, 'Thanks, everyone – I've really enjoyed being with you today'.

Sometimes during Circle Time you can ask students to nominate a student (never a close friend) for an award that week. For example, the teacher might say, 'Today I want you to nominate a student who has shown a recent improvement in work or behavior' or 'I want you to nominate someone who is always kind or hardworking'. If the teacher tries this approach, it is important that she devises categories that cover all the positive qualities of all the children and that she has a system to make the selection fair. Be sure to keep records of who is chosen from week to week so that all the children eventually get a turn. The names of the nominator and nominee and positive behavior can be posted on the board. During the rest of the day the class and teachers watch out for the positive behavior that has been nominated.

During these Circle Times students can also be encouraged from time to time to share something they feel proud about. For example, the teacher might say, 'Jamila tell the group about your reading today'. Jamila may respond, 'I feel proud because I worked hard and finished reading my book'. This ability to reflect one's own performance is an important aspect in the development of self-evaluation.

For young preschool and kindergarten children, we find it helpful if the child passes a stuffed bear to the person who is going to receive the compliment. Thus children who have difficulty verbally expressing a compliment, can still give a non-verbal compliment to another child by giving them the bear to hold. Also songs can be a fun way to introduce compliments. One song we use in Circle Time is 'Hello Peter, how are you? Compliment a friend and we'll clap for you.' Then as soon as the child gives a compliment to someone the class claps for him.

Doubling the Impact

Regardless of whether you're trying to reinforce academic skills or social skills, and regardless of whether the reinforcer is non-verbal attention or verbal praise, the task of teaching a child a new be-havior is a long and laborious one. For the fastest progress, you would reinforce the positive behavior every time it occurs, but that is an impossibility given the realities of the classroom. Still, it should be the goal to reinforce desired behavior as often as possible in the beginning. If there is more than one adult in the classroom, they can discuss in advance their behavioral goals for each child and decide what reinforcers they will use. This kind of strategic planning dra-matically increases the speed with which students will progress towards those goals. In addition, teachers can double the impact by building on each other's praise and by encouraging parents to cele-brate their children's successes.

To Sum Up

- Pinpoint what it is you like about the behavior and be specific in your praise.
- Praise with sincerity and enthusiasm, and in a variety of ways. Make a big deal out of it.
- Don't wait for behavior to be perfect before praising.
- Praise individual children as well as the whole class or small groups.
- Use praise consistently and frequently, especially when a child is first learning a new behavior. Remember, it is the most powerful form of positive recognition you can give a child.
- Children who are inattentive, highly distractible and oppositional need frequent attention and praise whenever they are behaving appropriately.
- Praise children according to your individual behavioral goals for them – including both academic and social behaviors.

- Don't stay behind your desk during independent work time; rather, circulate around the room giving recognition for positive behaviors.
- When you give a direction, look for at least two students who are following the direction – say their name and restate the direction as you praise the fact that they are following it.
- Develop a concrete plan for how you will remember to provide consistent praise such as a sticker on the clock or your watch, coins in your pocket, timer, etc.
- Focus on students' efforts and learning, not just the end result.
- Focus on students' strengths and areas of improvement.
- Express your belief in your students' abilities.
- Do not compare one student with another student (or sibling).

References

Brophy, J. E. (1981) On praising effectively, *The Elementary School Journal*, 81, 269–75.

Cameron, J. and Pierce, W. D. (1994) Reinforcement, reward, and intrinsic motivation: a meta-analysis, *Review of Educational Research*, 64, 363–423.

Martens, B. K. and Meller, P. J. (1990) The application of behavioral principles to educational settings. In T. B. Gutkin and C. R. Reynolds (eds.) *Handbook of School Psychology* (pp. 612–34), New York: Wiley.

Walker, H. M., Colvin, G. and Ramsey, E. (1995) *Antisocial Behavior in School: Strategies and Best Practices*, Pacific Grove, CA: Brooks/Cole.

Wyatt, W. J. and Hawkins, R. P. (1987) Rates of teachers' verbal approval and disapproval: Relationship to grade level, classroom activity, student behavior, and teacher characterstics, *Behavior Modification*, 11, 27–51.

Chapter Five

Using Incentives to Motivate Students

In the previous chapters we discussed the importance of teacher attention, praise and encouragement for everyday use in the classroom. However, when students have difficulty with a particular behavior or area of learning, praise and attention may not be strong enough reinforcers to motivate them. Learning to read, learning to write and learning socially appropriate behavior are slow and arduous processes, and sometimes children feel they are not making any headway.

Making Learning Tangible

One way of making learning tangible is to use tangible markers such as stickers or tokens, special rewards and celebrations to give students concrete evidence of their progress. Tangible rewards also provide extra incentives for children to tackle difficult learning areas, and can sustain a child's motivation until a positive relationship has been developed with the teacher that will make praise and attention more motivating. Positive results from using such incentive programmes have ranged from increasing classroom participation, on task work, co-operative behaviors, and improving spelling and maths accuracy, to reducing serious behavior problems (e.g. Rhode, Jenson and Reavis, 1992). When using incentive programmes to motivate students to learn something new, it is, of course, important to continue providing social approval as well. The impact is greater when both types of rewards are combined and each serves a different purpose. Social rewards should be used to reinforce the efforts children make to master a new skill or behavior. Tangible rewards are usually used to reinforce the achievement of a specific goal.

Incentive programmes involve planning in advance with a student which behaviors will result in a reward. This type of programme, which is like a contract, is recommended when you wish

94

to increase a rare behavior or a behavior that is particularly difficult for a student to learn. Let's look at a concrete example.

Transition Tickets

A teacher was having difficulty with her class of 7- to 8-year-olds whenever they came in from break. As students came into the classroom they poked, pushed and teased each other and took a great deal of time getting settled down to their classroom work. She found she was yelling at them constantly and that it took about 30 minutes before the class was finally engaged in their work. In fact, she noticed that any transition, be it from break or lunch or gym, was difficult for her students to manage without conflict. Her goal was help her students transition more smoothly to their work without a lot of classroom disruption. To achieve this, she planned a 'transition ticket system' with her students. First, she wrote the work assignment on the board so that when the students entered the class they would know exactly what to do. For example, she might write on the board, 'Start writing in your dialogue books' or 'Get out your reading books and read the first page of chapter 3' and so forth. Whenever she noticed students settling into their desks and following the directions on the board she gave them a transition ticket which was coloured coded for the week. These tickets were kept in a special box inside the students' desks.

Transition tickets were given out every time the students entered the class during the day so they had an opportunity to earn up to four tickets a day. On Fridays each student counted their tickets and traded them in for a prize if they had ten tickets. If they had over fifteen tickets they got a second prize from a special box. The teacher discussed with the students the kind of treats or prizes they would like to earn. For example, some items included pencils, erasers, sugarless gum, hard sweets, marbles, jelly beans, football cards and bubbles. The special box included such things as lunch with the teacher, line leader at break, choosing an activity for gym, choice of classroom treat, opportunity to bring a special item from home to share with class and so forth. In addition to counting each student's individual tickets, the teacher counted the total number of tickets the entire class earned each week and posted these on a large thermometer on the wall. She promised that when the entire class had earned 2000 tickets (top of thermometer) they would have a celebration. The teacher found that when she focused her attention on those students who were settling into work with her praise and attention coupled with giving out a ticket, the class soon settled down quickly without her yelling. Moreover, everyone enjoyed the game and planning their classroom celebration.

In this example, it is noteworthy that this teacher was specific about the problem behaviors and the positive ones with which she wanted to replace them. She chose specified periods of the day to focus on these behaviors and offered her students several opportunities a day to be successful and earn a ticket. Another significant aspect of this example is that it is developmentally appropriate for 7–8 year olds, who love to collect and trade in things. Moreover, children this age have the developmental capacity to wait a week before trading in their tickets. Later, when transitions were going smoothly, this teacher expanded her ticket system for other goals (based on individual student needs). Each student collected tickets which were akin to money vouchers which could then used to buy items at a school market day (children bring things they want to sell on market day). Another time when her budget for prizes was small, she set up a system whereby students put their tickets in a special raffle jar. At the end of the week there was a raffle and tickets were drawn for a prize. This teacher was successful because she tried to make the programme fun for her students by involving them in the planning of their rewards and celebrations.

However, for younger preschool children (3–5-year-olds), the incentive programme will need to be simpler with the opportunity for children to earn something immediately. For example, the teacher may stamp a card for each student (or give stickers) for specified behaviors which occur during the day, such as whenever s/he notices them sharing or helping another. At the end of the day each child can see how many stamps s/he has earned for being a helper and feel proud as s/he shares the successes with parents.

It is important to remember that incentive programmes will only work as long as you:

- give them for achieving a particular standard of performance (not simply for doing an activity)
- choose effective incentives
- make the programmes simple and fun
- monitor charts carefully
- are persistent and follow through with your agreement
- revise the programme as behaviors change
- periodically change the rewards and make them novel and interesting

- set consistent limits concerning behaviors which will receive rewards.

Once students learn the new behavior, incentive programmes can be gradually phased out and teacher praise and encouragement used to maintain it.

While incentive programmes may seem simple, there are in fact many pitfalls to be avoided if they are to be effective. In the first part of this chapter, we will discuss some of the erroneous objections that have sometimes been raised to using incentives with students, and in the second part we will discuss some common problems teachers encounter when trying to set up these programmes. Based on research regarding incentive systems we will describe the most effective and practical approaches to making them work (Cameron and Pierce, 1994; Elliott and Gresham, 1992; Stage and Quiroz, 1997; Walker, 1995). We will discuss a variety of ways in which teachers provide extra incentives to motivate children to learn social and academic skills.

Some Questions Teachers Ask

Don't Incentive Programmes Set Children Up for Failure in the Future Because They Become Hooked on External Rewards and Fail to Develop their Internal Motivation?

Sometimes teachers worry that incentives such as tickets, stars and pizza parties will lead to students becoming 'hooked' on external rewards and will not serve them well in the long run – because the children do not develop internal motivation and therefore are not able to function in future classes where teachers may not use incentive programmes. They worry that students will learn to manipulate the system and learn to respond to simple requests from teachers by saying, 'What am I going to get for it?'

Actually there is no research evidence that this happens if incentive programmes are implemented appropriately (Cameron and Pierce, 1994). It is important to emphasize that incentive programmes are not a substitute for other means of motivating students: building meaningful relationships with students, reinforcing them with attention and praise, stimulating their interests in certain areas, and so on. Incentive programmes are merely an adjunct strategy for the student who has some particular social or academic difficulty, who is resisting or avoiding trying or who is unresponsive to other reinforcers.

Because tangible rewards are immediate, they are also useful for getting a whole class quickly under control so that they will attend to what is being taught. The idea behind these incentive programmes is to gradually phase them out as children gain the confidence and skills that will strengthen their internal motivation to persist. Incentives might be thought of as a kind of *external scaffolding* to help children until they can do it on their own.

How Can You Set Up Incentive Programmes for Some Children in the Classroom and Not for Others? It's Not Fair. Won't This Cause Other Well Behaved Children to Misbehave in Order to Get the Rewards?

Teachers may be concerned that it is unfair to give rewards to some children and not to others. Actually, the issue here is that it is really more fair to individualize our teaching strategies according to what individual students need because every child has different abilities. Just as a doctor prescribes according to what medicine is most appropriate for a given illness, so the teacher must determine the specific learning needs of each of her students.

What about the problem of other students misbehaving to get the reward? This is rarely likely to happen, especially if the teacher has explained the programme to the class in a straightforward manner. For example, the teacher might say, 'Jessie has had some difficulty at times staying in her seat. She and I have worked out a special programme to help her stay in her seat. Everyone wants that don't they? And we are going to give her a special cheer if she can make her goal.' Here the teacher elicits student support for the programme and explains its purpose to the students thus reducing competition or jealousy from other students.

Should You Send Home Notes with Both Happy and Frowning Faces?

A common strategy used by teachers is to send home daily behavior charts with stickers of happy faces for good behaviors and frowning faces for misbehaviors. In general, we recommend you do not mix your reinforcement and your punishment systems – in this case, combining both kinds of stickers on the same chart – as the negative feedback (frowning face) will negate the positive feedback (happy face). In fact, the attention given (either by the teacher or the parent) for a frowning face may end up being greater and therefore more reinforcing than the attention given for a happy face. This is especially true for children with behavior problems who tend to be focused more on criticism than on praise or approval.

Another possible side effect of frowning faces is that some parents may become angry and resentful towards the teacher for sending home a negative report and may even blame teachers for the problem. Sending home negative feedback in the form of frowning stickers might also result in parents responding to the frowning stickers by punishing the child for misbehavior. Parents may punish out of frustration with their child or a feeling they are 'supposed to do something' about the teacher's note about the misbehaviors. This results in the child receiving a double punishment – from home and school. In addition, the parents' disciplinary action would be so far removed from the time the child's actual misbehavior occurred, it will have little effect on the misbehavior. Moreover, such a reaction from parents will only damage the parent–child relationship. Teachers should emphasize that when sticker behavior charts are sent home, it is the job of the parents to be supportive and encouraging of their children's successes and to refrain from commenting on the blank spaces where no stickers were earned (sometimes parents may punish a child for earning only five or six out of seven happy faces). Thus parents will give their children the consistent message that they believe they can succeed and that they want them to try their very best at school. Teachers can assure parents that they will handle any misbehavior as soon as it occurs at school and will quickly move on to a new learning experience so that the child can be successful.

When Do You Begin to Involve the Child in Evaluating his or her Day?

While incentive programmes do give students concrete feedback about their successes, teachers should still encourage children to reflect about how they did that day. For example a teacher might have a thermometer showing the range from calm (blue for cool) to overexcited (red hot) and the child might point to how he thought he did during the day. This would give the teacher an opportunity to give specific feedback on times when the child successfully calmed down. Similar thermometers might be used for anger or level of involvement in classroom activities. Children with behavior problems will often focus on their mistakes during the day; by reviewing the positive effort made by the child (for example, times

My Self-Encouragement Bubble

I'm a good problem-solver.
I'm good at maths.
I can face up to the problem and solve it.
I'm not a quitter.
I can cope with this.
I can calm my body down.
I'm good at sharing.
I can wait.
I am very helpful.
I am a friendly person.
I am good with words.
I ignore noises around me.
I can go to my seat without being asked.
I do what's best for myself.
I am incredibly brave.
I love to share my things.
I'm a good leader.

when the child successfully earned a sticker) the teacher can help the child learn to make more positive attributions about his day. Another self-reflective approach is to have children complete a form called *a self-encouragement bubble* for various things that occurred during the day regarding such things as friends, school work and frustrations. This can be completed verbally and transcriptions taken down by the teacher or alternatively, the teacher can ask the student to do drawings for each category.

Establishing Objectives

Be Specific about Appropriate Behaviors

Teachers sometimes set up tangible reward programmes that are vague about which appropriate behaviors will result in a reward. For instance, Billy is disruptive in class, he can't sit still in Circle Time, pokes the other children next to him and constantly interrupts the teacher's discussions with the students. Billy's teacher says to him, 'When you are good in school, you can pick a reward' and 'If you behave well at Circle Time, you can have a treat'. The teacher refers to a vague trait, 'goodness', but is unclear about what specific behavior will earn Billy a reward. If you aren't clear about the behaviors you want, your students are unlikely to be successful. Billy may even, in all innocence, demand a treat because he thinks he was good at school while the teacher felt his behavior was bad. He might argue, 'But I was good. I want a treat!' Indeed, he thought he was good because he shared once with another child and tried to behave. Unfortunately, his teacher's view of 'good' is more rigorous.

The first step in setting up an incentive programme is to think clearly about what misbehaviors are bothersome. How often do they occur, and what appropriate positive behaviors can be substituted for them? If, like Billy's teacher, you want your 3–5-year-old to be less disruptive at Circle Time, you might say, 'If you sit quietly by my side and keep your hands in your lap, while we have Circle Time, then you can earn a special sticker'. Or, 'Every time you put up a quiet hand without blurting out we are going to give you a sticker in this box'. Here the positive behaviors are described clearly for the child. Being specific also makes it easier for you to know whether or not you should follow through with a reward.

Make Steps Small

One reason many incentive programmes fail is that teachers make the steps or behavioral expectations so big that their students feel that earning a reward is impossible and give up trying – or don't even try in the first place. In the 'Circle Time' example above, if Billy was four years old, very active, in the habit of jumping out of his seat constantly and interrupting every 2 minutes, it would be unrealistic to expect him to stay by the teacher's side quietly for very long. Thus, a programme that involved earning a sticker for staying seated quietly for a 20-minute Circle Time discussion would be doomed to failure.

A good reward programme incorporates the small steps required to achieve the goal. First, observe how often the misbehavior occurs for several days. This baseline will be key to establishing the right steps for planning an incentive programme. Then choose the specific behavior you want to work on first. For example, if you notice that Billy can sit for 5 minutes, then this would be the first step to reinforce. The programme would involve giving Billy a sticker every 5 minutes he sits still and keeps his hands in his lap. In this example, the teacher starts with physical sitting as her first priority, and after she has gained success with the child sitting, she will move on to other goals such as teaching him how to put up a quiet hand instead of constantly interrupting verbally. With this approach Billy has a good chance of being successful and earning some stickers. Once he can sit still for 5 minutes without a problem, you can make the reward contingent on sitting for a little longer. Remember, the idea is to progress with small steps towards the desired goal.

A note of caution here, if Billy is, by temperament, very hyperactive you will progress slowly and will need to adjust your expectations for how long you can expect him to sit still at this age. Ten minutes may be the most he can realistically ever be expected to achieve. Consequently, if Circle Time in your classroom is usually 15 to 20 minutes, you will want to give a child such as Billy an appropriate way he can move around without causing disruptions. For example, after he has achieved his 5 or 10 minute goal for sitting, he is permitted to get up and go to a special place in the room called 'Billy's wiggle space', where he can move around quietly. Then, when he is ready he can come back to the circle and sit down and have an opportunity to earn another sticker for sitting still.

Pace Steps Correctly

The opposite problem occurs when teachers make the steps too easy. In this situation, the students are not motivated to work for the reward or they undervalue it because they get it so often. This is rarely a problem in the beginning since most teachers make the steps too big. However, it can become a problem as the programme continues. For instance, after a few weeks let's say Billy is consistently getting a sticker for every 5 minutes sitting at Circle Time. Unless the teacher makes the programme more challenging by asking him to both sit still and put up a quiet hand before receiving a sticker, the stickers may lose their reinforcing value.

A good rule of thumb is to make it fairly easy to earn a reward when children are first learning a new behavior. Initially, they need repeated successes to appreciate the rewards and the teacher's approval, and to understand they are capable of the desired behavior. Then you can make it a little harder. Gradually, the rewards are spaced further and further apart (intermittently) until they are not needed at all. Ultimately, teacher approval can maintain the behaviors. Be careful, however, sometimes teachers who are feeling successful with their programme step it up too quickly, and students then regress in frustration at their inability to succeed. Constant monitoring of the correct pacing of the steps is one of the keys to successful incentive programmes for changing behavior.

Choose the Number of Behaviors Carefully

Programmes sometimes fail because too many negative and difficult behaviors are tackled at once. We have seen highly motivated teachers start reward programmes involving stickers given throughout the school day for compliance to teacher directions, not teasing peers, quiet hands up, staying seated, not poking and for working hard. Such programmes are too complex. The pressure to succeed in many different areas of life may seem so overwhelming that children give up before starting. Another drawback of this approach is that it requires constant monitoring by the teachers all day long. Simply observing a student's compliance to teacher requests throughout a day will require a tremendous amount of effort because these situations occur frequently. Remember, if you cannot realistically monitor your student's behavior and follow through with consequences, even the best-designed programme is bound to fail.

There are three main things to consider when deciding how many target behaviors to help children learn at one time: the frequency with which each behavior occurs; your student's developmental stage; and what is realistic for you to carry out. With regard to frequency, remember that behaviors such as non-compliance, interrupting, touching others or jumping out of seat may occur often and therefore will require much teacher supervision. This means that realistically you will not be able to focus on more than one such behavior at a time.

The second important point to consider is the developmental ability of your student. Young children require easily understandable programmes that focus on one or two simple behaviors at a time. Learning to be compliant to teacher requests or to share with another child are major developmental tasks for a young child. Each will require many repeated learning trials, time and much patience on the part of the teachers. However, as children mature (school age and adolescent), tangible reward programmes can become more complex because older children understand and remember them better. In addition, problem behaviors at this stage usually occur less frequently and are easier to monitor. For a school-age child, therefore, it would be possible to establish a successful programme that included points for remembering to bring in homework, helping put away sports equipment at gym and settling down quietly to work when returning from break.

Evaluation of how much monitoring you can realistically expect of yourself is the third factor in deciding which child behaviors to focus on. Even if you have a co-teacher or assistant, it is difficult to monitor a behavior such as following teacher directions, throughout the day. This will be true, particularly if you have a class of thirty children including three or four children who are on incentive programmes for particular problems. Therefore, you will want to choose the time of the day when you can focus on the behaviors you want to increase. For instance, many children have difficulties during the unstructured or free play times, and this may be the time you want to really focus on praise and incentives for co-operative and sharing behavior. Or, for a child like Billy, you might focus on Circle Time to teach him the expected behaviors and later in the year expand to helping him with pro-social behaviors during other times of the day. Some teachers like to focus their incentive programs on difficult times such as transition times or break or unstructured play times. None the less, the key aspect is that you set up a programme that is realistic and that you can find the time to follow through consistently with the praise and rewards.

Focus on Positive Behaviors

Another problem occurs when teachers focus exclusively on negative behaviors. Teachers can clearly identify the negative behaviors they want to eliminate, such as fighting, interrupting, poking,

Behavior plan: Jenny

Negative Classroom Behaviors to Use	Occasion	Desired Behaviors	Specific Reinforcers
Poking, touching other students	In line	Keep hands to own body	Responds well to praise – does not like to be hugged
Speaks without raising hand	Small group discussion	Raise a quiet hand	20 coupons for quiet hand equals choosing book for story time
Talks while directions are given	Large classroom	Listen quietly when directions given	Use listening self-monitoring sheet – 10 points per day = choosing special activity at time
Off-task, daydreaming	Independent work time	Pay attention and concentrate	Happy grams for on-task work

running, disobeying, loud voices and disturbing others during work time in class. Their incentive programme outlines the rewards that their children will receive for going an hour without fighting, poking or interrupting. So far, so good; but the programme hasn't gone far enough. While it tells students clearly what they should *not* do, it neither describes clearly the opposite behavior you expect nor rewards the appropriate replacement behavior. Rather it is rewarding the absence of negative behavior. Thus, inappropriate behavior receives more teacher attention and behavioral description than appropriate behavior.

It is important to identify the positive behaviors that are to replace the negative behaviors and to include them in the incentive programme. For example, programmes should include rewards for the presence of cooperative behaviors such as sharing, taking turns and playing quietly with a peer, keeping one's hands to oneself, talking with a quiet voice in class, putting up a quiet hand, waiting a turn, working attentively on a project, coming into class and sitting down quietly, using words when angry and following teacher directions. It is critical that the positive behaviors be spelled out as clearly as the behaviors that are to be eliminated. In the behavior plan for Jenny which we discussed in Chapter 4, the teacher now adds some incentives to her praise planning.

When to Individualize Programmes

In the 'Transition ticket' example, it was appropriate to set up an incentive programme that involved the entire class since many of the students needed help with this problem. However, sometimes it is not helpful to do an incentive programme with everyone in the class, in fact, it might even decrease some students' motivation. For example, a teacher was concerned because some of her students were not reading books. Therefore she set up an incentive programme which involved giving a reward to every student who finished reading two books per month. The danger for those students who were already reading and motivated by their own enjoyment of reading is that setting a limit on two books may actually decrease the number of books they would try to read.

Rather, incentive programmes should be tailored according to the needs and abilities of the particular student who is having difficulty completing the assignment. For example, if a student has reading or learning difficulties, you might want to provide incentives for that student for trying to read each day for 15 minutes. Moreover, you will want to be sure that this child is given books that are not too advanced for his level of reading and that address some of his special interests. For example, if he is a child who loves dinosaurs, he can be offered books about dinosaurs. The goal for such a child will not be completing a certain number of books per month, but rather providing the encouragement so that s/he continually is engaged in the process of trying to read. On the other hand, if you have a student who is capable of independent reading but simply does not organize himself sufficiently to get any reading done, then the incentive programme might be set up for completing a certain number of pages during a set period of time each day. It is essential that teachers understand the nature of the child's behavioral difficulties because only then can you design effective incentive programmes.

Choosing the Most Effective Incentives

Once you have chosen which target behaviors you want to increase or decrease and have decided on the appropriate stages or steps in which to accomplish this, the next task is to choose appropriate rewards or incentives. Tangible rewards can include stickers, stars, points, stamps, small prizes such as pencils, books, bookmarks, decals, or special privileges such as lunch with the teacher, a chance to put on a magic show or play with a particular puppet, the opportunity to sit in a beanbag chair or visit another classroom for lunch, and so on.

It is important to remember that what is a positive reinforcer for one child may not be for another – some children crave praise and adult attention, others are wary of adult approval and would rather work for stickers or sweets, others like to earn special privileges. For many young children (ages 4–6 years), stamps or stickers on a page are rewarding in themselves, making it unnecessary to provide additional material rewards. As children get older, saving up coupons or stickers and trading them in for something desirable adds to the incentive programme by providing double reinforcement as well as by developing their ability to remain motivated in the face of delayed gratification. One way to get to know what might be particularly reinforcing for a particular child is to send home an interest survey to parents to get some information about the child's interests, hobbies and what things are especially reinforcing for the child. Parents can be very helpful to teachers in determining what incentives will motivate their child.

Some Ideas for Making Learning Tangible

- Putting 'I can' notes in a can on student's desk.
- Having students make accomplishment albums.
- Fill in one statement for student's self-encouragement bubble each day (e.g. 'I can go to my seat without being asked').
- Students applauding each other's accomplishments.
- Using positive Time Out (visit to principal for special accomplishment).
- Teaching self-approval (pat oneself on the back).
- Phone call to parents to tell of student's accomplishments.
- Compliment cards and charts.
- Playground raffle tickets for co-operative behavior.

Inexpensive Items

- Points, jelly beans, stickers (which can be traded in for prizes).
- Stickers or pin-on badges with messages (e.g. Well done for being a good listener, I was helpful today, I keep the playground rules, I join in well with others).
- Transition tickets which go in a raffle for a prize.
- Special prize boxes.
- Pencils, erasers, markers, scissors.
- Small notepads.
- 'Cool' stickers (e.g. scratch and sniff stickers).
- Football cards.
- Bubbles.
- Crisps, crackers, sugarless gum.
- Surprise notes.
- Bubble bath, small soap.
- Art supplies – sequins, glue stick.
- Postcard.
- Puzzle, mazes, 'brain teaser', joke.
- Stamp.
- Play dough.
- Beads.
- Posters.
- Mystery prize (a prize put in a decorated envelope or box).
- Spin the wheel of fortune for a prize.
- Photocopy voucher.
- Canteen voucher.

Special Privileges

- Lunch with teacher.
- Read student's favourite book to class.
- Work on favourite activity.
- Choose special video for class to watch.
- Field trip.
- Invite special visitor to class.
- Share a talent or hobby with class.
- Pick from fish bowl chance to win a prize.
- Choose which seat to sit in that day.
- Chance to eat lunch with another class.
- Being teacher's helper for the day.
- Line leader.
- Homework pass (ten compliment cards = homework pass for one night).
- Listen to 5 minutes of favourite music with class.
- Extra computer time.
- Extra 10 minutes of break on Friday.
- Play board game.
- Five minutes of conversation time where students can sit anywhere they wish and chat at the opening or closing of the day (as long as no one is left out).
- Disco time.
- Class visits.
- Opportunity to help a younger child in another class or work with a secretary.

Special Awards and Celebrations

- Win special 'award bear' to take home.
- Wear special button, ribbon or tie acknowledging the child's achievement.
- 'Top dog' award – soft toy dog given to child who wins award.
- 'Feather in your cap' award – feathers which are mounted on walls around the room.
- 'Citizen of the week' award.
- Popcorn or ice-cream party.
- Compliment chart – teacher keeps track of compliments given to students.
- Mystery super hero student.
- Get to become wizard happy – that is to wear the wizard hat and cloak and make a special wish.
- Giant of the week – a quality such as helpfulness or patience is selected for the week. The teacher and other children watch for this quality in others and nominate this student.

Be Sure your Incentives Are Age Appropriate

For 3–5-year-old children your incentive programme should be clear, simple and playful. Children of this age love to collect different stamps and stickers or perhaps even earn a little prize from a surprise grab bag. There is no need to complicate the system for young children with reward menus or trading things in for bigger prizes. Just receiving the sticker coupled with your encouragement and seeing their sticker chart fill up is all the reward they need.

Once children have learned the concept of numbers and understand the notion of days in a week and of time passing (around 6 years and up), they like to participate in programmes where they collect things and trade in things. This is the age when 'collections' start – remember all those collections of football cards, rocks, coins and stamps. At this age children can be offered the chance to collect stickers and trade them in later for a bigger prize.

Choose Inexpensive Incentives

Believe it or not, we have seen reward programmes that have bankrupted their teachers' classroom budgets for the year. Even when schools can afford more expensive incentives, use of these is not necessary and it teaches children not to expect big rewards for their successes. The emphasis is not placed on the magnitude of the reward, but rather on the satisfaction and pride felt by both the teacher and child at the child's success.

In general inexpensive or no-cost things are more powerful reinforcers anyway. Young children often like to earn time with teachers, such as having lunch with the teacher, choosing the book to be read in class, being line leader, bringing something from home to share and helping the teacher with a special project. Small food items such as raisins, crisps, sweets, or choosing their favourite snack can also be appealing. Young preschool and kindergarten children are happy with collecting stickers and stamps and don't need to trade them in for other prizes. Older children like to earn special privileges such as extra computer time, a homework-free night, choosing the playground activity, being team captain and so forth.

Special Recognitions and Celebrations

One powerful and inexpensive motivator for many students is to have 'special recognition' awards. These may be given to a student who has shown particularly dramatic improvement in some area, or who has shown improvement in a particularly difficult area, or who has completed some special achievement. While we often think of awards as being for academic achievement, special recognition can be awarded for social behavior too. When students receive positive recognition from others, especially teachers and classmates, they begin to feel capable and believe they can successfully contribute. When possible, these awards should be recognized by the principal. For example, the student may go to the principal's office to shake his or her hand or be given the award in front of an assembly of students. Notice of these awards should be sent home to parents so they can be informed of their child's successes.

Top Dog Award

One example of this is the 'top dog' award – 'top dog' can be a soft toy animal that sits on the desk of the student who has been the best citizen for that week. When children get to be 'top dog' they get to be first in line and go to lunch first because they have shown they are responsible. The goal of being 'responsible' or 'best citizen' may be defined differently for each child, in line with their individual goals.

Feather in your Cap

Another example of this, is to earn a feather in your cap. Children can earn a 'feather' from the teacher for saying something nice to someone or doing something nice for someone else without being asked. The feather is a picture of a feather which says, 'This is a feather in Johnny's hat earned because he helped in maths'. The teacher sticks these feathers on the wall in a vertical column starting at floor level; when the feathers for the class reach the ceiling, then the whole class earns a celebration. This system rewards co-operation and the social skill of praise. It might also be used for academic achievements.

Golden Acorn Award

A variation on the feather method of encouraging students is the growing tree. At the beginning of the year the class creates a huge barren oak tree. Then every time a student improves or reaches a particular target goal, s/he receives a blooming leaf with the words, 'I have learned to . . . ' and puts this leaf on the tree (also a note is sent home to tell parents of the achievement). Five leaves on the tree lead to a student getting a golden acorn which meant she had earned the 'golden acorn' award. If the child chooses, she can sit on the golden chair and receive questions about her hobbies, interests and life experience (or some other celebration). Three acorns lead to a golden squirrel which leads to an even bigger celebration. This system can be individualized for students to focus on their own particular targeted goals based on their learning needs.

Compliment Chart

A third example of a way to recognize students is called the compliment chart. Here the teacher has a chart posted in the classroom and records whenever the class receives a compliment from a teacher or parent or student. Once the students achieve a certain number of compliments they also earn a celebration. Another version of this is to give out compliment cards to individual children. The teacher might set up a contract with students, for example, when the class gets ten compliment cards they earn a homework-free night.

Involve Students in the Incentive Programme

Occasionally teachers choose tangible rewards that are more reinforcing for themselves than for their students. A related problem is teachers who take too much control over the programme. We have seen elaborate charts with pictures pasted on them and fancy stickers chosen by the teachers, not the children. Unless children are given some control, the programme is likely to fail. The goal of a tangible reward programme should be to teach your students to take more responsibility for their own behavior. If they sense that you are unwilling to delegate some control, they may dig in their heels for a fight, in which case their focus is shifted from the pleasure of co-operation and good behavior to the satisfaction of winning a power struggle by escalating their bids for negative attention.

Find out what is most rewarding for each of your students. You can do this by priming yourself with lots of ideas for rewards, just in case they don't have any to start with. However, try hard to get your students to come up with their own suggestions. You might say to a reluctant child, 'You like having playing with the computer. How about putting an extra 15 minutes of computer time on your list?' And remember that a reinforcement menu does not need to be completed in one discussion but can be added to over time as your students think of other things to work for. If you use stickers, ask students what kind of stickers they like (e.g. dinosaur stickers, sports, etc.) and ask your students to be involved in drawing up charts and deciding how many stickers particular items are worth. Older students love the possibility of earning a homework free night or the chance to bring something to share with their classmates. Get students involved in the *fun* of the game and excited about how to earn the items.

Calculate Daily and Weekly Rewards

Sometimes teachers not only make the rewards too big and expensive, but they also make the time interval until their students can earn them too long. Suppose Billy's teacher says, 'When you get 100 stickers for sitting still during Circle Time, we will have a class party'. Depending on how many stickers can be earned in a given day, it may take Billy a month or longer to earn the reward. Most children aged 4 to 6 will give up if they don't receive a reward on a daily basis. And certainly Billy will! But even older children, aged 7 to 9 years, who are inattentive and impulsive by temperament will not be able to wait more than a week to earn a reward. These hyperactive children live 'in the moment' and part of their developmental difficulty is an inability to anticipate consequences and see ahead to a future goal (Barkley, 1996). They need far more immediate reinforcement to learn from their experiences.

To set a realistic value on your rewards, first determine how many stickers, points or stamps could be earned in a day if your student was 100 per cent compliant with the programme. For instance, Tom, a 7-year-old, is a shy, withdrawn and anxious child. He is usually alone in the class, rarely says anything in class discussions and appears to have no friends. Let us say your goal is to help him participate more in class and to foster some positive peer friendships. Thus you set up a programme where Tom can earn stamps for putting up his hand and suggesting an idea in class, asking the teacher a question and helping another child with something. Based on your baseline observations you calculate that probably the most he will earn in one day is six stamps. Tom's reinforcement menu should therefore include small items worth four stickers, so that when he is on target with two-thirds of the positive behaviors in one day, he can choose something from the list. It would also be a good idea to have other items ranging in value from eight to fifteen points so that he could choose to wait two to three days before cashing in his stamps to receive a larger reward (e.g. time on the computer). Waiting for Tom to get 100 points for choosing a field trip would take seventeen days if he was perfect every day. If he was successful two-thirds of the time, 100 points would take twenty-five days. The key to setting up effective reinforcement menus is not only a creative list of incentives for your students to earn, but also a realistic price for each item, based on the child's usual daily salary of points or stamps. On the other hand, teachers who use points or stickers for compliance to teacher requests may find that their students can earn as many as thirty points a day. The price of items for their students would therefore be higher than for a child who can only earn four a day.

Note that for an isolated child such as Tom, it would important also for the teacher to be prepared to praise and encourage other children in the classroom when they play with Tom so that he gets more opportunities for social interaction. The teacher might also share with the students that when Tom earns a certain number of points there will be a classroom celebration, thus all the children will become invested in Tom's success with the programme.

Appropriate Behavior, then the Reward

What is the difference between a bribe and a reward? Consider a teacher who says to the screaming student, 'Eliza, you can have this book if you'll stop screaming'. Or a teacher whose student refuses to do what she asks, who says, 'Sunjay, I'll give you this snack if you put those toys away afterwards'. In these examples, the book and the snack are bribes because they are given *before* the desired behavior occurs and are prompted by inappropriate behaviors. The teachers are teaching their students that if they behave badly, they will be rewarded.

Rewards should be given for positive behaviors *after* they have occurred. It is helpful to remember the 'first–then' principle. That is, first you get the behavior you want and then your student gets a reward. In the example, Eliza's teacher could set up a programme to help her with her screaming and she might say, 'Eliza when you go a whole Circle Time speaking up politely (without screaming), I will let you choose the book we read at story time'. The teacher first gets the desired behavior and then gives the reward. In the second example, Sunjay's teacher might have said, 'When you put your toys away this morning, you can choose your favorite snack for snack time'. A good reward system is analogous to being successful in school or

Student Name				
Monday	Tuesday	Wednesday	Thursday	Friday

college. That is, you receive grades for completing courses and eventually a certificate or degree for finishing a series of courses.

Use Tangible Rewards for Everyday Achievements

Some teachers save tangible rewards for their students' special achievements such as getting As on a report card, or doing an outstanding drawing, or reading a particularly difficult book, or going the whole day without interrupting or getting out of their seat and so forth. This is actually an instance of making the steps towards the final goal too big. Not only do the teachers wait too long to give the rewards, but they save the rewards for perfection. This gives their students the message that everyday behaviors, such as trying out a new colour combination in a drawing, or trying to read a book out loud to the class when you are poor reader, or stopping yourself from interrupting too much, don't really count.

Think about giving small, frequent rewards. Certainly you can plan rewards for special achievements, but you should also use them for smaller steps along the way, such as rewards for the student who has shown the most improvement in reading, or for the student who has risked trying something new, or for the student who has worked hard to stay calm in class. Only by rewarding the effort of students can the larger goals of good grades, consistent compliance, or good relationships with friends be accomplished.

Replace Tangible Incentives with Social Approval

Teachers often worry about using too many tangible incentives. They are concerned that their students will learn to behave correctly only for a payoff instead of developing internal controls. This is a legitimate concern and it could possibly happen in two kinds of situations. The first involves the teacher who is 'sticker dependent', giving stickers or points for everything the child does but forgetting to provide social approval and praise. In essence, this teacher is teaching the child to perform for payoffs rather than for the pleasure both teacher and child feel about the accomplishments. The second situation arises when the teacher does not plan to phase out the tangible incentive programme and maintains the behaviors with social approval. In other words, the students are not given the message that the teacher expects they will eventually be able to accomplish the task or perform the behavior on their own without rewards.

The use of tangible rewards should be seen as a temporary measure to help students learn new behaviors which are particularly difficult. They must be accompanied by social rewards. Once you have taught the new behaviors, you can gradually phase out the tangible rewards and maintain them with your social reinforcers. For instance, Sonja was put on a sticker programme because she threw tantrums when her mother brought her to preschool and would not let her mother leave without a huge struggle. Sonja enjoyed earning the stickers and her tantrums occurred less and less often over the subsequent weeks. Next Sonja's teacher might say, 'Now that you are coming to school and leaving your mum like a big girl, and earning lots of stickers, let's make the game more fun. Now you have to be calm for two days when your mum leaves before earning a sticker.' Once Sonja is successful on a regular basis for two days, the interval can be extended to four days, and so forth,

Coming into Class Calmly without Disruptions

	M	T	W	TH	F
9.00–9.15					
10.30–10.45					
1.00–1.15					
2.30–2.45					
TOTAL:					

A stamp means coming into class and sitting down at your desk and starting your work right away without teasing or poking.

On Fridays we will count everyone's individual stamps:

    12 stamps = prize from grab bag
    16 stamps = one prize plus special prize
    1500 stamps for whole classroom = celebration ice-cream party

until stickers are no longer necessary. At that point, her teachers may want to stop using stickers or save their use if necessary to help her with a different problem behavior. She could say, 'You remember how well you did several months ago learning to go to school like a big girl with the sticker game we played? Well, let's help you learn to share with your friends by using stickers.' Thus, reward programmes can be phased out and begun again later for different behaviors when necessary.

An important aspect of a reward programme is the message that accompanies the reward. Teachers must clearly communicate that not only do they approve of their student's success, but they also recognize that the child's effort – not the payoff, *per se* – is responsible for the success. In this way, teachers help the child to internalize successes and take credit for them. For example, Sonja's teacher says to Sonja as she gives her the sticker, 'I'm proud of you for coming into school like such a big girl. You've worked hard and you must feel good about it. You are certainly growing up.' Here Sonja's teacher gives the student the credit for her accomplishments, not the sticker. Moreover this example points out that this teacher is relying more on her social relationships with Sonja than the sticker system.

Have Clear and Specific Reward Menus

Another common difficulty in reward programmes is that the rewards are too vague. A teacher says to a student, 'When you do what I ask you to do and earn lots of points, you can get a prize'. The child asks, 'What is the prize?' and the teacher responds, 'Well, you'll see, there will be something, if you get lots of points'. In this example, the teacher is vague about the reward and about how many points it will take to earn it. The result is that the student will not be very motivated to earn points.

Effective reward programmes are clear and precise. You and your students should draw up a chart that includes the rewards you have agreed upon and the value of each item. This chart should be posted in a place where everyone can see it. Younger children who do not read do best with charts that contain pictures of target behaviors and rewards. The child can help by drawing the pictures him or herself or by cutting out pictures from magazines.

Use Team and Group Incentives as Well as Individual Incentives

We often lament the power of peer pressure, yet peer pressure can be a powerful tool in the hands of teachers, a tool for motivating students. As was seen in the example above, in addition to the individual incentives there is a classroom incentive (ice-cream party) for the collective work of the entire classroom. This incentive has the effect of promoting class co-operation. Or sometimes children can be motivated by group competition – the teacher divides the class up into small groups or teams of four to six students, and the teams compete to earn an agreed-upon reward for a particular behavior. For example, the team who earned the most points for a particular accomplishment (e.g. coming up with the most solutions to a problem, getting ready first to go to lunch, being on task, following classroom rules, etc.) may win the privilege of drawing from a fish bowl the winning ticket for a prize. Or teams of children may save up points to earn the privilege for being the first team to draw a card to decide where they will sit the next week. This approach works well for school-age children who enjoy the fun of a competition as long as the teacher helps every team to be successful over time. Moreover, the teacher can set up the game so that it is possible for several teams to win, that is by rewarding all teams who achieve a certain goal such as particular number of points.

For 3–5-year-olds the teacher can still reinforce co-operative teamwork behavior by various means such as putting a teddy bear on the table for the team of children who gets ready to leave school first. Actually this has been used with older children as well.

Team Games

Small group games can be used to focus on positives and to celebrate group and individual efforts in learning and behavior. For example, one teacher set up the following team approach to help her class become calmer, quieter and more task focused. She began by setting up classroom teams consisting of five students per team who were seated together at a table. Each of the teams had a badge with their group motif (e.g. animals, plant name). Once her class had settled into its new groupings she explained that points could be gained by the groups for the following behaviors:

- lining up without pushing
- settling in their group quickly and quietly after recess
- co-operating in their group
- leaving their table clean and tidy
- staying at low levels (white and green) on the noise meter
- staying on task with their work in their chairs.

She explained further that as the group points added up they could be traded for a range of rewards. If all the groups achieved a common target (e.g. 500 points) then the whole class could have a treat. Sometimes teachers can enhance points gained by having an audible timer go off at random times during the day. The group most on task at the point the timer goes off gains extra points. Please note that it is important in these systems that the teacher clearly establishes that s/he is the umpire and the only one who can decide if a group has earned a point.

One novel way of implementing this approach is to give each team a board game or poster which has drawing of a maze or road or team sport on it. In our school, we have developed Wally's football game. Every time the small group (or team) gets a point they can move up one foot space on the football board game. When the group moves ten spaces each group member gets a jelly bean or token. When they move twenty spaces, each group member gets a sticker or stamp. At thirty spaces, they can have 5 minutes extra recess. At forty spaces which brings them back to the beginning they can play a board game or do an activity of their choice (quietly) or spin the wheel of fortune spinner for a reward. It is important that each group gets to ten in their first session so that they experience some success. When every team gets back to the beginning then the class plans a party.

Dinosaur Patrol

Another group classroom incentive system we have found effective for use with young children is called 'Wally's green patrol'. The idea is that all the children are striving to stay in 'green patrol' – that means they are following the rules of the classroom. At the end of a

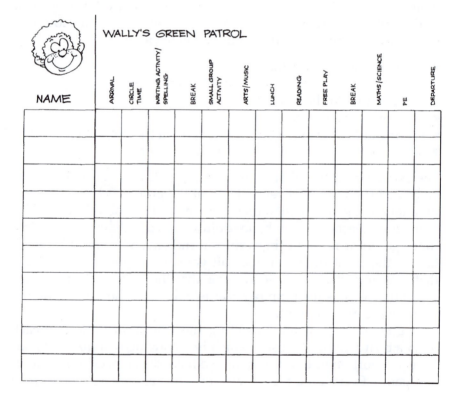

defined period (every half-hour or during certain periods of the day such as for reading period or free play) the teacher reviews to see if the classroom has all stayed in 'green patrol'. If so, there is a special Wally reward green patrol card that goes on a chart. (The chart may be set up with velcro so cards are easily applied.) When the whole class earns a defined number of these green Wally patrol cards, there is a special class reward, such as a pizza party or special event. The teacher can use this system to remind young children of the expected behaviors – for example, 'What do we have to do to stay in green patrol?' This system may also be used to provide incentives for individual children. They can contract with a teacher to earn a certain number of 'green patrols' for the day – for example, with eight greens in a day the teacher might say, 'This has been a green day – just excellent' or if the child earns six out of eight that day, the teacher might say, 'Almost a completely green day, I'll bet you can earn seven greens tomorrow!' Another advantage of this system is that it is 'portable' – the child can earn green cards from other teachers at break, on the bus, or at lunch.

Have a Varied Menu

Some reward programmes rely on a fixed reward menu. That is, the teachers and students set up a menu during one discussion and do not revise it for the next three months. The problem with this approach is that, at the beginning, children often aren't sure what they want to work for. They may think of more interesting items later on.

Make your reward menus flexible and varied. Encourage your students to include a variety of items, such as time with you, special privileges, inexpensive toys, outside activities and treats. Of course, the key is to discover what will be most motivating for them. Appealing and varied menus give children options as their interests and moods change from day to day. Moreover, it is important to evaluate menus every few weeks and permit them to add new things to the list as this will help keep them interested in the programme after the initial novelty wears off.

Be Positive

What happens if you put a lot of effort into setting up a reward programme for a particular child but your student fails to earn points? You may be tempted to respond by criticizing or lecturing the student on why s/he should try harder. Unfortunately, not only would this give the child a discouraging message about his or her ability (which could become a self-fulfilling prophecy), but the negative attention and ensuing power struggle could inadvertently reinforce misbehavior or non-compliance with the programme. In other words, the student would get more payoff for not doing the programme than for doing it.

If your student fails to earn points or stickers it is best to calmly say, 'You didn't get one this morning but I'm sure you'll earn one this afternoon, I'll be watching, I'm sure you can do it'. If you are going to predict the future, it is helpful to convey a positive expectation. However, if your student continues to have difficulties earning points, make sure that you have not made the steps too unrealistic.

School-Wide Incentives

In addition to using these programmes for individuals, teams and whole classrooms it is even possible to set up a school-wide incentive plan. This can be accomplished by developing a laminated matrix of 1 to 200 squares which can be posted on the principal's door next to a list of the school rules. The principal announces over the intercom that there will be a mystery motivator for the first class to fill in a column or row with coupons. Next the principal gives out ten coupons (each marked with a number from 1 to 200) to each teacher per day that the teacher can award to a student for following a particular school rule (e.g. walking in the hallway, helping someone). When a student gets one of these coupons they take it to the principal's office and the secretary helps them mark the correct number with the classroom name on the matrix. The impact of this for the individual student can be increased by having the secretary call the student's parents or send home a card letting the parents know about the child's success as a member of the Principal's 200 Club! On Friday the principal announces the class who wins the mystery motivator prize.

Playground or Cafeteria Raffle Tickets

School-wide planning for improving co-operative behavior not only includes the classrooms and hallways but also the other areas where students congregate such as bus queue, cafeterias and playgrounds. Another school-wide incentive idea is a raffle with tickets given out by the staff supervising playgrounds and lunch times as well as giving bus drivers a book of raffle tickets. Whenever the staff member observes a student being co-operative and helpful s/he hands out a raffle ticket with a positive comment, 'You were very thoughtful in helping that younger child with her bike'. The ticket stubs are collected and a draw is made at morning assembly. A team of teachers organise the prizes, presentations and rules for giving out tickets. For example, tickets were not to be given out for students who 'set up' positive behaviors but rather for student actions which were spontaneous.

Other Principles of Effective Incentive Programmes

Use Rehearsal to Explain Expected Behaviors

Once you have clearly identified the positive behaviors that you will put on your incentive programme, it is important that these behaviors be explained clearly. With young children it is not enough just to talk through the expected behaviors, but rather they need to be modelled and practised or rehearsed. Practice enables recall and short-term memory. For example, you can have the students practise putting up

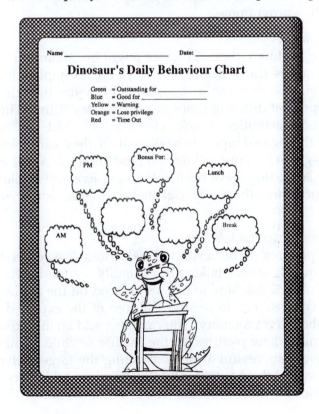

Name _____   Date: _____

Dinosaur's Daily Behaviour Chart

Green = Outstanding for _____
Blue = Good for _____
Yellow = Warning
Orange = Lose privilege
Red = Time Out

PM
Bonus For:
Lunch
Break
AM

a quiet hand or moving to their seats without talking or touching others before the timer goes off. As these expected behaviors are practised the teacher can be supportive and give positive feedback.

Make your Incentive Programmes Fun and Playful

There are all sorts of ways to make incentive programmes fun for children. Here are some examples.

Tic tac toe (noughts and crosses)

A teacher plays a tic tac toe game with her class. First she specifies the behaviors she expects such as everyone sitting quietly in a circle by the time the buzzer goes off, or everyone helping to put snack away by the time the break bell is rung and so forth. Each time the class achieves the agreed upon goal then she gives the class an X on the tic tac toe game. When the class gets a straight line they earn 10 minutes of free play or some special activity which they have chosen. This type of tic tac toe game could also be used individually on a student's desk or for a small group of students on their table as an incentive programme.

Colour-in pictures

For young children, their successes might be coloured in on a picture at various times during the day. For example, children are given a picture showing a dinosaur with some thought balloons which represent different times during the day (Circle Time, break, small group activities, snack, etc.). If the child (or classroom) achieves the agreed upon behaviors then they can colour in the balloon – green for outstanding and blue for good. At the end of the day they see if they have been able to get five green coloured balloons which earns them a special sticker, a maze or a prize of some sort.

Use cartoons of expected behaviors

Cartoon pictures of the expected behaviors (e.g. quiet hand up, working quietly at seat, talking in a friendly way and giving compliments to others, listening to teacher) placed on the students' desks can be a concrete cue to remind children of the expected behavior and aid short-term memory. You can even add an incentive chart to the bottom of these pictures for the teacher or child to fill in whenever they are successful at demonstrating the target behavior. We also like to add the positive self-talk statement which accompanies the behavior for those students who are able to read.

Surprise rewards
Children love surprises! For example, a teacher gets out her toy microphone and says, 'Announcing the greatest class in the universe, for cleaning up the playground so stupendously you are awarded an ice-cream party!' Turning in transition tickets for a chance to win something from a raffle is also motivating for children because of the delight of a surprise reward.

Another incentive programme which has a surprise element built in is the 'mystery super hero' game. Here the teacher picks three students' names out of a hat and tells her class she has three names but she isn't going to say who they are. Then she explains that she will be counting everytime she notices these particular students helping someone, putting up a quiet hand or working hard on an assignment. If by the end of the day these mystery students have each earned ten points they will be the mystery super heroes and

Student Name				
Monday	Tuesday	Wednesday	Thursday	Friday

Student Name				
Monday	Tuesday	Wednesday	Thursday	Friday

can choose a special activity for the class to do. The advantage of this system is that every child in the classroom thinks s/he might be one of the names picked so it encourages everyone to work hard. Moreover, if one of the three doesn't achieve the goal of ten, the teacher does not need to identify that person.

Dot to dot game
Another fun incentive game is for the teacher to play dot to dot with the whole class or with groups of students or an individual student. In this game, each time the student, small group or classroom accomplishes a specified target behavior the teacher fills in one dot to dot number. When the drawing is completed the class or student earn a celebration such as extra computer or recess time on Friday.

Spinner wheel of fortune game
One playful way to determine the reward a child will receive for achieving a behavioral goal is to allow him or her to spin the wheel of fortune. The spinner has the possibility of landing on a number of possible rewards. Each of these may be given more or less space on the pie diagram (i.e. more expensive items being smallest wedge in

pie). Some rewards listed on the pie might be 10 minutes of extra break, 5 minutes of extra computer time, choosing the book for the class to read, treat from the magic grab bag, choice of music to listen to during quiet time, popcorn party, and homework pass. It is a good idea to laminate these spinners and use washable marker so you can change the rewards throughout the year.

Wheel of Fortune

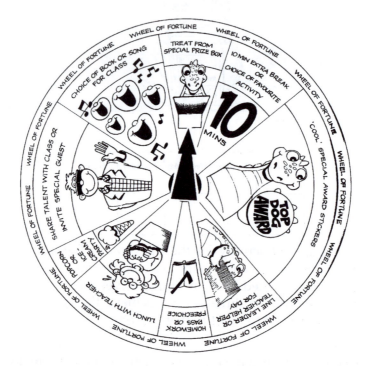

Mystery motivators

Perhaps because of the surprise element, we have found that children of all ages love the idea of working for a mystery motivator (Moore *et al.*, in press; Rhode, Jenson and Reavis, 1992). The teacher writes down on a piece of paper what the mystery motivator is and puts the paper in a large, decorated envelope. Next this envelope is put in some very visible place in the front of the classroom (e.g. taped on the board). The teacher then tells the students that if they earn a certain number of stickers or points that they can open the mystery motivator. The teacher can also remind children when they are on the verge of misbehaving by saying, 'Remember the mystery motivator'.

For example, the mystery motivator could be used for teaching the classroom rules. The teacher does this by preparing a pile of happy faces on cards which have been laminated. Whenever she notices a student following one of the classroom rules (e.g. quiet hand up, going to seat quietly, helping someone, etc.), she puts a happy face in a jar on her desk. She says to the student, 'you went straight to your seat, you earned a happy yes face for everybody'. Then at a certain point in the day when an agreed upon number of happy faces have been collected, she permits the mystery motivator to be opened. Mystery motivators can include any of the things outlined above. You can add to the fun of this by writing or drawing the mystery motivator with an invisible pen which can only be revealed when a special marking pen is scribbled on top of it (i.e. Crayola Changeables).

Programmes such as the one described here can be used with whole classes, teams or with individuals for clearly defined behaviors.

Keep Incentive Programmes and Discipline Programmes Separate

Some teachers create tangible reward programmes and then mix in punishment. For instance, a student may receive stickers for sharing and have them taken away for fighting. The stickers then take on negative rather than positive associations. This approach can be even more problematic if the child is left with a negative balance. If the only prospect is to earn stickers to get out of debt, all the positive incentive for good behavior is gone. The natural outcome is for the child to become discouraged and abandon all efforts to change.

Keep your rewards programme separate from your discipline programme. Removing earned points or rewards as punishment will defeat the purpose of the programme, which is to give attention to appropriate behaviors. If you want to use privilege removal as a discipline technique, keep any privileges you foresee withdrawing (time off recess, computer time) off your reward menu. (See Chapter 7 for information on privilege removal.)

Keep Control of your Programme

There are several ways you can lose control of your reward programme. The first is by paying for 'almost' performance – that is giving rewards to your students when they haven't earned the required points or stickers. This usually happens because they argue for them, claiming they've done everything required. Unfortunately, it undermines the rules of the contract as well as your authority. It is also likely to result in your students escalating their begging and debating with you over the attainment of points. Instead of a behavior problem being solved, a new one is created. Lack of follow-through can be a second problem. This happens when your students have behaved according to the programme but you fail to notice the behaviors or you forget to give them the stickers or to allow them to trade them in at the agreed time. If the rewards are given very late or in an inconsistent manner, their reinforcing value is minimal.

Tangible reward programmes require a lot of work on the part of teachers in order to be effective! You must consistently monitor your students' behaviors in order to determine whether they have earned stickers or points. Only give stickers if you have actually observed these behaviors (not when they claim to have done them out of your sight). If you and a student are working on high frequency problems such as not listening or following directions, then a great deal of vigilance will be required. Rewards are most effective if they are given *immediately* after the desired behavior is performed. Also, in order for these programmes to work, you must be a consistent limit setter. All children will test the limits and try to see if they can get rewards for less work. That's natural, but it means that you must prepared for this testing, stay committed to the programme and ignore arguments, debates or pleading when your students have not earned enough points. Finally, you need to keep control of the rewards. Prizes and stickers should be hidden and awarding points and stickers determined by you, not your children. (See Chapter 6 for more information on how to set limits and ignore misbehaviors.)

Use 'I Can' Cans on Children's Desks to Teach Positive Self-Talk

Put an empty can on each child's desk and label it the 'I can' can. Whenever you notice the child sharing, co-operating, helping, being friendly write these behaviors out as 'I can' statements and put them in the can for the child to take home. For example, 'I can help others', 'I can listen to the teacher well', 'I can cope with this conflict', 'I can sit in my seat without rocking', 'I can move quickly to my seat without disturbing others', 'I can stay in my seat until the egg timer goes off', and so forth. Doing this helps the child challenge negative self-talk and rehearse positive self-statements and positive behavior at school. If these notes are reread at home with parents, the impact is doubled.

Sharing Successes with Parents – Happy Grams and Awards

When a child's success at school is shared with that child's parents, another reinforcer comes into play – namely, parental attention and approval – and the child gets a 'double dose' of reinforcement. Teachers can send home notes, special awards or 'happy grams' (or make phone calls) throughout the year announcing their child's special accomplishment or just to tell them about a particularly good day. Not only does this kind of gesture work wonders for your relationship with the student and parents, it also is a form of teaching, for it shows parents you want them to recognize what their child has accomplished. And it also helps strengthen parents' involvement in their child's school experience. Moreover, you are building up what might be seen as a 'positive bank account' with that student and parents which creates a trusting relationship

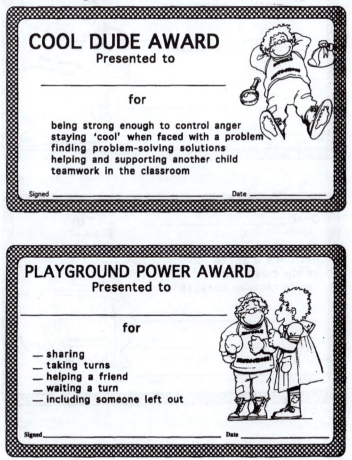

COOL DUDE AWARD
Presented to

_____

for

being strong enough to control anger
staying 'cool' when faced with a problem
finding problem-solving solutions
helping and supporting another child
teamwork in the classroom

Signed _____ Date _____

PLAYGROUND POWER AWARD
Presented to

_____

for

— sharing
— taking turns
— helping a friend
— waiting a turn
— including someone left out

Signed_____ Date _____

between teacher and parents. If it becomes necessary to discuss a behavior problem concerning their child, parents who have a positive relationship with you will be more open and more able to collaborate with you in addressing the problem.

An additional benefit of sending home awards or compliment notes to parents about some positive aspect of the child's behavior or attitude is that it helps the parents focus the *child* on his or her successes, thus preparing the child to behave in similar ways the next day.

Attention: _____
Parent's Name

I'm very proud to announce that

_____
Student's Name

has made an AWESOME IMPROVEMENT
in our classroom because

_____

_____

_____

Signed   Date

To: _____
Parent's Name

CONGRATULATIONS!
I'm pleased to announce that

_____
Student's Name

had a GREAT DAY because

_____

_____

Signed   Date

To Sum Up

- Identify one to two positive behaviors you want to increase first. These may be contracted with the whole class or set up as individual goals according to children's particular needs.

- Explain to the class or individual child which behaviors will result in a reward.

- Select the incentives. Stars and stickers can be good motivators for 3–5-year-old children. Older children like to earn points, tickets or chips and trade them in for something they have chosen on a reinforcement menu.

- The reinforcement menu should be planned in advance with children – it should be specific.

- Allow young children to earn rewards daily. Older school-age children should earn something every few days.
- Don't reward 'almost' performances.
- Be sure to fulfil your end of the agreement.
- Always combine tangible rewards with social rewards, such as labelled praise and encouragement.
- Remember, what is a meaningful reinforcer for one child may not be reinforcing for another child. Individualize the incentives as much as possible.
- If you use charts to keep track of progress, review the charts every day with your class.
- Set a goal to increase the number of positive notes and phone calls you make home to parents and children each week.
- Write on the board the names of children who make a special achievement – either academic or social. This reinforces good behavior and is a reminder to all the class of the expected behavior.

Some Dos and Don'ts

Do

1. Clearly define the desired academic and social behaviors.
2. Identify small steps towards the goals.
3. Gradually increase the criteria for the reward (make it challenging).
4. Begin by choosing only one or two behaviors to work on.
5. Focus on positive behaviors.
6. Choose inexpensive rewards.
7. Offer rewards that can be earned on a daily basis.
8. Involve students in choosing the rewards.
9. Give the reward *after* the behavior occurs (first–then).
10. Reward everyday achievements and successes.

Don't

1. Be vague about the desired behaviors.
2. Make the steps too big for the child.
3. Make the steps too easy for the child.
4. Create complex programmes involving too many behaviors.
5. Focus on negative behaviors.
6. Offer expensive rewards, or rewards that cannot be furnished immediately.
7. Use rewards that take too long to earn.
8. Choose rewards that are not motivating to the child.

9. Offer rewards as bribes.
10. Be stingy with social rewards.

References

Barkley, R. A. (1996) Attention deficit/hyperacitivity disorder. In E. J. Mash and R. A. Barkley (eds.) *Child Psychopathology* (pp. 63–112), New York: Guilford Press.

Cameron, J. and Pierce, W. D. (1994) Reinforcement, reward, and intrinsic motivation: a meta-analysis, *Review of Educational Research*, 64, 363–423.

Elliott, S. N. and Gresham, F. M. (1992) *Social Skills Intervention Guide*, Circle Pines, MN: American Guidance Service.

Moore, L. A., Waguespack, A. M., Wickstorm, K. F., Witt, J. C. and Gaydos, G. R. (in press) Mystery motivator: An effective and time efficient intervention, *School Psychology Review*.

Rhode, G., Jenson, W. R. and Reavis, H. K. (1992) *The Tough Kid Book*, Longmont, CO: Sopriswest, Inc.

Stage, S. A. and Quiroz, D. R. (1997) A meta-analysis of interventions to decrease disruptive classroom behavior in public education settings, *School Psychology Review*, 26, 333–68.

Walker, H. M. (1995) *The Acting-Out Child: Coping with Classroom Disruption*, Longmont, CO: Sopriswest, Inc.

Chapter Six

Managing Misbehavior: Ignoring and Redirecting

The proactive strategies discussed in the first five chapters will prevent many classroom behavior problems from occurring. However, in spite of the best proactive classroom management on the part of teachers, misbehavior will still occur. When a student disrupts the classroom with misbehavior, your responses are likely to be scattered, inconsistent, and sometimes merely reactive unless you have established a clear discipline plan. A discipline plan is fundamental to proactive classroom management. A classroom discipline plan means not only that rules and expectations are clearly delineated, but also that it is clear to every student exactly what the consequences will be if the rules are broken or expectations are not met.

In general, research has shown that teachers are more likely to rely on punitive or negative consequences in the classroom than on positive techniques when responding to discipline problems (for review see Bear, 1998; Hyman, 1997; Martens and Meller, 1990). This is true despite the widespread recognition of the limitations and negative effects of punishment, especially when used as the primary strategy of response. However, less severe consequences and less punitive strategies should always be tried first. This is called the 'law of least disruptive intervention'. In the discipline plan, consequences should be organized in a hierarchy from the least disruptive intervention to the most disruptive. For example, when a rule is broken the first time there will be a verbal warning, the second time a privilege will be withdrawn, the third time a Time Out may be given, the fourth time the child has a talk with teacher at break and so on. By making sure that students are familiar with the discipline plan and understand the consequences, the proactive teacher ensures that students know exactly how the teacher will respond to misbehavior. The consistency of the teacher's follow through with this discipline plan increases children's sense of security. A discipline plan enables students to anticipate consequences as the natural outcomes of inappropriate behavior. The major alternatives before resorting to negative consequences such as loss of privileges and Time Out are the strategies of ignoring, self-monitoring, re-directing, and reminders or warnings.

The following pages will help you develop a discipline plan for misbehaviors starting with the least disruptive interventions and leading to more disruptive negative consequences which are discussed in Chapters 7 and 8.

Ignoring Misbehavior

One major strategy for reducing inappropriate behavior in students is ignoring it. In one sense ignoring misbehavior is unnatural, for there is a natural tendency for teachers to attend to students who are out of their seat or being disruptive or argumentative. However, teacher attention only reinforces that behavior. Ignoring can be a powerful tool for modifying behavior, since it deprives the child of the attention all children want. While ignoring is highly effective, it is also probably the hardest teaching strategy for teachers to actually carry out. The following discussion will help you deal with some of the problems that teachers encounter when trying to ignore their students' minor misbehaviors.

Choosing Behaviors to Ignore

Minor inappropriate or low-level attention seeking behaviors such as whining, teasing, arguing, eye rolling, pouting, calling out and trantrums (i.e. behaviors that are not dangerous or hurtful to other children or adults) can often be eliminated if they are systematically ignored. Sometimes teachers feel ignoring is not discipline. In fact, it is one of the most effective techniques that can be used with students. Teachers who ignore their students when they behave inappropriately give no payoff (or power) to the student for continuing the misbehavior. By not giving the misbehavior attention, the teachers are also not engaging in the power struggle with the student. As ignoring is consistently maintained, students will eventually stop what they are doing. Moreover, if students receive praise and encouragement for the opposite prosocial behaviors (e.g. speaking politely, sharing, co-operating, and controlling their temper), they will learn it is more beneficial to behave appropriately than inappropriately.

There are also some child behaviors that are irritating to teachers but cannot actually be controlled by children. For example, the hyperactive child may not be able to stop his wiggling and fidgeting in his seat or the impulsive child his mumbling under his breath or the language delayed child his stuttering. These behaviors certainly should not be punished and need to be ignored by teachers. Attending to them will only make them worse and will cause other children to attend to them as well.

Avoid Discussion and Eye Contact

Sometimes teachers think they're ignoring their students' misbehavior when they are actually giving them considerable attention. They may have stopped talking to a student but continued glaring, grimacing or in other ways letting the student know that the misbehavior is affecting them. Some teachers ignore by avoiding eye contact with the student but continue to make critical or sarcastic comments. In both instances, the misbehaving student is successful in receiving attention and, perhaps, a powerful negative emotional response as well.

Effective ignoring occurs when you are able to neutralize your reaction to what your student is doing. Your facial expression should be neutral, you should avoid eye contact, and stop all discussions. Ignoring also involves moving away from the student, especially if you have been in close contact. Just as the most powerful form of positive attention includes a smile, eye contact, verbal praise and physical touching, the most powerful form of ignoring is a neutral expression, involving no eye contact, no communication and a turning away of the body.

Use Consistent Ignoring – Be Prepared for the Misbehavior to Get Worse at First

Sometimes well-intentioned teachers start to ignore misbehavior such as tantrums or arguments without being prepared for the student's possible response. Most children will initially react to ignoring with an increase in negative behaviors to see if they can get their teacher to back down. For instance, 5-year-old Hanook wants to play with the long bubble-maker but his teacher says he cannot have it. He cries about this for several minutes and insists on grabbing it from her. Finally the teacher takes the bubble-maker and putting it on a high shelf proceeds to ignore his protests. Hanook escalates his demands and tantrums to see if he can get the bubble-maker back. This tantruming goes on for ten more minutes until the teacher, exasperated and worn down by the crying, says 'All right, you can have it!' By giving in for the short-term benefit of making life more peaceful, the teacher has created a long-term problem: Hanook has learned that if he tantrums long and hard enough, he will get what he wants. Thus, he has been reinforced for inappropriate behaviors.

Remember, when you first start ignoring a misbehavior it will usually get worse. In fact, if the student's behavior gets worse when you begin to ignore, that is a signal to you that the strategy is working! You must be prepared to wait out this testing period if the behavior is to improve. If you give in, your students will learn that behaving inappropriately is an effective way to get what they want. The example of Hanook and his teacher is not unlike an experience you may have had with a vending machine. You put your change in for a soft drink, but don't get one and can't get your money back. You press the return button several times and when this doesn't work you try the drink button again. Depending on how thirsty or cross you are, you may persist in pressing the buttons and even try banging on the machine. Finally, if no soft drink appears, you give up and move on to something else because there has been no payoff for your banging. However, if by some stroke of luck a soft drink pops out during your banging, then you know that the next time you can't get a soft drink, the trick is to bang hard and long enough. Children can learn to be persistent. This is one of the reasons that ignoring is so difficult for teachers to carry out. All children will test their teacher's ignoring skills by escalating their misbehaviors. If you decide to use this technique you must be prepared to wait out this period by remaining firm in your resolution to ignore.

Ignore and Distract

Choosing to ignore misbehavior doesn't mean that there is nothing positive you can do to improve the situation. In fact, failure to provide distractions or suggestions for alternative, more appropriate behavior can lock teachers and children into a power struggle and cause the children to prolong the misbehaviors. Consider this scenario: Johnny asks his teacher if he can use the paints. When his teacher refuses permission, Johnny starts yelling and screaming. His teacher effectively ignores this tantruming by walking away and in a couple of minutes the screaming subsides. At this point, Johnny's teacher fails to notice his quiet behavior or to distract him with something else to play with. Johnny, feeling ignored, begins to scream again, in an attempt to gain his teacher's attention.

Use distractions to reduce your student's reaction to being ignored or being denied something. Distractions are particularly useful with 3- and 4-year-olds, but they also work with older children. For example, once Johnny stopped screaming, his teacher could have prevented further outbursts by giving him attention and suggesting some other interesting activity he might like to try. In another example, a student starts whining when told she can't use the computer. The teacher ignores her until she stops whining and then asks her if she wants to help clean the fish tank. The idea is to ignore her secondary misbehavior in response to being told she can't have something, and then distract her as soon as she starts behaving more appropriately. Of course, if she misbehaves again in response to the distraction, you will need to resume ignoring.

Another way to combine distraction with ignoring is to distract *yourself* from your student's inappropriate behaviors. You can do this by talking to another student, or involving yourself in something else. If you are ignoring your student who is having a tantrum, you may want to go over to other children who are playing quietly and comment on their activity or their ability to co-operate. If your student thinks you have been distracted, he or she will quickly stop misbehaving. Then you can turn your attention back to the student and praise this or her first co-operative behaviors.

Move Away from the Student but Stay Nearby

It may seem reasonable to ignore your student's misbehaviors by walking to the other side of the room. This can be an effective technique if the child is clinging and physically demanding attention. However, the difficulty with going too far away is that you won't be able to pay attention to and reinforce the appropriate behavior as soon as it returns. When ignoring, it is best to physically move away by standing up and walking to a part of the room nearby. This way you can monitor your student's behavior and reinforce him as soon as he stops misbehaving. For example, as the teacher is going around the room assisting students, Freddie calls out from across the room, 'Miss, hey Miss!' The teacher realizes that if she goes over to Freddie or asks him to wait, she will be giving attention to his calling out so she decides to tactically ignore it. She doesn't look at him or comment on his behavior and continues to work with several students. Freddie calls out again, 'Miss, come on, I need your help, please! I only want to ask a question.' The teacher continues ignoring and moves on to help another student. Freddie sulks for a while and then begins to do some writing. At this moment she goes up to him and casually asks, 'Can I see your work?' and reaches for his book. She simply and quietly reminds him, 'Remember to put up a quiet hand and wait, then I will happily come over'.

Ignoring Teaches Self-Control

Some teachers do not use ignoring because they feel it is disrespectful to their students and harmful to their self-esteem. They are concerned that this approach will damage their relationship with their students. Other teachers do not ignore because they feel it does not punish their student enough for the misbehavior. They say, 'How can you ignore behaviors like swearing or yelling? These behaviors need punishment.'

Research indicates that ignoring is an effective discipline approach because it maintains a positive teacher–student relationship based on respect rather than fear. If you can ignore screaming or swearing instead of responding with yelling or criticizing the student, you show your students that you can maintain self-control in the face of conflict and anger. And because you don't get upset by these behaviors, students soon realize that they have little effect or payoff and learn that there is no value in continuing to use them.

Teach Other Students to Ignore

Sometimes ignoring backfires because even though the teacher ignores the student's misbehavior, the other students give it attention by laughing at and teasing the child. If this is happening, your ignoring will not work because the student is still managing to get attention for his misbehavior from his peer group. If other students are responding and giving attention to a particular child's misbehaviors, they need to be taught the wisdom of ignoring their friends' tantrums and arguments when they occur. Teachers can say to the tantruming student's classmates, 'We can best help Jeremy right now if we ignore him until he has got himself under control'. It is helpful for teachers to practise and role-play ahead of time with students how to ignore certain behaviors. For example, students can be taught not only how to ignore the child who has tantrums in response to a teacher request but also how to ignore their classmates if they tease or make fun of them.

Limit the Number of Behaviors to Ignore

Whereas some teachers have the problem of ignoring too rarely, others ignore too much. Such teachers effectively ignore their student's initial misbehavior but then they continue to withhold attention, support and approval for several hours or even days at a time. A related problem occurs when teachers deal with too many misbehaviors at once; whining, yelling, screaming, arguing and messy work, for example. Ignoring so many things will cause children to feel neglected and leave teachers feeling overwhelmed. Not only will they find it difficult to be consistent in their ignoring, but they will find it hard to remember to give attention for the opposite, positive behaviors.

It is important when ignoring that you identify specific behaviors to focus on. Choose only one or two to systematically ignore at any given time. By limiting yourself this way, you can more realistically expect to be consistent in ignoring the misbehavior every time it occurs. As well, you will be able to observe and monitor the effects this discipline technique has on the particular behavior.

Certain Student Behaviors Should Not Be Ignored

Some teachers ignore *all* their students' misbehaviors, regardless of the type, severity or the setting in which they occur. This is not an appropriate approach for behaviors that are verbally abusive or physically destructive to children, themselves, other people or property. It is also inappropriate for behaviors such as lying, stealing, non-compliance or forgetting to do homework.

In most circumstances, annoying behaviors such as whining, pouting, screaming, and tantrums can be dealt with effectively by ignoring. On the other hand, dangerous or abusive behaviors, including hitting, verbal abuse, running away and damaging property must not be ignored. Bullying a classmate or stealing, which provide students with immediate benefits while inconveniencing or harming others, should not be ignored either. In these situations a stronger consequence, such as a Time Out, loss of a privilege or a work chore, needs to be used in order to change the behavior. Therefore, it's important to select the behaviors you are going to ignore with care. Also remember that ignoring an inappropriate behavior will only be effective with those students for whom teacher attention is the primary reinforcement. Thus the teacher will need to have worked very hard building a positive relationship with that student first before ignoring will be effective.

Pay Attention to Positive Behaviors

Some teachers become so engrossed in their teaching that they fail to pay attention when their students speak nicely, share toys, solve a difficult problem or work quietly. If these positive behaviors are ignored, they will disappear. Teachers often develop a reflex response, reacting to students only when they get into trouble. This negative cycle of paying attention when they misbehave and ignoring them when they are behaving appropriately actually increases the frequency of misbehavior.

If you use ignoring, it is crucial that you plan carefully to give attention and praise to pro-social behaviors, particularly those that are the opposite of the one you are ignoring. If you have decided to ignore whining, for instance, you should make a conscious effort to praise the student whenever he or she speaks appropriately. 'I really like it when you use your polite voice', you might say. It's important to focus on the positive behavior you want to see replace the problem one. If you are concerned that your student is grabbing and hitting, you need to praise her frequently for sharing and playing nicely.

Another effective strategy involves combining ignoring and praise in a group of two or three students. When one child is misbehaving, give your attention to the one demonstrating appropriate behaviors. Imagine a different scene with Peter throwing Lego on the floor, while Jamal is building something carefully with the Lego. Your natural instinct is to focus on the child who is misbehaving: 'Peter, don't do that'. However, this would reinforce Peter's inappropriate behavior. If instead, you ignore Peter and praise Jamal, Peter will probably begin to behave more appropriately because he sees that co-operative behavior gains attention and misbehavior doesn't.

Give Back your Attention as Soon as Possible

Once in a while teachers may be so distressed and angered by inappropriate behaviors that they cannot focus on good behaviors. It's important to remember that as soon as the student stops misbehaving, you should quickly return your attention (within 5 seconds) and praise some appropriate behavior. Only by combining the withdrawal of attention for inappropriate behaviors with consistent attention for appropriate ones will you reverse the cycle of negative attention for negative behavior. So, just as soon as the misbehavior stops, begin to smile, praise, look at and talk to the student.

Use Subtle Ignores with Secondary Behaviors

Teachers can be too dramatic in the way they ignore their students. If a youngster begins to sulk, pout or mutter, or roll their eyeballs, the teacher may make an exaggerated gesture of pulling away and disregarding the misbehavior. This can be almost as reinforcing as giving attention for the misbehavior because it shows the student she has been able to produce a strong emotional response in her teacher.

Although it is advisable to withdraw physical contact, eye contact and verbal contact when ignoring, it is also important that you neutralize your emotional reactions and be subtle. If the student is whining, you should matter of factly look away and perhaps comment to another student about something else that's going on. This is effective because it reveals no hint that you are affected in any way by your student's whining.

It is very helpful to use this subtle ignoring for the non-verbal secondary behaviors which often accompany a child's reaction to a teacher's command or request to do something. For example, you have asked two students to clean the hamster cage and while they have co-operated with your request and are starting to clean the cage, they are also moaning, whining, sulking and sighing as they do the task. Here the teacher needs to focus on praising their compliance to her request and ignoring the other secondary and less important misbehaviors. If, on the other hand, the teacher were to respond to their low grade challenging misbehaviors by saying, 'I don't like your attitude and your snotty tone of voice' then s/he would be fuelling this response with her attention. Remember it is not necessary nor realistic that your students enjoy doing chores or following your directions.

Stay in Charge

Mary, the teacher, is running late and it is time for the children to go to break. Several students are dawdling and won't put on their shoes. She is so frustrated that she finally says, 'If you don't hurry up and get ready, I'll leave without you!' When the children keep on dawdling, she walks out of the classroom. Of course, she waits there, though she may hide for a bit around a corner of the hallway.

Teachers who take ignoring to an extreme and threaten to leave their students believe that the fear caused by their leaving will mobilize the children into being more compliant. While such threats may get the children out of the door, they have several long-term disadvantages. In order to continue to be effective, all threats need to be backed up with the threatened consequence. Once your student realizes you are only pretending to leave, s/he will respond with similar threats: 'Go ahead and leave me. See if I care!' You are then left in a powerless position because your student has called your bluff. If you don't leave, you're not following through. Yet leaving isn't really an option since it is not safe to leave a young child in the classroom alone. The emotional hazard is also great as threats to abandon children make them to feel insecure and create further problems of poor self-esteem. Furthermore, you are teaching the students a powerful strategy to use in relationships when faced with conflict. Students may begin threatening to run away or may leave school to test the power of this tactic for getting what they want.

Never threaten to leave or abandon a student, no matter how great the temptation. Think about other strategies that are effective in helping them to be more compliant. Perhaps if you can ignore the behavior that makes you feel so cross that you are ready to leave them, they will begin to behave more appropriately. If you can't use ignoring, you may need to try another discipline technique such as loss of privileges or work chores. While these strategies will take more of your time in the short run, they will teach your students that your relationship is secure, regardless of occasional conflict. These strategies are far preferable because they are based on respect rather than on the fear of abandonment.

Conclusions about Ignoring

If you decide to use ignoring, you must be determined to ignore the student at all costs until the misbehavior stops. Consistency is the essence of ignoring. When your student throws a tantrum you may be tempted to give in. However, each time you do so you actually make the misbehavior worse because you teach her that she can outlast you. The next time, the tantrum will be louder and last longer. Therefore, you must continue ignoring until the behavior changes.

Remember also that ignoring is not likely to affect how your student behaves unless a positive relationship has been built up between the two of you. The first task in any plan to change behavior is to increase your attention and praise for positive behaviors. Although ignoring will decrease annoying misbehaviors, it will not increase positive ones. To do this, it must be combined with social approval for good behavior as well as teaching about appropriate behaviors when your student is behaving well.

Encourage Self-Monitoring for Disruptive Behaviors

One common problem that all teachers face is the student who blurts out the answer in class instead of waiting and putting up a quiet hand. The teacher's least intrusive strategy for reducing this disruptive behavior would be to praise the students who have quiet hands up, answer only students who have a quiet hand up, and occasionally remind students that you will only respond to them when they have their hands raised and are quiet. Given that the teacher has taken these preventive steps consistently and the child still is yelling out in class, then it may be necessary to go to a higher level of discipline in the hierarchy such as a planned ignoring or a warning of consequences.

Remember always to have a positive incentive programme in place first before using ignoring. A self-monitoring chart can often be helpful for inattentive and impulsive children (who act before they think) and prevents the need to use negative consequences. For example, for the students who have difficulty with blurting out responses in class, you can implement a picture of a *quiet hand up sheet* at their desks. With this strategy, you give the students a picture chart which not only reminds them of the behavior they are working on but also permits them to record every time they put up a quiet hand. You may even want the students to record their talking out as well. At end of the morning you can review with them how many quiet hands up they have recorded. You can contract with them regarding how many quiet hands up they will get in the afternoon and offer an incentive for achieving a certain goal. The teacher says, 'When you get five quiet hands up and only one blurt out you can choose the activity for break'. This strategy is very useful for helping a child learn to monitor his own talking out behavior.

If this is a problem for the whole class you might consider a blurt out thermometer. First, you get a baseline of how often your students are blurting out in the morning. Let us say you find they are blurting out thirty times a morning. Next you show your students a thermometer numbered from one to thirty and challenge them to get only twenty blurt outs. Then each time there is a student who blurts out you circle the number on the thermometer but make no

Student Name				
Monday	Tuesday	Wednesday	Thursday	Friday

further comments (to avoid giving undue attention to blurting out). You will find that your students will not exceed twenty and most classrooms get lower than the goal you set. The next day you might set the goal lower to fifteen blurt outs. Of course, you can never expect zero blurt outs so your baseline might never go below five or six. You might set up a celebration or incentive for when the class consistently achieves blurt outs of less than ten for three days in a row. (Again your expectations will vary depending on whether you are teaching 3–5-year-olds or older children.)

In the case of preschool children it is probably unrealistic for teachers to be concerned about blurt outs and quiet hands up since it is developmentally normal for 3–5-year-olds to be more impulsive and to have difficulty waiting. With this age children, your goal may be simply to encourage their participation and attention. Gradually as you respond primarily to quiet hands up and reinforce this behavior (and ignore blurt outs) you can begin to help these children learn that this is expected classroom behavior.

Redirecting Misbehavior

It's very important for teachers not to ignore students who are withdrawn or off task during classroom activities. While withdrawn behavior is non-disruptive to other students and may be less of a problem for teachers, it is a significant problem for such students because they are not involved in what they should be doing and therefore not learning what they should be. If the teacher ignores this behavior, it sends the message to the students involved that the teacher doesn't care and has low expectations for them. On the other hand, punishing a child who is off task but non-disruptive is unnecessarily severe and may be counterproductive. Instead, the teacher should redirect distracted students, giving them the opportunity to become involved in a more productive activity.

Many minor non-disruptive student misbehaviors can be handled unobtrusively by effective use of teacher redirection. This redirection can be non-verbal, verbal or physical in nature. The advantage of this approach is that it doesn't draw attention to the student's misbehavior from other students and doesn't disrupt the classroom work being carried out.

Use Non-verbal Signals and Prompts and Picture Cues for Redirecting

Many teachers have certain non-verbal signals or prompts that they use consistently and that have a clearly established meaning regarding particular rules for behavior. Examples are an upheld hand with two fingers raised, or turning the lights off and on, or tapping on a small glass jar or rhythmic clapping, all of which may signal 'quiet down'. Another creative way for the teacher to indicate to her classroom that she wants their attention is to begin to draw the eyes, ears and emerging face on the chalkboard. When the teacher finishes drawing the smile on the face all the eyes and ears of the students  should be on her. A thumbs up or wink can also quickly acknowledge that students quieted down when this request was made.

Teachers may want to establish special non-verbal signals for particular children to help them remember specific behaviors that are expected of them. One commonly used approach by teachers is the 'stare'. Catching the student's eye implicitly says, 'You need to get back on focus'. Although no words are used, this non-verbal and non-confrontational communication redirects the child to pay attention – and without drawing attention to him as an overt verbal command would. Another example for the child who has his feet up, or is swaying backwards on his chair, is for the teacher to signal ('four on the floor please') with a non-verbal simulation of chairs legs – four fingers pointing down.

For young children, the use of rules stated in the form of pictures or visual cues that symbolize the appropriate behaviors are very

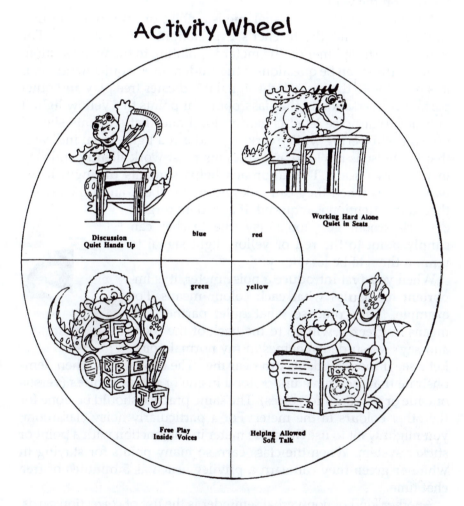

Activity Wheel

Discussion
Quiet Hands Up

blue

Working Hard Alone
Quiet in Seats

red

green

yellow

Free Play
Inside Voices

Helping Allowed
Soft Talk

powerful ways of redirecting or reminding students about the rules. For example the teacher could have a picture showing quiet work being done, or quiet hand up, or a student staying in seat, so that when some students are talking or out of seat or forget to put up a quiet hand, the teacher can simply point to the visual cue to remind them of the rules for the activity, 'Remember our rule for asking questions?' Additionally, most teachers have rules posted on the wall. One non-verbal way of redirecting a child is simply to point to the rule on the wall.

Another example of a visual cue is a noise or activity meter that cues children into the teacher's expectations for an activity. For example, if the spinner on the meter is pointing to the white section, it means there can be questions if the student uses a quiet hand up; if it is pointing to the green light signal it indicates free play and quiet partner conversation in the classroom; if it points to a yellow light it indicates that noise level is getting loud and that students should use soft whispering while working, and a red light signal indicates that the noise is too loud and students must work silently and stay in their own seats. This approach helps students distinguish between times when they can talk and move about and times when their total attention is required. If a student forgets or a classroom gets too noisy, the teacher can simply point to the red or yellow light signal to remind them to be less noisy.

Noise Meter

When you first introduce a noise meter, it is important to discuss what each colour means. For example, 'Let's practise what quiet partner talk means in green. I will go to the back of the room and say two students' names in my normal voice. Let's see if those students can hear me.' The children can then demonstrate that they have understood inside or partner voices (versus outside or playground voices). The same practice should be done for the other colours in the meter. For a particularly noisy classroom, you might want to use the noise meter in conjunction with a point or sticker system. When the class earn so many points for staying in white or green they can earn a privilege such as 5 minutes of free chat time.

Another kind of non-verbal reminder is the use of correction cards. Here the teacher does not say anything to the student but passes him or her a correction card. The card could say 'remember quiet hand up' or 'now is the time to stop' or 'keep working'. For use with

Working hard

Quiet hands up in class

Stop - look - think - check

Listening to teacher

younger children, it should have a picture of these messages on the card. This approach is beneficial because it helps the teacher to talk less about the negative behaviors and avoids distraction of other students. Of course, if a teacher is using correction cards, they are advised to use compliment cards as well. These cards may be given out for the pro-social behavior that is being strengthened.

Other examples of visual prompts are:

- Squeeze imaginary ball (get it together).
- Raise hand with two fingers apart (for quiet down).
- Dark room (lights off and on for transition to recess).
- Thumbs up (good job).
- Wink (working hard).

- Musical sound for transition.
- Picture cue – such as red light for 'absolute quiet', yellow stop light for 'quiet talk while working', green light for 'free play'.
- The 'stare' – catching the child's eye.
- Correction card (e.g. stop signal, quiet hand up signal).
- Compliment card.
- Volume turning down signal with thumb and forefinger (turn down noise).
- Four fingers pointing down (to signal four legs on the floor).
- One finger pointing down and moving in a circle (to indicate turning around).
- Give me five (ears open, eyes on teacher, hands in lap, mouth closed, feet on floor).

Remember, students with attention deficit disorders, impulsivity and language delays are visual learners. Picture cueing for rules, routines and transitions will be very helpful to these students because of their short-term memory problems.

Use Physical Redirection to Practise, Divert and Diffuse

Young preschool children may need to be physically walked through the motions of the behavior that is expected of them in order to understand the verbal instructions. Even for young children who do process verbal instructions well, walking them through the actual behaviors you expect will often help them learn more quickly than if you tell them verbally and wait for them to respond. For example, if the child is wandering out of Circle Time you may just gently redirect him by taking his arm and leading him back to his seat. It may not be necessary to even give a verbal command.

Another type of physical redirect is to ask a disengaged or hyperactive student to do something to help you. This might mean asking them to put away the books, collect the papers, tidy up the book corner, or help you get the snack ready. Such a request allows the child a legitimate opportunity to move around and engages him in some useful activity giving him or her a sense of involvement and responsibility. Sometimes it is also helpful to give very fidgety children something to do with their hands, such as knitting or squeezing a rubber ball, etc. These approaches divert and diffuse the disruption before it comes a problem or gains attention from peers.

Positive Verbal Redirection

There is a real art to redirecting a disruptive student verbally without being confrontational. Sometimes a teacher can signal a child to stop by simply mentioning the student's name while you are teaching a lesson. This gives minimal attention to the misbehaving child and is often enough to get a child back on track without resorting to consequences.

Try to avoid negative verbal redirections such as, 'Didn't you hear what I asked you to do?' or 'You weren't listening and were talking to your neighbour'. These redirections do little to help the child become more productive. Instead for the child who is daydreaming and off task, the teacher might say, 'May I see what you have done so far?' For the student who doesn't seem to be listening, the teacher might say, 'Jessie will you tell me what the instructions are?' For the student who is chatting, 'Face this way please' or 'Having trouble, need a hand?'

One type of ineffective verbal redirection is 'why' questions. For example a student pushes in line and pokes another child and the teacher responds with, 'Why did you do that?' Or, a child is procastinating with her work and the teacher says, 'Why is it taking you so long? Why are you out of seat?' Why directions are counterproductive because they draw the teacher into unnecessary dialogue and imply a criticism of the child. Moreover, children don't usually understand why they have behaved the way they did, neither do adults for that matter! It is likely is that when you ask a child why he did something, he will withdraw or deny the problem. Instead, focus on what you saw and give direct feedback, 'I saw you pushing in line, remember our rule for respect?' or 'You are have trouble doing your work. Can you finish it before lunch or do you need to stay in at break?'

Of course, one of the most effective positive redirections is through the use of proximity praise. When the teacher praises the students who are working hard, paying attention and following directions, this praise serves as a reminder or verbal redirection to the students who are not engaged in these behaviors.

Be Firm and Direct

For some disruptive behaviors, a clear and unambiguously assertive response (without aggression and screaming) is the most appropriate strategy. For example, verbal put downs that are intended to abuse and hurt. If you hear a vicious or loud put-down from a student in your class for the first time, stop immediately and say firmly, 'Jeff! (pause) This is serious. That is a put-down and put-downs hurt. That is unacceptable. We have a rule for polite language and I expect you to use it. Our class is a positive language zone. Now, class, back to work.' It is not helpful to continue on with a lecture about teasing or disrespectful behavior or to force apologies at this time because students probably need a cooling off time before they can learn anything more from the experience.

Use Other Students to Help with Redirection

For the highly distractible, hyperactive or disengaged student, re-directing is a constant process. Such students should be seated near to the teacher so it is easier to redirect them unobtrusively. However, it is not always possible to arrange this physical proximity because sometimes the teacher may need to work with a small group of children for a while. When this is the case, it can help to pair the distractible child with another student who is self-directed and focused. Proximity to a positive peer model can help keep the distractible student on task.

Reminders and Warnings of Consequences –
'Remember our Rule for'

Positive reminders are particularly useful strategies with impulsive or distractible students who have difficulty remembering what is expected of them. For example, the teacher might say to the class at transition times, 'Remember we sit on the mat when we go in class, thanks' or 'Remember before we leave the class we put our pencils in the container, slide our chairs under our desk, and check the floor for rubbish'. For the student who is blurting out or talking loudly the teacher might say, 'Remember what our rule is for asking questions?' or 'Remember the rule for working noise?' or 'Remember our rule for manners?' Reminders given in a positive tone of voice can quickly redirect students away from disruptive behavior back to classroom rules and routines. 'Remember' is a nicer way of saying this than 'Don't forget' which reminds them of what not to do.

Another type of verbal redirection which can be used for handling inappropriate behavior without resorting to negative consequences is the use of warnings. A warning is essentially a reminder of the consequences of breaking a rule or deviating from a protocol. As we said in the beginning, teachers need to establish a discipline plan that lays out the consequences of not following the rules and procedures, and students need to be informed from the beginning of the school year what the discipline plan is. But they also need to be periodically reminded of the details of the plan. Reminders about the rules and the consequences can be helpful – especially for distractible children who easily forget not only what they are supposed to be doing, but what the consequences are for not doing it. For example, the teacher might say, 'Alice you need to stay in your own seat and work by yourself for this assignment. If you talk to your neighbour again you will lose one minute of break'. Or, Jeff, who has already been reminded of the 'no put-down rule', it may be necessary to add a warning of the consequence, 'Jeff! In our class we have a rule about respectful language. If that happens again, it will result in a Time Out.' Or, for the child who constantly forgets to clear up his desk before break, the teacher might say, 'Remember if you haven't cleared up your desk area, you will have to stay back at break'. In many cases a simple reminder or warning of the consequence will be all that is needed to stop the undesirable behavior. The other advantage of this approach is that the warning is expressed as a choice which fosters the child's sense of responsibility.

Sometimes the teacher can give the warning in the form of a slip of paper which is placed on the student's desk. For non-readers, it might have a picture of Dinosaur working hard to denote staying on task and in seat or Dinosaur with quiet hand up to remind student of not blurting out with questions. For readers, it might simply remind them of the rule.

Counting is a kind of warning; it implies that some consequence will follow. For example, the teacher says, 'When I count to five I want you seated please'. Then when the child sits down the teacher says, 'That's great you are quiet now. You have made a good choice and are really helping me out, because we concentrate better on our work when it's quiet.' Commenting that a child has made a good choice is a nice way to phrase the positive feedback.

Calling Students Aside

It is helpful to redirect some off-task students, particularly the attention seeking and oppositional ones, more privately and away from their audience. For example, as the teacher is walking around the room she notices Sally grabbing the art materials from the other two students at her table. The teacher says, 'Sally can I see you a minute?' and as Sally is walking over the teacher resumes her attention to helping some other students. Once Sally has reached her, she privately asks her, 'What is our classroom rule for sharing?' Sally states the rule and the teacher praises her understanding. Then says, 'Good, now I will be watching you for all the times you are sharing'. By taking Sally away from her audience, it minimizes the likelihood she will show off, and she will have no audience to perform for. Also the teacher's approach of turning back her attention to other students while Sally is walking over to her is effective because she is avoiding a confrontation, ignoring any secondary non-verbal behavior on the part of Sally (such as eye rolling and sighing), and minimizing the attention given to her disruptive behavior.

Be Specific

Be sure that you are being specific with students about your expectations. Sometimes teachers are too general in their approach. For example, a teacher says to an inattentive and highly distractible child, 'Ally you need to work for 15 minutes but if you aren't good you can't go out for break. Do you understand?' Let's say that during the next 15 minutes, Ally got up to sharpen her pencil and whispered to her neighbour, does she get to go out for break? The problem with the teacher's approach here is that it is not clear what behaviors she expects. Rather the teacher should say, 'Ally you need to do two things in the next 15 minutes in order to go out for break today. You need to stay in your seat and not whisper to anyone around you. Can you tell me what you need to do to go out for break today?' By verbally rehearsing the specific behaviors expected of her she is more likely to remember them, and if she breaks one of these rules then it is clear that she has lost her break.

Reinforce the Expected Behaviors

As we have discussed earlier, it will be important to have a well-developed reinforcement system for teaching students the expected behaviors. For example, for the distractible student it would be important to praise and label the student every time he or she is concentrating hard on his work. This will help the student to know what behaviors are required when one is concentrating and paying attention.

Another reinforcement strategy for a distractible student would be to use a 'sand timer' (or 'tornado tube') filled with sand or rice and which can be tipped over. A behavior programme for such a student might be that for every time she has remained seated and working while the sand runs through the timer, she gets a sticker on a chart on her desk. When she gets ten stickers, she gets to choose a special activity of her choice (e.g. computer, drawing, etc.). (These 'sand timers' and 'tornado tubes' can be made out of two large plastic lemonade bottles.)

Conclusions

We have seen that when a student shows minor annoying mis-behaviors such as blurting out, butting in, distracting others, talking out of turn, wandering out of seat, or procrastinating at work you can use a variety of strategies to redirect the student. For example, you can ignore the students doing these things and respond to only the students who are putting up a quiet hand or who are working hard, 'Thank you Carey for putting up a quiet hand. What is your question?' You can use a rule reminder such as, 'Remember our rule for quiet hands up?' You can give a clear direction of the expected behavior, 'Hands up without calling out please'. You can use a non-verbal signal such as demonstrating quiet hand up with a finger on your mouth. You can take the student aside and briefly review the rule, 'What is our rule for respect?' If you have tried all these things and the student still continues the misbehavior, you will need to warn the child of the consequence and follow through with a nega-tive consequence if it continues. Chapter 7 discusses natural and logical consequences for misbehavior.

To Sum Up

- Choose specific student misbehaviors (low-level attention seeking behaviors) to ignore and make sure they are ones you *can* ignore.
- Praise the opposite pro-social behaviors in your student.
- Avoid eye contact and discussion while ignoring.
- Physically move away from your student.
- Use subtle ignoring especially for non-verbal secondary behaviors.
- Be prepared for testing – remember when first ignoring the mis-behavior often gets worse before it gets better.
- Be consistent.
- Return your attention as soon as misbehavior stops.
- Combine distractions with ignoring.

- Limit the number of behaviors to systematically ignore.
- Teach other students to ignore minor misbehaviors.
- Encouraging self-monitoring when possible.
- Don't ignore withdrawn behavior – use redirections to engage student.
- Use non-verbal signals and picture cues for redirecting.
- Young children benefit from physical redirection at times.
- Positive reminders are particularly useful for impulsive or distractible students.

References

Bear, G. G. (1998) School discipline in the United States: prevention, correction and long-term social development, *School Psychology Review*, 2 (1), 14–32.

Hyman, I. A. (1997) *School Discipline and School Violence: A Teacher Variance Approach*, Boston: Allyn and Bacon.

Martens, B. K. and Meller, P. J. (1990) The application of behavioral principles to educational settings. In T. B. Gutkin and C. R. Reynolds (eds.) *Handbook of School Psychology* (pp. 612–34), New York: Wiley.

Chapter Seven

Managing Misbehavior: Natural and Logical Consequences

No matter how consistently you use ignoring, redirecting and warnings or reminders as strategies for dealing with inappropriate classroom behavior, and no matter how consistently you reinforce appropriate behavior, there are still times when children will continue to misbehave. In these cases, their misbehavior needs to be dealt with by imposing a negative consequence.

A negative consequence is something the child does not want, such as being last in line, losing break, getting Time Out in the classroom, missing free time or a special activity, or loss of a privilege. Consequences do not have to be severe to be effective. The key is consistency, not severity. Consequences must be applied consistently rather than varying according to the situation. They must be applied uniformly – that is, they must be the same for everybody. And they must be applied promptly – that is, immediately after the misbehavior. For this reason, it is a good idea to avoid establishing consequences that are inconvenient to enforce.

Consequences are a way of holding children accountable for their behavior. Students must be familiar with the discipline plan in advance so that they can see the negative consequences as the direct result of their behavior. Whenever possible, consequences should be presented as a choice the child has made – for example, 'You hit Carl; you have made the choice to go to Time Out for 5 minutes'.

Negative consequences should be:

- consistent
- applied uniformly
- applied promptly after the misbehavior if possible
- convenient to enforce
- presented as a choice the child has made
- non-punitive and reasonable
- related to the behavior.

In the next pages we will discuss several types of negative consequences which have been shown in the literature to be effective (Brophy, 1996; Stage and Quiroz, 1997).

Natural and Logical Consequences

Sometimes there is a consequence that arises naturally out of the situation and minimizes classroom disruption. A natural consequence is some negative outcome that would result from the child's misbehavior without any intervention on your part. For example, if Ryan did not want to wear his coat out to break, then he would get cold. A logical consequence, on the other hand, is a negative outcome that results from the child's behavior because the teacher set it up that way. For example, in one particular preschool the rule was that teachers pour out the milk for the children at lunch. However, one day Bruce poured his own milk and spilled it. A logical consequence when Bruce asked for more milk, was for his teacher to say, 'At school the teachers pour the milk so today for lunch you will have to drink water'. A logical consequence for Seth not staying at his desk and for bothering the other students is to have to sit up front at the teacher's desk. A logical consequence for fighting to be the first one in line is to be sent to the back of the line. Consequences work best when there is an inherent connection between the misbehavior and the consequence.

Examples of Natural Consequences

- If a student forgets her school books or homework, she will not be able to have her paper marked.
- If the student uses up all her glue on one art project there won't be any left for another project.
- If the student doesn't come in for snack on time, there might not be any left.
- If the student refuses to eat the school lunch, he or she will be hungry.

Examples of Logical Consequences

- If the student can't use the scissors safely, they will be taken away.
- If water is spilled all over the floor, the student will be responsible for cleaning it up.
- If the student doesn't wear a bicycle helmet, s/he'll not be able to ride the tricycle that day.
- If the student can't use a quiet voice in the library, then s/he will have to leave.

- If student can't stay at her seat during study time, she will have to sit with the teacher.
- If the student doesn't stay in the playground at break, s/he will not be allowed to go to the next break.
- If the student keeps blurting out in class and arguing with the teacher, s/he will be given an appointment card to stay in at break to discuss his or her concerns with the teacher.
- If the student breaks a classroom rule, her special animal (which belongs to the child) is removed for break or she may lose some of her Golden Time (special activity she has signed up for).
- If the student can't stop distracting and bothering other students at his table, then he will need to sit away from the others.
- If the student procrastinates and does not do the work in class time, then he will have to be kept back to do it on his own time (time when other students are doing special activities).
- If the student pushes in line at lunch, then s/he will be directed to the back of the line.
- If the student chooses not to work in the place designated by the teacher, s/he will be kept back at break to discuss the issue (good for the big child who refuses to move).
- If the student continues to call out after warnings and reminders, s/he has to leave the discussion.
- If the student breaks or damages something, s/he will have to complete a job to 'earn' money to replace it (e.g. sharpen pencils, tidy book shelves, share books, clean fish tank, etc.).

Natural and logical consequences are most effective for recurring problems where teachers decide ahead of time how they are going to follow through. This approach can help children to learn to make decisions, be responsible for their own behavior and learn from their mistakes. In the following pages, we will discuss some of the problems that can occur when setting up logical and natural consequences and effective ways to overcome them.

Be Sure your Expectations Are Age Appropriate

Most natural and logical consequences work best for children 5 years of age and older. They can be used with younger children, but teachers must first evaluate carefully whether the children understand the relationship between the consequence and the behavior. For instance, if Alexandra is not ready to be toilet trained but she is made to clean her underpants, she may feel unduly criticized.

Moreover the logical consequence is an undue punishment. However, to refuse dessert or snacks to a child who has refused to eat dinner is an appropriate consequence since the child learns that not eating dinner causes hunger. Of course, natural consequences should not be used if children may be physically hurt by them. For example, a 3–5-year-old should not be allowed to experience the natural consequences of sticking a finger into an electrical outlet, touching the stove or running into the road.

When thinking through the natural consequences that may result from your students' inappropriate behaviors, it's important to be sure that your expectations are appropriate for their age. Because of the cognitive skills involved, natural consequences will work better for school-age children than for 3–5-year-olds. Logical consequences that young children do understand are 'if–then' statements. For instance, 'If you don't keep your chewing gum in your mouth, I will have to take it away'. Or, for a child who points scissors at someone, 'If you can't use the scissors carefully, then I will remove them'. In these examples, the logical consequence of not using something properly is having it removed.

Be Sure You Can Live with the Choices

When attempting to carry out natural and logical consequences, some teachers find it difficult to allow their students to experience the outcomes of their actions. They are so sympathetic towards their students that they feel guilty for not coming to their aid and may intervene before the consequence occurs. For instance, a teacher tells Angie, a 5-year-old, that the natural consequence of dawdling and not being ready for gym on time will be to miss gymnastics that day. However, the teacher can't bring herself to let Angie miss gymnastics and dresses her instead when the time comes to enforce this. Such over-protectiveness can handicap children by making them incapable of handling problems or mistakes.

When using consequences it's important to think about the pros and cons of applying this technique to particular misbehaviors. Be certain that you can live with the consequences and that you are not giving idle threats. In the example above, the teacher should have first considered whether or not she would be willing to follow through and let Angie miss gymnastics if she continued to dawdle. Failing to follow through with an agreed consequence will dilute your authority and deprive your children of opportunities to learn from their mistakes.

Consequences Should Be Fairly Immediate

The natural and logical consequences approach doesn't work when the consequences of misbehaviors are too distant. The natural consequences of not brushing teeth would be to have cavities. However, since this might not occur for five to ten years it would not be effective. Permitting youngsters not to do homework until the end of the year report card shows they have failed is another consequence that is too delayed to have any influence on their daily study habits. Such long-term consequences may instead lead children to feel hopeless about their abilities.

For 3–5-year-old and school-age children it's important that the consequences closely follow the inappropriate behavior. If Dan doesn't bring in his homework he will have to do it at break. Or if Kimmy damages another child's book, then it should be replaced as quickly as possible and she should have to help pay for it through chores. In this way, Kimmy and Dan will learn from their inappropriate behavior and will probably behave more appropriately the next time.

Give your Student Choices Ahead of Time

Sometimes teachers use this approach in a punitive way, not letting their students know the possible consequences in advance. Robbie's teacher comes up to him one morning and says, 'You haven't completed your homework again, so you're not going on the field trip today'. He is given no warning and does not have the choice of deciding to do his homework or miss his field trip. Not surprisingly, Robbie will probably feel resentful and will probably not see himself as responsible for the consequences of his behavior. Instead, Robbie's teacher could say, 'Since you are having a hard time getting homework done, you can use break time to get it done'. Or he might say, 'Either you give in your homework every day this week or you will have to miss the field trip to do it'. It is up to the child to decide how to respond.

Let's take another example. Christina has been chatting and distracting other students during quiet work time. The teacher says, 'Christina I have asked you twice to work quietly. If you continue to talk out and distract others, you will have to work at a separate table.' Christina protests, the teacher repeats the choice and walks away. When Christina settles down the teacher says, 'That was a good choice Christina you are working hard now'.

These approaches which emphasize the language of choice give students the sense that their behavior is their responsibility and they have some self-control over how to behave. Eventually students understand, through experiencing the consequences, that it is better to respond positively rather than negatively.

Consequences Should Be Natural or Logical and Non-punitive

Occasionally teachers come up with consequences that are not logically or naturally related to an activity or are too severe. Consider the bus driver who says the student can't come on the bus for two weeks because of misbehaving on the bus one morning. While the bus driver might argue that it is a logical consequence for a youngster who has been misbehaving, this approach is too punitive. For example, it may mean the student stays at home from school for two weeks because the parents have no transportation available. Furthermore this results in the student falling behind in school and jeopardizing his academic learning. When consequences are too harsh or lengthy, children will feel resentful and perhaps even retaliate against such consequences. They will be more likely to focus on the cruelty of the teachers than on changing their own behavior.

A calm, matter of fact, friendly attitude is essential for deciding upon and carrying out consequences. The natural consequence of not wearing a coat when it's cold outside is to become chilled. The logical consequence of misbehaving on the bus might be to miss break that day. These consequences are not degrading and allow the student an opportunity to make a different decision in the immediate future. Instead, they help children to learn to make choices and to be more responsible.

Strive for Certainty of Consequence Rather than Severity

Sometimes teachers impose a consequence such as staying in after school or missing break for a teacher chat and the student runs away to avoid taking the consequence. It is important that the teacher remains calm, since chasing or yelling at the child will reinforce the oppositional behavior. Instead, later in the day the teacher can call the student out of class for a discussion and complete the consequence. In this situation it is more important that the certainty of the consequence be enforced rather than the severity or immediacy.

Involve your Student Whenever Possible

Some teachers set up a natural and logical consequence programme without involving their students in the decisions. This may well cause the children to feel cross and resentful. Instead, you should consider this an opportunity for you and your students to work together to promote positive behaviors, allowing them to feel respected and valued. For instance, if your students are having problems fighting over the computer, you might say, 'You seem to be having trouble agreeing on who's turn it is to use the computer. You can decide either to take turns using the computer or it will not be available for use today. Which would you prefer?' Involving your students in the decision making about consequences often reduces their testing when there is a problem and enhances their co-operation. Or, let's say Erica is having trouble working quietly with Anna. You might say, 'Erica if you're having a problem working here with Anna, would you prefer to work separately?' This message is given as a choice and a chance to choose a better response. If Erica continued to be noisy after this, then the teacher would ask her to move to a different table.

Be Straightforward and Friendly – Avoid Arguments

Sometimes students vehemently argue or deny that they swore, blurted out or talked loudly. Be careful not to undermine your consequence programme by becoming angry, argumentative or critical with your students for being irresponsible. This will only reinforce their behavior. Avoid taking their protests as bait and be straightforward and assertive about the consequences. For example, 'Ben I heard you call him a butt head'. Ben denies doing this but the teacher reiterates, 'We have a rule for respect and I expect you to use it'. Ben continues to argue and deny having said the word and the teacher avoids arguing, 'I heard you, go back to your seat and I'll see you at break'. The teacher walks away allowing the student to cool off. Later the teacher will discuss this incident with Ben and work out whether an apology is in order. The rule will be restated as well as the consequences.

It's important to be straightforward and assertive about consequences, to be prepared to follow through with them, and to ignore your students' protests or pleading. If they refuse to accept consequences, you should use Time Out or the loss of a privilege, whichever best fits the situation. Remember, your students will try to test the limits, so expect testing. But it is important not to lecture or criticize them or offer sympathy after the consequence occurs. Instead, once it is completed, they should be given a new opportunity to be successful.

Consequences Should Be Appropriate

One common trap occurs because teachers are so angry that they impose a consequence that lasts too long and is unduly punitive. Consider the teacher who says to Cary, a disrespectful 8-year-old student, 'That's it now, I've had enough, you will miss break for a week'. Later the teacher realizes her dilemma. She has actually punished herself for now she has to monitor Cary in her classroom all week. Moreover by removing break for a week she will have to come up with some additional consequence if Cary's misbehavior continues on a different day. On the other hand, if she doesn't follow through with this consequence then Cary will not believe her in the future and will test harder. In another similar example, 4-year-old Ben rides his tricycle on an area of the playground where he is not allowed to go. The logical consequence would be for the teacher to prevent him from using the tricycle at the next break. Locking it up for a month, however, would be excessive and bound to make Ben feel cross and resentful. Moreover, it wouldn't allow him any new opportunities to be more successful in handling his tricycle responsibly. Although some people believe that the stronger and longer the punishment, the more effective it will be, the opposite is actually true.

A more appropriate consequence for the disrespectful student would be to lose break for the morning period and then look for any chances to compliment her for polite language in the next period. In Ben's case a more appropriate consequence would have been to restrict his use of the tricycle for one break period and then allow him the chance to be successful in the way he rides it at the next break. If 4-year-old Kathy is using crayons and starts colouring on her desk, a logical consequence to present her with might be, 'If you can't keep the crayons on the paper, then I will have to take them away'. If she continues to colour on the desk, then the crayons would have to be removed. However, they should be returned within half an hour to give her another opportunity to use them appropriately. The principle is to make the consequences immediate, short and to the point, and then to quickly offer your student another chance to try again and be successful.

When in Doubt about the Appropriate Consequence Use Deferment

Sometimes you are so angry with a child you can't think of an appropriate consequence and you run the danger, like Cary's teacher, of imposing too severe a consequence. If this happens you should first calm yourself and defer making a decision. For example, Cary called her teacher a 'doo doo head', and her teacher responded, 'I'm so angry right now I don't know what I am going to do. Please go to the back of the room and sit at the table until I decide what to do.' The teacher then proceeded to pass out the papers and get the rest of the students involved in their work. Then when she was calm she approached Cary and said, 'Cary calling me names hurt my feelings, you know we don't use that kind of language in the classroom. Are you ready to go back to work now?' This teacher's approach is effective because she models a respectful response as well as how to calm down before trying to solve a problem. If the teacher had threatened Cary or sent a note home or sent her to the principal's office it probably would have escalated the situation and given more power to the child's misbehavior.

Other Consequences

Moving the Child

Another effective response to misbehavior is to take the child away from the situation s/he is disrupting or the situation that is stimulating or reinforcing the misbehavior. This usually stops misbehavior by decreasing the attention it is receiving from other children. This strategy also gives the student a chance to calm down and get back on track. For example, a teacher is conducting a reading Circle Time but one boy repeatedly makes noises and pokes the child next to him. She has used signals to remind him of his need to have a quiet mouth and to keep his hands to himself and she used frequent proximity praise, praising the other students for paying attention and working hard. She has also used her most engaging teaching strategies but he continues to disrupt the reading time. Finally she warns him he will have to leave the group and go to another table if the poking continues. His misbehavior continues and after another warning she sends him away from the group to sit alone at a nearby table. This is different from Time Out in that the student can still continue working and participating in the classroom activities but not at a table with other students.

Perhaps a less disruptive strategy would have been to first try moving him to sit next to the teacher to help with the reading. The potential danger of this response after repeated reminders is that sitting next to the teacher would actually reinforce the mis-behavior. However, if the teacher had moved him up closer earlier on in the sequence of misbehaviors it would have allowed her to monitor his behavior more closely and to give him a legitimate way to show off some of his leadership skills. (It would be import-ant that this leadership role be offered as a result of appropriate behavior not misbehavior.)

If the boy had refused to go to the table to sit alone by saying, 'No! I'm not going,' the teacher could use deferrment by saying, 'If you don't go to the table, you will have to stay behind at break'. Then continue on with the lesson and leave the choice up to the child.

Loss of Privileges

Another type of negative consequence is for the student to lose some privilege. The privilege that is removed may depend on the teacher's assessment of what the child usually likes to do. If a stu-dent doesn't like to go out to break or to gymnastics then removing break or gym that day will not be likely to have much impact. In fact, it might even be reinforcing as the child gets to avoid some-thing s/he doesn't like. If you know that the student loves to work on the computer, then losing computer time can be very effective. Other privileges that might be removed are loss of free choice time or Golden Time (a special activity the child has signed up for) and being restricted to a particular area of the room, loss of time with other students, inability to be line leader and so forth.

One creative programme was set up by a kindergarten teacher we worked with. She allowed all her students to bring in their favourite toy or teddy bear on Mondays. If the students didn't have a toy on Monday they were allowed to pick one out of the teacher's special toy box. The students could play with these special toys before school started and during special free play periods during the day. During the rest of the day they were placed on the top shelf of a bookcase. The teacher explained the rules for these special toys, that is, the children were not allowed to swap, trade or sell them or they would lose a privilege for two days. Next if a child broke a class-room rule during the day the teacher would say, 'Your teddy needs to go to calm down for 3 minutes, so you will need to wait 3 minutes at break before you can play with your teddy'. Thus the students would lose the privilege of playing with their favourite toy as consequence for breaking a rule. A similar idea for older students is losing Golden Time for breaking a Golden Rule. Students sign up for a special activity to do during Golden Time. If the child breaks a rule, they lose a minute or two of this time. This means that during Golden Time they have to sit and look at a sand timer until the time they lost is past. The important aspect to this approach is that the special activity is something truly special!

Staying Behind after Class

As can be seen in the examples described above one of the consequences often used by teachers is to have the student stay back after class or to miss break. A widely used practice regarding 'detention' after class is to make the student sit and do nothing during this time or to write 100 lines over and over. This consequence is problematic because it is not connected logically to the misbehavior, denies the child's rights to be socially accountable and only serves to demonstrate the power of the adult to coerce the child. It is far more effective to connect the stay back experience with the student's efforts to repair the situation. For example, during the stay behind time the student can be asked to fix the damaged item, clean up the mess that was made, write an apology, explain what rule was broken, do a problem analysis (i.e. describe the problem, solution, consequences, a better solution – see Chapter 9 for a description of this), finish the work not completed or think of a different solution. This can be a very useful way to teach students about responsibility and accountability as well as consequences.

Avoid Group Detentions

Sometimes teachers keep the whole class in from break for a detention in order to punish a few students' misbehaviors. Teachers should avoid doing this because it erodes the goodwill of the entire class. Students who are unfairly punished feel let down by their teacher.

Avoid Putting Names on the Board for Negative Behaviors

Sometimes teachers will put a child's name on the board 'in blue' to indicate that the student has misbehaved. They think that this approach serves to warn the misbehaving child. However, this approach is not recommended because it focuses teacher and peer group attention on the misbehaving student and may actually reinforce their negative identity or reputation in the classroom. Instead if teachers put students' names on the board we suggest it be for being a 'hero' or 'outstanding student'. One of the key principles of a classroom discipline plan is that it be non-humiliating, non-confrontational, limits the amount of attention the misbehavior gets and, when possible, gives the student an option for making a better choice as soon as possible.

Give Appointment Cards for Planned After-Class Chats

One non-confrontational strategy for the older defiant student is to give out teacher appointment cards (which are made up ahead of time with time, place and reason for appointment). Let us say you have a student who is hostile, sarcastic and constantly argues with you about the required work to be completed or is throwing a pouting tantrum because he can't play on the computer that day. Instead of arguing or trying to reason with him at that moment, you can respond simply by giving him an appointment card which tells him when he can meet with you after class to discuss his concerns. You might say, 'I can see that what you are saying is important to you so I am going to give you an appointment time when we can talk about it privately. At 1.15 today we can meet in my office to discuss your concerns about . . . '

This approach has two benefits for the child. First, it avoids a confrontational or public discipline approach in front of the rest of the students and de-escalates or breaks the cycle of negativity between the teacher and student. If the teacher had persisted in discussing the issue at the time the student was being oppositional, her attention could potentially have reinforced the student's misbehavior. Moreover, the teacher disrupts the rest of the class in order to pursue this discussion. Secondly, at the time a child is misbehaving s/he is usually angry and defensive, and unlikely to benefit from a teacher discussion or may perceive it as punitive. Instead, teachers should have these discussions at a neutral time when both the teacher and student are calm and use them to collaborate and to develop a plan for coping more effectively with the problem.

There are a number of basic relational skills to remember when having these one-to-one after-class chats.

1. Start by acknowledging how the student might be feeling. For example, 'I can see you are upset about missing some of break time, and I won't keep you long. I need to speak to you about . . . '

2. Focus on the specific behavior that occurred in the classroom such as the calling out, butting-in, wandering, being 'rude' in tone and attitude and so on.
3. Invite the student's feedback on what you have said. 'Can you think of a different way to respond if you have a bad day again? How can you let me know without yelling at me?'
4. Avoid arguing or haranguing, stay focused on the primary issue or rule broken.
5. Work on an agreement about future behavior.
6. Finish with brief reminder and separate amicably. For example, the teacher says, 'I appreciate you staying in to tell me that. Indeed we all have bad days but we've got a right in our classroom to polite and respectful behavior. Next time let me know so we can see if there is some way I can help. See you later.'

Avoid Sending the Child to the Principal's Office

One frequently used consequence by teachers is to send the misbehaving child to the principal's office. In fact, in some schools teachers will use this strategy as many as four or five times a week, even for annoying misbehaviors or student insubordination. It is usually the gradual build up of these minor misbehaviors during the day that leads to the eventual use of an office referral. However, this consequence should not be used for these relatively minor misbehaviors. If used at all, the principal's office should be reserved for misbehavior that is so disruptive that the teacher can't teach at all. In the short run sending a misbehaving child to the office frees the teacher from the stress of the disruptive child for a while, but in the long run it may actually increase the child's misbehavior. Many children get reinforced when they go to the principal's office by the attention of the secretary or the principal or the reaction of their peer group. Moreover, if office referrals are overused, the administrator will be deluged and unlikely to do offer any real help to the student. Instead it is likely to be far more beneficial for the child if the teacher continues to use proactive strategies such as incentives, warnings, redirection, self-monitoring approaches, ignoring, loss of privileges and in-class Time Outs to manage misbehavior. In addition, sending students to the principal's office to scare them into submission confuses students' perceptions of the role of the principal, who becomes an evil power.

Calling Parents

Another approach that is used by teachers is to threaten a child that his or her parents will be called if she continues to misbehave. This approach will usually only work for the child who has a good relationship with his parents and fears their disapproval and disappointment. For the child with multiple family problems and a negative relationship with his parents it is unlikely to work and may even result in the child getting excessive punishment from his parents, thus making his defiance worse. These are the children who are practised at getting punished and almost seem to become immune to it. This does not mean that parents shouldn't be invited in for a meeting to plan a programme to help a problem child but threats about calling parents should be used sparingly and wisely.

Avoid Sending the Child Home or At-Home Suspensions

Sometimes teachers believe that at-home suspensions are the most severe consequence they can use for disciplining the student's disruptive and aggressive behavior. While this approach might provide temporary relief for the teacher, it is actually an inappropriate consequence for the young child for several reasons. First, the consequence is too lengthy and does not allow the child the opportunity to try again and to learn more appropriate behavior. Secondly, it is perceived as a form of abandonment by the student and will severely set back any trust in the relationship between the student, family and teacher. Thirdly, it has the possible ramifications discussed earlier of an angry parent excessively punishing the child for the suspension, particularly if it means the parent's job is jeopardized. Fourthly, in all likelihood a working parent will be unable to get child care on such short notice and will be forced to leave the child at home unattended. Leaving an aggressive child who has few self-management skills unsupervised at home is highly likely to lead to future behavior problems. The problem has simply been transferred from the school to the streets. Finally, for a child who is having difficulty in school, staying at home may be much more appealing than struggling in the classroom setting, and at-home suspension may actually serve to reinforce the child's negative school behavior. It is far more effective for the teacher to handle the problem immediately with a Time Out or a form of in-school suspension such as loss of break or loss of extra school privileges that day.

However, if the behavior is so extreme that suspension is felt necessary then the decision should be made by a team and not by the individual teacher. It is also important to be careful not to give special hero status to the suspended student. In addition school work should be sent home so the student does not fall behind.

In-School Suspension

If a suspension is deemed necessary then the school should consider an alternative in-school suspension rather than an at-home one. This means that the student is withdrawn from the home classroom activities for part of the day and is asked to do his classroom work by himself.

Some Other Principles of Discipline

Avoid Interrogations and Sermons – Be Succinct and Respectful

How often have you encountered a scenario similar to the following. A teacher observes Elonzo throw a handful of dirt at another child on the playground. She calls him over to her and says angrily, 'What did you do?' Elonzo, thinking the teacher has not seen the action, replies, 'nothing'. Now the teacher is even angrier and retorts, 'You are lying, I saw what you did, why did you do that?' Elonzo shrugs his shoulders and looks at the floor and says, 'So what!' The teacher replies, 'Don't you speak to me in that tone of voice. Look at me.'

There is tendency for adults to want to make children admit their mistakes and to force them to tell you why they misbehaved. However, it is hard enough for an adult to admit a mistake let alone a young child and rarely does a child understand why s/he did something. Moreover these sorts of interrogations usually lead to the teacher moralizing and preaching about how the child's misbehavior will affect his future in school and so forth. Finally, in the example above, the teacher is actually teaching her student to be more disrespectful by her own tone of voice and blaming attitude.

Try to avoid interrogating a child about what he did, especially if you directly observed it. Avoid asking why he did it, and preaching for it only serves to escalate the situation. Instead, directly and politely acknowledge the child's misbehavior and enforce the consequence. For example, the teacher could say, 'Elonzo I saw you hit Ricardo with the dirt, you need to miss the rest of break and stand next to me'. In a discipline confrontation, children generally only hear the first 20 seconds so you should be as succinct as possible. Additionally, the teacher is modelling respect by remaining calm and polite.

Avoid Emotional Intensity and Escalation

Too much emotional intensity or shouting when disciplining can also escalate children's misbehavior. Taking the example of Elonzo, the teacher might have responded to his lying by lecturing and shouting, 'Shut up. You are in big trouble now. You are getting a detention. Why can't you stay out of trouble for once in your life? You are going to be expelled from school one day. With that kind of behavior where do you think you will end up, eh? Unemployed, that's where!' Elonzo probably begins to tune out his teacher at this point and may be thinking to himself that this is just one more teacher who is mean and doesn't care about him. He might even retaliate, 'See if I care, you're a lousy teacher and I hate this school'. The teacher may react, 'Don't you talk to me like that!' and so it continues.

Try to avoid emotional responses to children's misbehavior for they only serve to escalate the conflict and probably gain the attention of the other children as well as fuelling Elonzo's desire to be defiant. Moreover, teachers' shouting teaches students to shout more and in the case of some students, it unsettles, unnerves and overly excites them. Instead, the teacher should respond calmly by saying, 'I know you probably wish you hadn't thrown that dirt, but you did throw it so now you have to miss the rest of break. I don't think you will do that again.' In this instance, the teacher de-escalates the situation. This calm, non-emotional response to misbehavior is key to a teacher's success in following through with consequences.

Remember to Develop Discipline Plans with a Behavioral Continuum

Sometimes teachers fall into the trap of setting up a comprehensive discipline plan to cure a child of all his misbehaviors. This approach is doomed to failure especially in the case of the child with multiple problems, for the expectations for him to change are too high. Let us take the example of Reed, an 8-year-old child who has a low level of tolerance for frustration and frequently storms out of the classroom swearing at the teacher. He then leaves the playground which results in a school suspension. A teacher who has a behavioral continuum in mind will realize that the first step is for Reed to learn how to stay in the class and a much later step is to manage his profanities. Thus his teacher sets up a discipline plan that gives him two points for staying in the classroom each day. He is allowed to mutter profanities, and she explains to the class that they will ignore his swearing while he is learning to calm himself down. She also gives him two passes to use each week which permit him to leave the classroom because he is feeling frustrated. During this time he is to go to the counsellor's office for 5 minutes and then return to class. If he uses this approach he gets one point. If he only needs to use one pass in a given week he gets three points. In this example we see the teacher planning a discipline approach which uses gradual steps and targets on one or two behaviors to encourage at a time.

The Importance of Teacher Supervision

Remember children with attention deficit disorders, impulsivity and aggressive behavior disorders have tremendous deficits in their social skills and lack self-management skills. This means that they will need constant monitoring and 'scaffolding' by teachers using all the proactive strategies outlined earlier as well as redirection, warnings and immediate consequences. This additional supervision and clear discipline can be seen by teachers as an investment not only in the problem child but the classroom as a whole because utilizing these approaches leads to a safe and caring environment. This kind of environment provides optimal social and academic learning for all students. None the less, these approaches take time, planning, patience and repetition. Most of all it requires a calm, respectful attitude.

To Sum Up

- Consequences do not have to be severe to be effective.
- Follow the 'law of least disruptive interventions' – use ignoring, self-monitoring, non-verbal and verbal redirecting, and warnings or reminders before negative consequences.
- Make logical or natural consequences immediate, non-punitive, age-appropriate, non-confrontational and short.
- Negative consequences should be tailored to the particular circumstances – something that will be effective with that particular

child because it deprives that child of something he or she particularly likes (loss of privilege) or something that is inherently connected to the misbehavior (logical and natural consequences).

- Consequences should never be physically or psychologically harmful to the child, nor should they humiliate or embarrass the child.
- When possible, present consequences as choice the student has made.
- Be friendly and respectful but firm – control your negative emotions.
- Be prepared for student testing when ignoring or when a negative consequence is enforced.
- Avoid sending students to the principal's office.
- Quickly offer new learning opportunities with immediate teacher attention for pro-social behaviors.
- Make sure your discipline plan is developmentally appropriate.

References

Brophy, J. E. (1996) *Teaching Problem Students*, New York: Guilford.

Stage, S. A. and Quiroz, D. R. (1997) A meta-analysis of interventions to decrease disruptive classroom behavior in public education settings, *School Psychology Review*, 26, 333–68.

Chapter Eight

Managing Misbehavior: Time Out

The student who displays physically or verbally violent behavior – for example, hitting another child or teacher, screaming so loudly that children cannot pay attention, lashing out and pushing over furniture, or persistently refusing to comply with anything the teacher requests – needs to be met with a more severe disciplinary strategy that will necessarily be more disruptive than those methods we have discussed so far. In Chapters 6 and 7 we discussed how some commonly used (and disruptive!) discipline strategies by teachers such as lecturing or yelling, putting a student's name on the board, or sending him to the principal's office have actually been shown to be ineffective (Bear, 1998; Martens and Meller, 1990). In fact, criticizing, arguing and shouting only result in students learning to shout at, criticize and argue with both teachers and peers. Reasoning with students or putting their names on the board while they are verbally abusive or non-compliant may provide teacher attention that actually reinforces the particular misbehavior or adds to the students' negative self-image. On the other hand, sending a student home for aggressive behavior may backfire if the student prefers to be at home. Additionally, sending a child home sometimes results in parental physical or verbal abuse that serves to compound the student's problems and alienate the parents from the teachers.

The task for teachers is to provide an ethical approach to discipline: one that teaches students that violent behaviors will not be tolerated, establishes positive expectations for future appropriate behavior, and conveys to them that they are deeply valued despite their mistake. Ideally this discipline plan should be a *whole-school plan* and not just an individual teacher classroom concern. All teachers have a role for caring for all students when outside the classroom and schools have a commitment to supporting all teachers in managing students with difficult behavior problems. Thus it is important that all school staff have a consistent discipline method.

Methods discussed in earlier chapters such as self-monitoring, ignoring, using logical consequences and loss of privileges are effective discipline approaches for many disruptive student behaviors. However, a Time Out or Calm Down strategy is reserved specifically for high-intensity problems, such as aggression towards peers or teachers and destructive behavior. It is also useful for highly non-compliant, oppositional or defiant children (any child who refuses to do what you ask him to do 75 per cent of the time or more falls into this category), since compliance is the cornerstone of a parent's or teacher's ability to socialize a child. Time Out is probably the most intrusive short-term consequence a teacher will employ for disruptive behavior. It can occur in the classroom as a formal, or semi-formal cooling off time or it can involve temporary removal from the classroom to another classroom or a specially designated area in the school.

Time Out is actually an extended form of ignoring in which students are removed for a brief period from all sources of positive reinforcement, especially teacher and peer group attention. Time Out offers several advantages over other time-honoured disciplinary practices such as lecturing or sending a student home, if it is carried out correctly. It models a non-violent response to conflict, stops the conflict and frustration, provides a 'cooling off' period for both students and teachers, and maintains a respectful, trusting relationship in which children feel they can be honest with their teachers about their problems and mistakes. Time Out also is also a time for children to reflect on what they have done and to consider other solutions, and fosters the child's development of an internal sense of responsibility or conscience. Time Out is more effective than sending a child home because it immediately follows the misbehavior and then allows for the child to quickly return to the classroom and to experience a new learning trial and a new chance to be successful. Sending a child home, on the other hand, usually occurs at least an hour after the misbehavior (after parents have been contacted), thus diminishing its power as a negative consequence. Moreover, a student who is sent home has no chance to come back into the classroom and reverse the behavior or repair the situation. Time Out provides the teacher with a chance to teach the student that dangerous behaviors will not be tolerated and will consistently result in temporary exclusion. This permits the rights of the non-disruptive students to be protected as well.

Steps to Setting Up Time Out or a Calm Down Time

Time Out means different things to different people and, like any discipline strategy, can be open to abuse if the protocols and philosophy of practice are not clearly described before and after its use. As a discipline process it should never stand alone and needs a school-wide policy which is well thought-out with backup and support.

There are a number of steps in setting up a successful Time Out (Brophy, 1996; Doles *et al.*, 1976; Forehand and McMahon, 1981; Gardner, Forehand and Roberts, 1976). These steps should be practised and role-played by teachers with other teachers in order that they should have a total understanding of them before actually carrying out a Time Out with a student.

STEP 1: Time Out Location

You need to carefully consider the Time Out location for your class. Preferably it should be a chair placed in an empty corner of the classroom (ideally a partition could serve to block its view from the rest of the classroom). It will also be necessary to have another room or classroom that can be used as a backup room in case the child will not stay on the chair. This room should be a safe place to be alone in, and as boring as possible. The place should have no books or toys or people walking by that the child can chat with. Although students should not receive any attention while they are in Time Out, there should *always* be an adult nearby to monitor the Time Out. In some cases teachers have made arrangements with another teacher (or a counsellor) to use their room as a backup location. A student will often not exhibit the same disruptive behaviors in another teacher's classroom. After being sent several times to the backup room, usually the student will learn that they prefer to stay in the classroom and sit on the Time Out chair. Time Out has been given many names, such as a Calm Down place or a Cool Off place. It is important it is not called the 'naughty corner' or 'naughty seat'.

STEP 2: Types of Behavior that Result in Time Out

You should decide which specific misbehaviors will result in Time Out. Behaviors that are absolutely impermissible, such as violent and destructive behaviors, or verbal abuse to the teacher or peers are good ones to choose. In the beginning, it's important to select the most disruptive behavior (i.e. physical violence) to work on. Then after several weeks, when these have been reduced, you can move on to another aggressive behavior, such as verbal abuse. Consistent defiance or non-compliance from a student is another case where Time Out could be used. In this case, the student should be given a

Time Out warning before actually being sent to Time Out. Violent behavior, on the other hand, should receive an 'automatic' Time Out (no warning). Time Out should never be used for minor disruptive behaviors such as calling out, coming late to class, clowning behavior, etc.

STEP 3: Time Out Length

A general rule of thumb is 3 minutes for 3-year-olds, 4 minutes for 4-year-olds and 5 minutes for children aged 5 and older. Research has shown in numerous studies that *Time Outs longer than 5 minutes are not more effective*. However, children should not be let out of Time Out until there has been 2 minutes of quiet, signalling that they have calmed down. This means that a child's first Time Out may last longer than 5 minutes if the child continues to yell or scream. Once children learn that they must be quiet to end Time Out, it will be possible to limit Time Out to 5 minutes. The main idea is to make it as brief as possible and then immediately give the student an opportunity to try again and be successful.

Sand timers or egg timers for keeping track of time in Time Out are essential. Most young children don't understand the concept of time, so they may panic when asked to sit still for any period of time. Focusing on the sand timer is not only calming but it provides a visual symbol of how much time is left.

STEP 4: Keys to Effective Use of Time Out

Give a warning unless the behavior was violent (aggression or destruction). Wait for the child's response to the warning and if he continues the misbehavior (or fails to obey), tell him in a firm, calm voice what he did that is unacceptable and that he must go to Time Out. It is important that the student know why he is being sent to Time Out. Here's an example for non-compliance:

Teacher: Seth, go to your seat and start working on your maths assignment please.

Child: (*wandering around classroom*) No, I don't want to and you can't make me.

Teacher: If you don't start your maths, you will have to go to Time Out.

Child: I won't do it, cool off.

Teacher: Seth, I asked you to start your maths assignment and you disobeyed. Go to Time Out now.

In this case there was a command, an 'if–then' warning and enforcement of Time Out. Hitting should result in an automatic Time Out. For instance, if you observe Seth hitting another student it would not be appropriate to say, 'If you hit Sally again, you will go to Time Out', as this would give Seth a second chance to hit another student. For example:

Teacher: Seth, you hit Johnny. Go to Time Out now.

STEP 5: Set a Timer

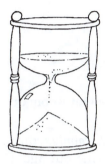 Once your student is in Time Out, you should set a timer for 3–5 minutes and leave the student alone. Two lemonade bottles (1 litre each taped end to end to look like an hour glass) with one bottle filled with sand can also be turned over to indicate the time passing. When the sand has passed into the second bottle this indicates the Time Out is finished. It is important not to talk to the student while he or she is in Time Out.

STEP 6: Repeat the Command

If you use Time Out for non-compliance, once Time Out is over, you should *repeat the original command*.

Teacher: Seth, start your maths assignment now.
Child: Okay.
Teacher: I'm pleased you are starting your work, you have made a good choice.

(If Seth refused to start his maths, then the entire sequence would have to be repeated. If Time Out is used for hitting or some destructive behavior, once Time Out is over, you should look for the student's first positive behavior that can be reinforced.)

Teacher: Seth, that's nice co-operating with your friend.

STEP 7: All Students Will Test the Time Out Procedure

Students under 6 years of age who refuse to go to Time Out can be gently but firmly taken to Time Out. Older children should have one minute added on for each refusal to go to Time Out *up to 8 minutes*. At that point a warning should be given to go to Time Out or lose a privilege – no computer, no break, extra homework.

Teacher: Seth, sit at your seat and start your maths problem please.
Child: No, I don't want to.
Teacher: If you don't start your maths assignment, you will go to Time Out.
Child: I don't care. You can't make me!
Teacher: That's one extra minute in Time Out.
Child: Who cares? I like it there anyway.
Teacher: That's 6 minutes now.
Child: So you can count, huh?
Teacher: That's 7 minutes. If you don't go now, you will have no break today.
Child: But that's not fair! (*walks to Time Out chair muttering unhappily*)
Teacher: Thank you, you have a made a good choice.

STEP 8: Refusal to Sit in Time Out – Use Backup Time Out Room or Another Class

If the child leaves the Time Out place in the classroom, *calmly return her* with a warning of a loss of a privilege: 'If you come out again before your time is up, you will have your computer privileges removed for 24 hours'. Or, alternatively you might warn the child that they will be sent to Time Out outside the class. Warn the student of this consequence by saying, 'If you get off the Time Out chair again, you will go to the Time Out room in Mrs C's class'.

It is always preferable to keep the child in the structural environment (classroom) whenever possible because the child will learn more. However, for the child who initially won't sit in the classroom Time Out or won't settle down after the warning has been given, it will be necessary to use the backup room or follow through with the deferred consequence. Do not send young children to the hall because they may run away.

STEP 9: Initially, Misbehavior Will Get Worse

Remember, when you first use Time Out with a child, the child's behavior will worsen before it gets better. Be prepared for testing.

STEP 10: Be Positive When Time Out Is Over

When Time Out is over, do not scold or lecture. Welcome the student back into the group – this welcoming reunion is critical! For example, you might say, 'Your Time Out is over now. Come on back to your desk. Let's try again. I know you can do it. Let's see, you were working on that maths problem, and I think you were close to getting the answer – let's look at that.' Immediately look for new learning opportunities at which your student can be successful.

Sometimes teachers think the student should decide when he or she is ready to come out of Time Out. We do not advocate this approach because in discipline situations it is important that the teacher be *in charge* of Time Out. The goal should be to return the child to the learning environment as soon as possible.

STEP 11: Prepare Other Students to Ignore Child in Time Out – Role-Play

It is important for the teacher to let the students know at the beginning of the year the rules of the classroom and under what circumstances Time Out will be imposed. Students should be taught to ignore a student while he or she is in Time Out and understand the importance of continuing with their work. If the students are making fun of a student who is in Time Out, this not only humiliates the student but peer attention may actually reinforce the student's misbehavior while in Time Out. It is helpful to role-play with puppets a situation where one of the puppets has to go to Time Out for breaking a class rule. While the puppet is in Time Out (calming down and deep breathing), the other students are coached how to ignore the puppet in Time Out.

STEP 12: Teaching Students the Meaning of Time Out and How to Handle Going to Time Out

As part of this initial teaching, you also need to explain to your students the meaning of Time Out. For example, you might say, 'If you have to go to Time Out, it is because you have made a mistake, and every one makes mistakes from time to time. Time Out (like Time Out in a competitive game) gives you a chance to calm down and think about what you have done. When it is over, you will have a chance to try again.'

In addition to helping students understand that Time Out is a time to reflect and gain control, we also teach students positive self-talk to use while they are in Time Out. For example, the teacher might say to the class, 'What will the student say to himself if he has to go to Time Out?' At that point the teacher can coach the words, 'Stop. Calm down. Think – I can calm down. I can do it. I can handle this. I can keep my hands to myself. I made a mistake but I can do better. I'll take a big breath. I'll try again.' Children with behavior problems often have negative, self-defeating thoughts when they go to Time Out such as 'My teacher hates me. I'm a failure. I can't do this. The other kids think I'm the worst kid. No one likes me.' Coaching them in positive self-talk to use while in Time Out helps these students to gain self-control and learn to calm down more quickly. Again, puppets and role-plays can help students practise the appropriate self-talk to use while in Time Out.

Sample Script for Teachers to Explain Time Out

First, explain to your students that aggressive behaviors such as hitting others, being verbally abusive and breaking objects will result in Time Out. For example, teachers might introduce a programme as follows:

'Class, I'm so proud of you for getting ready so quickly in your seats today. Now, I want to help you be more successful controlling your anger. It is normal to get angry, but I can't allow you to hurt others so I am going to help you learn to control your anger by putting anyone in Time Out who hits someone. You will have to go to Time Out in the chair in the corner of the classroom for 5 minutes. And you will have to be quiet for at least 2 minutes before you can get off the chair. If you can't calm down in the chair you will have to go to Miss Smith's class for Time Out. You can help yourself get calm in Time Out by using your 'turtle technique'. In addition, I am also going to keep track on this chart of any times I notice students staying calm in frustrating situations and talking about their feelings in an acceptable way. When your class earns thirty-five points we will plan a party.'

STEP 13: Be Sure your Classroom Environment is Positive

Remember Time Out will not work unless the teacher has worked hard to develop a positive relationship with the student and has set up a classroom environment that is highly rewarding for the child. What makes Time Out an effective discipline strategy is the loss of teacher approval and attention, and the contrast between a rewarding classroom environment and the far less rewarding Time Out environment. Research has shown the most effective teachers in managing hostile-aggressive students are those that use discipline such as Time Out, warnings and loss of privileges sparingly and combine them with a variety of positive strategies (Brophy, 1996; Steinberg, 1996).

STEP 14: Informing Parents about the Use of Time Out

It is important at the beginning of the year for teachers to explain to parents their discipline plan, including when and how they will use

Classroom Time Out for Destructive Behaviors for 4- to 6-Year-Olds

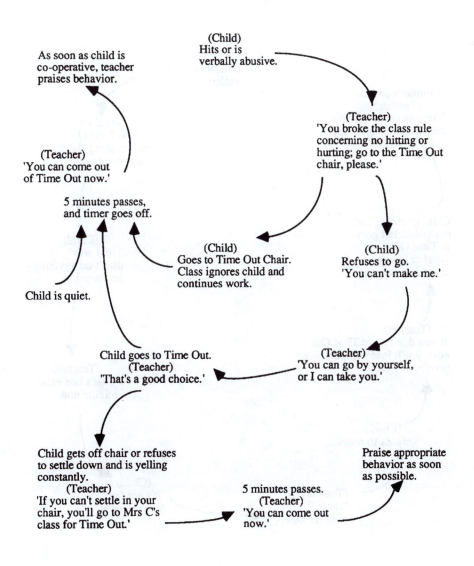

(Child)
Hits or is verbally abusive.

(Teacher)
'You broke the class rule concerning no hitting or hurting; go to the Time Out chair, please.'

As soon as child is co-operative, teacher praises behavior.

(Teacher)
'You can come out of Time Out now.'

5 minutes passes, and timer goes off.

Child is quiet.

(Child)
Goes to Time Out Chair. Class ignores child and continues work.

(Child)
Refuses to go.
'You can't make me.'

Child goes to Time Out.
(Teacher)
'That's a good choice.'

(Teacher)
'You can go by yourself, or I can take you.'

Child gets off chair or refuses to settle down and is yelling constantly.
(Teacher)
'If you can't settle in your chair, you'll go to Mrs C's class for Time Out.'

5 minutes passes.
(Teacher)
'You can come out now.'

Praise appropriate behavior as soon as possible.

Time Out ethically. It is wise to list the specific destructive child misbehaviors that will result in Time Out and to ask parents to sign their permission for its use under these circumstances. Post the Time Out procedures on the wall next to the Time Out chair. Ideally this discipline plan should be a whole-school policy applicable to all students in the school.

Classroom Time Out for Destructive Behaviors for 6– to 8–Year–Olds

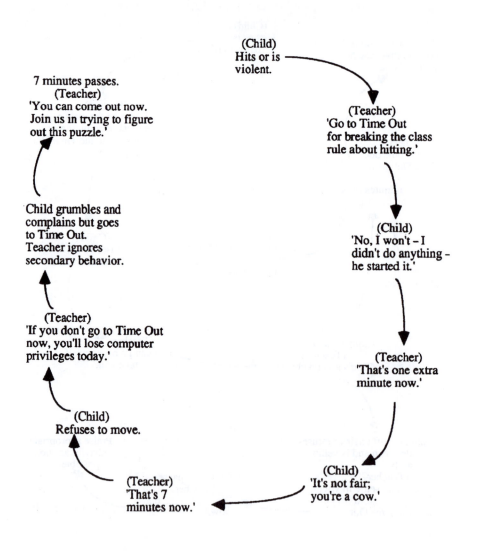

(Child)
Hits or is violent.

(Teacher)
'Go to Time Out for breaking the class rule about hitting.'

(Child)
'No, I won't – I didn't do anything – he started it.'

(Teacher)
'That's one extra minute now.'

(Child)
'It's not fair; you're a cow.'

(Teacher)
'That's 7 minutes now.'

(Child)
Refuses to move.

(Teacher)
'If you don't go to Time Out now, you'll lose computer privileges today.'

Child grumbles and complains but goes to Time Out. Teacher ignores secondary behavior.

7 minutes passes.
(Teacher)
'You can come out now. Join us in trying to figure out this puzzle.'

Pitfalls to Implementing Time Out

There are many pitfalls to be avoided in the use of Time Out. On the following pages, you will find some of the problems you may encounter and ways to overcome them.

Criticisms and Angry Responses

It can be extremely difficult to keep your cool in the face of blatant non-compliance or aggressive behavior from a student. Sometimes teachers criticize students or accompany Time Out with insulting or hurtful statements. A few examples include 'Why can't you do something right for once? Go to Time Out', 'I'm fed up! You never listen to me! Go to Time Out', 'You've been terrible today. Go to Time Out', 'How many times do I have to tell you to stop?' These criticisms are more likely to result in children refusing to go to Time Out or responding in kind. Teachers may then respond with more angry and passionate responses, resulting in an escalation of bickering.

It is understandable that teachers feel hurt and angry when their students misbehave or challenge their authority. However, in order to avoid an escalation of negative exchanges, teachers must decide to refrain from criticisms and be polite and calm at the very time their students are being impolite and agitated. Try to minimize talk about the misbehavior, for this will only escalate your own anger. Try to keep your facial expression neutral. This also means *not* lecturing a student after a Time Out. Sometimes teachers feel they have to remind students why they had to go to Time Out – 'You were put in Time Out because you hit. Remember hitters are not allowed in this classroom.' This is rubbing the child's nose in the mistake. Once Time Out is over, you should view this as a clean slate or a new learning trial – a chance for the student to try again and be successful!

Delayed Responses

Sometimes teachers put up with annoying behaviors for a time then suddenly explode with anger as the limits of their tolerance are reached. 'You get into Time Out now!' There are several problems here. First, this means the students don't receive feedback until teachers are boiling with anger and are about to lose control. Second, students receive no warning and consequently have no chance to correct their behavior. Finally, it may be unclear to a child why he is being sent to Time Out (because the other ten times he poked his neighbour, the teacher didn't give a consequence). This approach only teaches students an explosive response to frustration.

You may not even be aware of the mounting anger triggered by certain behaviors until you explode. If this is the case, try to think about and monitor your reactions to particular misbehaviors. If you find that certain behaviors elicit a strong emotional response, you may decide that it isn't possible for you to ignore this behavior for very long. This is a good time to present your students with the 'Three Strikes and You're Out Rule'. For example, tell them that interrupting three times will result in a Time Out. The first time a child interrupts you might say, 'That was your first interruption', then, 'That was the second interruption', and finally 'That was your third interruption. Go to Time Out'. This warns your student that the behavior is inappropriate and alerts you to your mounting annoyance level. With this approach, you are clear about exactly what type of behavior will result in Time Out and you model an effective, calm and rational approach to a problem behavior.

Expecting Remorse

Some teachers believe that in order for Time Out to be effective, it must result in a child expressing remorse over the misbehavior. They also feel the child doesn't learn from the experience, if he doesn't apologize. If these things don't happen, they may mistakenly think Time Out isn't working and stop using it. They may consider a more extreme form of punishment, such as informing a parent or suspension, because those are more likely to result in tears and expressions of remorse. However, as we have seen, excessive punishment, even when it eliminates undesirable behavior in the short run, tends to cause more problems in the long run. Also, these punishments do not teach children to problem-solve or cool down so that they can cope in a more successful way. Tears and apologies may satisfy a teacher's need for 'just desserts', but they don't necessarily reflect effective discipline.

Don't be surprised if your students tell you Time Out doesn't bother them, and don't be fooled. They're only bluffing (remember the Brer Rabbit trick!). Remember, the purpose of Time Out is *not* to get revenge or produce remorse, but rather to stop the misbehavior and withdraw the reinforcing effects of negative attention from teachers and peers. It provides children with a cooling off period and a chance to think about what they have done.

MANAGING MISBEHAVIOR: TIME OUT   189

Prolonged or Abortive Time Outs

It's easy to believe that longer Time Outs are more effective – especially if your students have done something really bad like lying or hitting or breaking something. Some teachers add time on whenever a student yells or misbehaves in Time Out. This is especially problematic if teachers are giving continual feedback during Time Out, 'That is one more minute for that scream', since this attention will actually *increase* the misbehavior. Overly long Time Outs tend to breed resentment in children, and the isolation imposed keeps them from new opportunities to learn from experience, to try again and be successful. Remember, with children, there's no need for the punishment to fit the crime.

The opposite response is also a problem. Sometimes teachers use Time Out for a minute and then let their students out when they bang on the door, cry or promise to behave. Unfortunately, letting children out when they are still misbehaving reinforces that particular inappropriate behavior. The message communicated is, 'If you kick (or cry or promise) hard enough, I'll let you out'.

The most effective Time Out need only be 5 minutes, provided there have been 2 minutes of quiet at the end. (Some children take longer to calm down than others.) Adding time on for more serious infractions or letting children come out of Time Out prematurely will reduce the impact of Time Out. In fact, these mistakes may even make children's behavior worse.

Overuse of Time Out

Time Out is frequently used for a variety of behaviors ranging from whining, to yelling and screaming, to out-of-seat behavior, to throwing, hitting and lying. Some teachers report using Time Out six to eight times a day with particularly difficult students. This overuse removes misbehaving children from opportunities to learn or demonstrate good behavior. It doesn't teach them new and more appropriate ways to behave. While frequent Time Out keeps children out of trouble in the short run, in the long run overuse can cause bitterness and make children feel that they can't do anything right.

If you are a 'Time Out junkie', make sure you are using it only for selected misbehaviors and not for minor disruptive behaviors such as sulking or avoiding a task or minor touching of another student (which can tactfully be ignored). For example, using Time Out for out-of-seat behavior or a chair for the hyperactive and inattentive 6-year-old will undoubtedly result in too many Time Outs and is probably expecting the child to do something she is not developmentally capable of doing. It would be more appropriate for such a child to have a 'wiggle space' or 'office' where she can go for a few minutes if she needs to move about. When the child is ready, she can rejoin the group without shame. In order to be sure this overuse doesn't happen teachers need to have a written list of the specific dangerous behaviors which will result in Time Out. Then whenever Time Out is used the initiating teacher needs to keep records detailing the behavior which set off the Time Out, what happened, how long it occurred and what follow-up behavior plans are being initiated for the student. Most importantly, you must ensure that you are spending more time *supporting, teaching and encouraging appropriate behaviors* than you are focusing on negative ones. Time Out will only work if there are frequent positive consequences and teacher attention for appropriate behaviors.

Remember do not judge the effectiveness of Time Out by reductions in actual number of times Time Out is used. Rather it is the reduction of the amount of time in Time Out that first signals whether it is working.

Lack of Follow-Through – Empty Threats

Occasionally teachers threaten Time Out without being committed to following through. They might say, 'Do you want a Time Out?' or 'You're asking for a Time Out!' or 'Are you ready for a Time Out?' These empty threats dilute the teacher's authority. Children come to believe that Time Out won't be used, and the result will likely be an escalation of resistance to Time Out when it is actually imposed.

It is more effective to use an 'if–then' statement than an empty threat of Time Out. 'If you don't stop on the computer, then you will have to go to Time Out.' Then follow through once you have given your student an opportunity to comply. Only mention Time Out if you have the time and energy to carry it out. Otherwise it's better to ignore the misbehavior.

Following through also means that you must be prepared to repeat the Time Out if your student doesn't comply after the first one is over. If Donna's teacher put her in Time Out for refusing to follow the directions, as soon as the Time Out is over, she must repeat the command. If Donna refuses again, the warning and Time Out must be repeated until she complies. If you miss this important part of the follow-through, your students may learn to use Time Out in order to avoid doing something they don't want to do.

Undermining Time Out through Attention

Some teachers inadvertently give attention to students while they are in Time Out. For instance, the child is sent to the principal's office – where the secretary gives him biscuits! Timmy yells in Time Out and Timmy's teacher responds to each yell with 'You must be quiet before you can come out'. Other teachers go in and out of the Time Out room, either to check on their student or to return them when they come out. All these actions defeat the purpose of Time Out and are very reinforcing for children.

There should be *no* communication with children when they are in Time Out. If you are likely to enter a Time Out area for fear that your student will break something, remove any breakable items from the area or find a new location. If you use a Time Out chair and your student manages to attract the attention of the other students, you may need to move the chair away from the rest of the classroom or have the student in another teacher's classroom during Time Out.

Physical Restraint

Sometimes when children repeatedly come out of the Time Out chair/area, teachers will resort to dragging them back to Time Out or physically restraining them in the chair. They may justify such physical restraint by saying that it was used as a last resort, or believe that since it works it must be all right. Unfortunately this 'the end justifies the means' approach defeats the purposes of Time Out by focusing only on the short-term goals of ensuring compliance and maintaining control. These short-term benefits of physical restraint are far outweighed by the long-term disadvantages: increasing children's aggression and providing a model for a violent approach to conflict situations. Such situations are much better handled by combining Time Out with a loss of privileges or a warning that Time Out will be served in another location. For instance, 'If you don't go back into Time Out now and stay until the end, you will lose break today' or 'If you don't do a quiet Time Out in here, you will have to finish your Time Out in Miss Day's classroom'. This technique models a nonviolent approach that maintains good relationships and respect with students.

Physical restraint is risky and not recommended for several reasons. First, the physical restraining and adult attention that necessarily accompanies restraint may actually contribute to reinforcing the oppositional behavior of the child who is being restrained. For

some neglected children, physical restraint may be the most inten-
sive adult attention they have had in their lives so they increase their
misbehavior in order to get it. Secondly, young children are quite
strong and many adults find that when they restrain children they
are sometimes holding the children so tightly that they might inadvertently hurt them. Certainly physically restraining a child or
dragging a child to Time Out is very stressful for the teacher and the
rest of the class. Thirdly, physical restraint teaches children to rely
on adults holding them in order to calm themselves down. Whereas
when Time Out is used, the child attributes his eventual ability to
calm down in Time Out to his own behavior. This ability of the child
to calm down by himself is a strategy that will be more beneficial to
him in the long run.

If you can't reasonably remove a child from his audience, when
significantly acting-out, then you remove the audience from the
child. The teacher can signal she needs a support teacher to supervise the acting-out child while the regular teacher calmly directs the
class outside to another area. The student needs to spend time away
from the class until he has settled down and is able to think and
renegotiate his entry. Fifteen minutes is the average length of time
for a student who needs to be sent out of class or for a class that
needs to be removed.

Refusals to Go to Time Out

When young children (ages 4 to 6 years) refuse to go to Time Out,
you can say, 'You can go to Time Out by yourself like a big boy (or
girl) or I will have to take you'. This choice is often enough to
motivate them to go by themselves. However, if they won't go on
their own, then you must calmly but assertively take them by the
arm and walk them to Time Out. If the teacher is firm and sure of
herself, this physical guiding to the Time Out will be successful.

If your students are old enough to have some understanding of
the concept of time (usually around 6 or 7 years) and they refuse to
go into Time Out in the first place, add an extra minute to Time
Out. For example, 'That's an extra minute for arguing and not
going to Time Out'. You can continue that up to 9 minutes. At that
point, give a warning about a loss of a privilege: 'That's been 9
minutes now, if you don't go to Time Out now, you will not be
allowed to play in the football game tonight'. Once the teacher has
followed through with the loss of an important privilege to the
child, the child will quickly learn it is better just to go to Time Out

in the first place. The advantage to this approach is that the teacher gets out of a power struggle with the student and the child has been given a choice: either he or she chooses to go to Time Out (for 10 minutes) or chooses to miss the football game.

If a privilege such as break or a football game or field trip is taken away, it is important that it is taken away the same day and only for the day. Longer punishments, such as taking away break or computer privileges for the week, are not more effective. In fact, just the opposite is true – children feel unfairly punished and get caught up in resentments towards the teacher rather than internalizing their role in the problem. Longer punishments remind the child all week of the misbehavior they did on Monday. Briefer consequences allow the child to have *fresh starts* and new chances to be successful. Moreover, if you take away the computer for the week and the child does something else that is inappropriate, you will need to remove a second privilege. A child can quickly fall into such a deep pit that he sees no way to earn himself out of trouble. Moreover, you soon have nothing else to take away. (See Chapter 7 for this discussion.)

Refusals to Come Out of Time Out

There are several forms of standoffs that can occur during the Time Out sequence. The first involves those children who refuse to come out of Time Out once it's over. Some teachers respond by letting their students stay in the Time Out room as long as they wish. This is inappropriate in the instance where Time Out is used as a consequence for non-compliance. In such cases, teachers are not following through with the original command and their students learn that they can get out of doing something by staying in the Time Out room.

If your student refuses to come out of Time Out, you should add 2 minutes to the Time Out. This can be continued for up to 10 minutes and then a privilege should be withdrawn. If your child is in Time Out for hitting, you can say, 'Your time is up. You can come out now'. If the child won't come out, you can give a warning, 'If you don't come out now and start your work, you will have to miss break'.

Other Power Struggles

Another type of standoff happens when a teacher refuses to talk to a child for lengthy periods of time after a Time Out. This is, in a sense, an extended Time Out. As mentioned earlier, this does not teach children how to deal with conflict in an appropriate fashion; rather, it teaches them to withdraw from conflict.

Refusing to speak to your students for long periods after misbehavior only escalates tension and anger. In this situation, you should think about what is bothering you, what behavior you expect, and then state this clearly.

Other Principles of Time Out

Hold Children Responsible

It's not uncommon for children to react strongly to Time Out, especially in the beginning. They may throw things, beat on a desk or a wall, or otherwise be destructive. If a student damages things during a Time Out, you can respond in several ways. First, the original command (if this is a Time Out for non-compliance) must be repeated. For example, if your student was in Time Out for refusing to do an assignment, then she will first have to do the assignment. Afterwards, she should be asked to clean up the Time Out room. If she has broken something, then she should be held responsible for repairing the damage if possible or should lose a privilege for that day.

Expect Persistence

A child yelling, screaming, swearing and banging on the wall during Time Out can be an exhausting experience for teachers. It's difficult to listen to children misbehaving without feeling anxious, depressed or angry. 'Will she ever stop this?' or 'What did I do wrong?' or 'It can't be good for him to get so upset'. Such feelings make it hard to complete Time Out for the full 5 minutes or to use it again. In a sense, teachers may suffer a 'hangover' from trying to use Time Out and avoid its use in the future. If this happens, students have been successful in getting teachers to back down from the rules.

Expect that Time Out will be difficult at times because all students test the limits. If you use Time Out for hitting, children are likely to hit again several times in order to determine if it is a predictable and consistent response. If they learn that you don't always respond to aggression with a Time Out they may continue to use hitting as a method of handling anger or conflict. In order to remain consistent and cope with the stress of enforcing a difficult Time Out try distracting yourself or call on the support of another teacher or the principal.

Don't Forget your Student in Time Out

We have seen Time Out used in the classroom where the child is put in Time Out or sent to the principal's office and then forgotten. The teacher did not put the timer on to signal the end of Time Out and became so engaged with the other children that the child in Time Out was forgotten. This can easily happen on the playground where there are so many children and few adults to monitor them. It is essential to remember to end Time Out on time to ensure that the child has a new learning trial.

Make Time Out or Calm Down Procedure a Certainty for Aggressive Misbehaviors

Often teachers feel they have no time to carry out a Time Out. They are busy teaching the rest of the class when their students misbehave. When confronted with doing a Time Out and stopping the classroom work, they decide to overlook or give in to the misbehavior. This makes the use of Time Out inconsistent and usually results in an escalation of inappropriate behaviors during these hectic periods. Remember, start by using Time Out consistently but sparingly for a few serious misbehaviors. You may experience a few tough days as your students test your commitment to the new rule, but in the long run your classroom will run more smoothly.

Plan for Time Outs on the Playground and in the Lunch Room

Since unstructured places such as playground break time and lunch rooms are the places where students are most likely to be aggressive, it is necessary to plan how Time Out will be implemented there. For example, schools might have specially painted benches or places where students are to go if they are given a Time Out. There needs to be adequate staffing in these areas to be sure that Time Outs can be successfully enforced. All Time Outs should be recorded in a monitoring book and followed up with the teacher. For more serious misbehaviors, students may need to be sent to the designated Time Out room in the school.

Support Each Other and Work Together to Manage a Difficult Time Out

Occasionally, while a teacher is doing a Time Out, another teacher or school personnel will disrupt the process by talking to the child or will argue about using Time Out. This makes it difficult to enforce Time Out and will result in the child seeing an opportunity to 'divide and conquer'.

Research has shown that conflict with students can spread into conflict between teachers. Consequently, if a teacher is doing a Time Out or Calm Down procedure, there should be an agreement that other teachers will be supportive. Teachers who share a classroom should be sure they have discussed, problem-solved and agreed on the following before they initiate Time Out:

- which behaviors result in Time Out
- how to determine who will take the lead in carrying out the Time Out
- ways for each to show support while supervising a Time Out
- how one teacher can signal to the other that he or she needs help to finish the Time Out
- acceptable ways to give feedback about the use of discipline
- where and who will take the student if the Time Out cannot be done in the classroom.

Ideally, if a teacher is alone in a classroom and has some difficulties enforcing Time Out there, then a backup team of supportive teachers should be 'on call' (with beepers) to be available to assist the teacher and help exit the child from the classroom to an alternative Time Out place. Schools should have a published emergency protocol or 'code red' procedure which is used whenever a teacher needs immediate assistance because of a very disruptive student who is a potential threat to someone's safety. If the teacher doesn't have an intercom then she should have a specially designated code such as a red card which can be given to a responsible student to take to the office to signal help is needed. Specially designated trained teachers need to be available to come immediately to the classroom should the code red be called.

These designated teachers need to be able to escort the extremely disruptive child to a Time Out room or 'calm down thinking area' room which is a safe, supervised place where s/he can calm down and refocus. Time in this alternative Time Out room should be as non-reinforcing as possible. In this room several posters can be placed on the wall that signal the student about the following:

1. Take big breaths and tell yourself, 'Stop, Calm Down and Think'.
2. Tell yourself, 'I can control this, I can calm down'.
3. Think about why you were asked to leave the classroom.
4. Ask yourself, 'What rule did I break?'
5. Think about a solution or way to fix things.

For the child who was sent out of the room for a Time Out who has eventually calmed down, s/he can be asked to complete a Time Out

Referred by: _____

PROBLEM-SOLVING SHEET

Name: _____   Date: _____

1.   What was the problem?

_____
_____
_____
_____

2.   How did you feel?

AFRAID   ANGRY   EXCITED   EMBARRASSED   SAD   OTHER

3.   What solution did you use?

_____
_____

Was it safe?   YES or NO
Was it fair?   YES or NO
Did everyone feel OK?   YES or NO

4.   **What are some different solutions you could have tried?**

_____
_____
_____
_____

5.   **What is the best solution?**

_____
_____

Is it safe?   YES or NO
Is it fair?   YES or NO
Will everyone feel OK?   YES or NO

6.   **What will you do now to make things better?**

_____
_____
_____

Signatures:
Student:_____   **Teacher:**_____
Parent: _____   **Principal:**_____

report (verbally or in writing). For young children who cannot read, pictures of the self-control management cue cards next to the Time Out chair can be helpful to remind them of the calming strategies (see Chapter 11).

It is important also that teachers do not perceive that calling for assistance is a sign of weakness but rather is the school policy regarding the way the school handles extremely disruptive students.

Remember There Is No Instant Solution

Some teachers claim that Time Out doesn't work for them. The previously discussed implementation problems may contribute to ineffective Time Out, or it may simply be that a teacher gave up too soon. It's a mistake to expect four or five Time Out trials to eliminate a problem behavior.

Time Out is not magic! Children need repeated learning trials. They need *many* opportunities to make mistakes and to misbehave and then to learn from the consequences of their misbehaviors. Just as it takes hundreds of trials for a baby to learn to walk, so it takes many trials for children to learn how to behave in a classroom. So remember, even when Time Out is used effectively, behavior changes slowly. Be patient. It will take your students at least eighteen years to learn all the mature adult behaviors you'd like to see.

Remember Time Out Does Not Teach Positive Behavior

Time Out is only a short-term solution for stopping the aggressive behavior. It does not offer students a chance to learn pro-social behaviors. It does not motivate students to do their school work. If our goal in managing classroom behavior is to help children make better choices, learn more acceptable behavior and to give them opportunities to be successful, Time Out will not, by itself, help further that goal. Rather, it is a last resort when other strategies such as praising, ignoring, redirecting, giving warnings, using logical or natural consequences and removing privileges have failed. In addition to using Time Out to reduce aggressive behavior, teachers will need to focus on developing behavior management plans that focus on teaching such students non-violent problem-solving approaches to manage conflict as well as appropriate social skills (see Chapters 9, 10 and 11).

Be Alert to your Own Need for 'Time Outs'

Teachers can be overly sensitive to their students' misbehaviors because they are exhausted, angry or depressed about the lack of apparent improvements in the students' behaviors despite their best teaching efforts. A teacher may also be angry or depressed because of events in his or her personal or professional life that are unrelated to the classroom. A teacher who becomes angry at a student may really be angry at the principal for assigning too many students to the class or for not assigning an aide. Or a teacher may become cross with her students for making noise because she is stressed about a personal situation at home (such as a sick child or a dissolving marriage). Depending on the mood and the energy level of the teacher, a student's behavior can seem cute one day and obnoxious the next.

Even the kindest and most well-intentioned teachers get frustrated and angry with their students. No one is perfect. The important task is to recognize the filters and mood you bring to your perceptions of your students, and to have strategies for coping with your own feelings. If you're depressed because of work problems, it may be a good idea take a Time Out yourself, away from the class in order to relax for a few minutes and gain perspective. If you're angry with your principal or co-teacher, you may need Time Out to problem-solve. In helping your students to be less aggressive and more able to problem-solve and handle conflict constructively, it is vital that you model the use of Time Out to manage your own anger and frustration.

Just as we talked about a teacher using a signal to alert school personnel that help is needed with managing a physically dangerous situation, there also should be a safety valve mechanism for a teacher to signal that she needs a 'break' or brief Time Out immediately. There must be a 'no blame' climate for this to operate well. For example, a teacher might use the code, 'there's a message for me in the office', to signal she needs a brief break. Or likewise, if another teacher sees that her colleague's classroom is in chaos, she might use a code signal, 'Can I borrow several of your students (the catalysts) for a few minutes?' and then have a chat with them about their behavior out of sight of the room. This short-term colleague support can be immensely helpful to maintain a calm attitude in the face some difficult student behaviors.

Developing your Discipline Hierarchy

As we have said, teachers need to have a classroom discipline plan or hierarchy of consequences for students' misbehavior. We have discussed the importance of using the least intrusive teacher interventions such as redirection, reminders, ignoring, warnings and self-monitoring approaches (covered in Chapters 3 and 6) to manage most student misbehaviors. However, when misbehavior continues despite the use of these proactive interventions then the teacher moves to a higher level in the hierarchy using negative consequences such as taking away privileges, giving work chores, setting up a logical consequence or planned discussions (covered in Chapter 7). Finally, for severe misbehavior such as aggressive or destructive behavior the teacher can use immediate Time Out or a Calm Down procedure.

Teachers should make their discipline plan visible in the classroom by posting it on the wall and explaining it to students as well as to parents in their initial orientation meetings. A sample hierarchy for disruptive behavior might look like this:

Sample Hierarchy for Disruptive Behavior

First time: Warning of Consequences
(*'I've reminded you to work quietly twice now, if you can't stop distracting your neighbour and talking out you will have to take time away by yourself'*)

Second time: Five Minutes Away from Group/or Yellow
(same day) Card Turned

Third time: Time Out plus lose 3 minutes of Break/Red Card

Fourth time: Time Out plus lose all of the Break

Or this:

Sample Hierarchy for Destructive Behavior

First time: 5-minute Time Out in classroom
(*'Chloe you've chosen not to follow the class rules, so it's 5 minutes in Time Out.'*)

Second time: Time Out in Time Out Corner/Chair in Classroom

Third time: Time Out (plus plan meeting with parents)

Fourth time: Time Out (plus stay in at break to make up work lost)

If Time Out cannot be completed in the classroom, the teacher needs to decide whether she will use a deferred consequence (i.e. loss of break) or procedures for having the student escorted to another classroom or room to complete the 5 minutes of Time Out.

The Green, Yellow, Red Light Card-Turning System

One effective method of setting up a discipline hierarchy which appeals to young children is the signal light card-turning system. The teachers post on a bulletin board small pocket envelopes (can be made from library cardholders) with all the students' names on them. In each pocket are placed three cards – a green, yellow and red card. The teacher uses this card system to indicate warnings and consequences for specifically identified misbehaviors. For example, a teacher might set up a system to eliminate hurtful comments to others and disrespectful speaking out in class. When Latasha says something impolite the teacher responds, 'Latasha, I want you to turn your card to yellow. You were speaking rude language to Jenny.' After Latasha has turned her card, the teacher remembers to look for times when Latasha speaks politely and to praise her. However, if she repeats the rude language, the teacher asks her to turn her card to red. In this case the teacher has explained that getting a red card means that Latasha misses morning break.

After break, any students' yellow or red cards are turned back to green, and they have a new learning opportunity and chance to be successful. However, the teacher will keep track of how many yellows or reds a student will get in a day. During the next period prior to lunch Latasha stays in green and the teacher says, 'You did a great job of staying in green, what did you do to stay in green?' Latasha responds, 'I spoke out quietly and politely when you called my name'. This verbal rehearsal of the appropriate behaviors helps the student remember what is expected of her. The programme will continue throughout the day with opportunities every hour or two for cards to be turned back to green and students offered a 'fresh start' with a clean slate.

This signal card-turning system may be set up for different disruptive behaviors such as for out-of-seat behavior, student non-compliance and defiant behaviors. The teacher may decide that hitting is an automatic red card for that period. The teachers may offer difficult students a personal challenge each day such as getting through an entire morning with no red or yellow cards or reducing the numbers of yellows from the day before and so on. Students may participate in the decision-making about how many

greens they think they can get that day. The teacher may want to add to the fun of this by challenging a whole class to get all greens for the reading period or free play period and so forth. He may offer an incentive to an individual student or class for meeting this challenge.

A note of caution: Be sure that such card-turning programmes are set up for the entire classroom – for example, for any child who is impolite or non-compliant or aggressive. Remember consequences should be applied uniformly – that is, they must be the same for the same misbehaviors regardless of who it is that misbehaves. Children will be quick to pick up on the unfairness of a teacher who gives consequences to some students and not others.

Developing a Behavior Plan for Individual Students with Problems

The interventions we have discussed in the previous chapters, as well as those described above, are generic teacher classroom management strategies to be used when any student in the class misbehaves.

BEHAVIOR PLAN

for

_____

Developed by: _____

Date: _____

This plan is to be created by teachers, therapists or counsellors working directly with a student or parents, and parents in collaboration with each other. This plan should be expanded over the year and then used to develop a transition plan for next year's teachers. Please be as specific as possible with examples.

I. Preventive Strategies

The following preventive strategies are particularly effective with this student:

> *For example: seating child near teacher with back to classroom when doing seat work; picture sequence chart on desk that outlines class schedule to help with transitions; allow for opportunities to move around; non-verbal cues and signals.*

II. Encouragement of Appropriate Behaviors

Targeted Positive Behaviors to Increase. The following positive behaviors have been targeted for additional support and reinforcement:

> *For example: hands to own body; concentrating on work; quiet hand up; following teacher's directions; sharing ideas with group; listening to others quietly; reading practice.*

Effective Motivators and Incentives. The following teaching strategies are effective in motivating this student and increasing his/her pro-social behaviors and academic success:

> *For example: frequent verbal praise which clearly describes the positive behaviors he/she has accomplished; praising nearby children when he/she is off task; behavior sticker chart which targets positive behaviors which child can earn stickers or coupons for – these are turned in for prizes whenever he/she earns 25; 'happy gram' coupons are given for special accomplishments; child likes to earn extra time on computer or chance to be teacher aid – teacher attention is a particularly powerful motivator; child also likes to be a leader of class activities and will work for this privilege.*

III. Decreasing Inappropriate Behaviors

Targeted Negative Behaviors to Decrease. The following behaviors have already been successfully eliminated:

The following behaviors are receiving some planned consequences in order to decrease their occurrence:

> *For example: interruptions during class; disengagement in class particularly during large group activities; non-compliance with teacher instructions.*

Effective Strategies for Handling Misbehavior. The following teaching management strategies are helpful with this student:

> *For example: clear non-verbal cues and reminders were helpful in redirecting him/her back on task for non-disruptive behaviors indicating disengagement; warning of consequences often prevented misbehavior from escalating; warning of Time Out for disruptive behaviors such as refusing to follow directions often stopped misbehavior; Time Out given for hitting immediately; Time Out consisted of chair in corner of room for 5 minutes; if he/she couldn't sit in chair, office was called and he/she went to classroom next door for 5-minute Time Out; loss of computer privileges if he/she had two or more Time Outs in one day.*

IV. Parent and Teacher Insights about the Student's Temperament and Interests – Tips for Connecting

> *For example: Interests – collecting football cards, ballet, etc. Temperament – likes hugs, squirms a lot and avoids eye contact but absorbs information readily, anxious about new events and sharing self, hates writing but computer helps; Family – has pet dog Ruffie, adjusting to divorce.*

IV. Plan for Collaborating with Parents: The parents would like to be involved in supporting their child's success in school and agreed that the following approaches would be mutually supportive:

> *For example: behavior sticker chart of positive behaviors sent home each day – child will trade these in for additional incentives from parents; parents will be supportive, positive and hopeful with their child – they will focus on his successes; discipline plan was agreed to by parents and they will avoid punishing bad days at school – as discipline would be administered at the time of misbehavior by teacher at school; telephone calls will be made to mother to tell her of positive behaviors; mother would like to participate in field trips or reading sessions in classroom; mother can help with transitions if this is a problem; parents suggested incentives which they have found motivating for their child; teachers and parents will try to communicate weekly by note, voice mail or e-mail.*

Plan discussed and agreed upon (date): _____

Plan to be re-evaluated: _____ (as necessary)

For the chronically misbehaving child, it will be important to develop an individual behavior plan because it will help the teacher to be more precise in how she focuses her attention and how she follows through with the agreed upon consequences. The behavior management sheet can be used to develop this plan.

Identify Negative Behaviors

First, you need to identify the specific negative behaviors that you want to reduce such as poking, blurting out, profanities, grabbing, wandering, or out-of-seat behavior, social withdrawal and so forth. It is important that these be defined clearly. For example, what is meant by disrespect? Some teachers might feel that the rolling of a student's eyeballs is disrespectful while others might focus on more overt disrespectful behaviors such as swearing or abusive name-calling.

Next choose which of these misbehaviors you want to target for intervention first. Once the target negative behaviors have been chosen, then observe and record their frequency, intensity and duration and the occasions or situations in which they occur. For example, are the specific misbehaviors more likely to occur in structured or unstructured times (i.e. on the playground, in the lunch room, or hallways, versus the classroom)? Do problems usually happen on particular days, such as Mondays after a stressful weekend at home? Are behaviors more likely to occur in the afternoons than the mornings? Do they usually occur with particular students? Do they occur under particular situations, such as when there is less teacher supervision? Or during transitons? What are the triggers that usually set the misbehavior off? For example, does the child misbehave when teased, rejected by a peer group, when left out of a discussion or when a learning task is too difficult or frustrating?

While keeping running records is not easy, this information will be critical for you in developing an intervention that is based on the specific needs of the student. For example, if the problem occurs more often in the afternoon, it may be necessary to set up a more frequent incentive programme at that time. Or, if the problems occur only in the cafeteria where adult monitoring is minimal, then the intervention may require additional monitoring during lunch times. If the problems primarily occur with particular students, then you may want to set up play groupings which separate these children. These records will also enable you to monitor any intervention strategies.

Why is the Misbehavior Occurring? (Functional Assessment)

Next formulate a hypothesis about why the child is misbehaving. The following checklist will help you to understand the child by thinking about why the child may be behaving in a particular fashion:

Understanding the Misbehavior

	Yes	No
Child uses the misbehavior in order to get attention		
Child is venting frustration with the misbehavior		
Child does not have the developmental ability to do other behaviors		
Child uses the misbehavior to avoid stress or some unpleasant task		
Child finds the behavior fun in and of itself		
Child is unaware of doing the behavior		
Child uses the behavior to obtain power over others		
Child uses the behavior to gain revenge		
Child has not been taught other more appropriate pro-social behaviors		
Child's home environment or past history has not taught the child predictability or the trustworthiness of adults		
Child's community endorses the behavior		
Child's behavior reflects child's feelings of inadequacy		

Understanding the child's motivation and self-awareness for the behavior is also key to developing an individualized and appropriate intervention plan for the child. For example, the child with attention deficit disorder or hyperactivity will not have the ability to sit still for long periods of time and may not even be aware of his twitching or muttering under his breath. It would inappropriate to discipline such a child who does not have the developmental ability or capacity to perform a more acceptable behavior. Or, on the other hand, the child who uses the misbehavior to gain power over or attention from others will need an intervention that permits him to earn power and attention for appropriate behaviors rather than for inappropriate behaviors. Or, the child who is easily frustrated or who avoids stressful and unpleasant situations may need to learn self-control strategies. The child who is dirty and smelly may need to be taught hygiene habits because there is no one at home who has instructed him in the importance of this social skill.

Target Positive Replacement Behaviors to Increase

For every negative behavior, you need to identify a positive behavior to replace it with. For example, for the child who is withdrawn and non-participatory in class, you might target joining in with peers and participating in classroom discussions as the prosocial behaviors to be increased. For the child who is impulsive, you might identify waiting with a quiet hand up or taking turns as important alternative behaviors to encourage. For the child who constantly needs teacher reassurance, the goal might be to do some aspect of the assignment by himself first. It is important that these targets are achievable (i.e. within the child's capability) and measureable. This step of identifying the positive goals or behaviors is key to the eventual effectiveness of a behavior plan. Striving to achieve negative goals, such as the absence of pouting or tantrums or blurting out, is not likely to be effective because it does not help the child to visualize the positive alternative.

Determine Specific Reinforcers for Desired Behaviors

Once the positive behaviors have been identified, the next task in planning is to identify the specific reinforcers that will work to motivate this child. Some students are responsive to teacher praise and encouragement while others are suspicious of it. Some students are motivated by a tangible reward while others will work for the opportunity to be the teacher's helper. Understanding the possible underlying motivation for the misbehavior can help you choose incentives that might more likely be effective for this particular student. Understanding the occasions in which misbehaviors occur can help you determine how often the incentive plan will need to be implemented. For example, the child who has more difficulties in the afternoons might need an incentive system based on 15-minute intervals, whereas in the mornings it might be based on 1-hour intervals. When determining reinforcers, try to brainstorm all possible proactive strategies which may work with this student as well as find out from the parents what they think will be effective incentives. (See Chapter 5 for discussion of incentive programmes.)

Select Specific Consequences for Negative Behaviors

Finally, the specific consequences for the specific misbehaviors must be decided and clearly outlined in the plan. For the child who blurts out but doesn't use profanities, you might decide to use ignoring in combination with praise for waiting with a quiet hand up. On the other hand, for the child who blurts out profanities, you might impose a mild consequence (such as loss of 2 minutes of break) in combination with points for polite talk. For the child with impulse control problems, you might decide to use Time Out for hitting, points for co-operation with others, self-monitoring and social skills training.

Once the plan has been agreed upon, a written implementation plan should be drawn up. That is, who will arrange for the incentives, record the data, call the parents, teach the social skills, set up the self-monitoring plan and so forth. A date should be set to re-evaluate the outcome.

Remember the student on an individual behavior plan is not getting special privileges by being on the plan. Rather the student is being given individual support in much the same way as a student with an academic problem would receive additional tutoring.

Keep Records of Progress and Analyse your Discipline System

As we have seen above, the behavior plan for an individual child involves a combination of different strategies (consequences and incentives) rather than a single solution. If the plan is working, there should be some reduction in the misbehaviors within several weeks. Although, as was mentioned with the ignoring and Time Out strategies, there will likely be some worsening of behavior before it improves. If the misbehavior does not decrease over time with consistent implementation of the plan, then the plan should be re-evaluated to be sure there are sufficiently strong positive incentives and to determine whether negative consequences are being used too often.

Your ability to analyse your discipline plan – to assess whether it is working to reduce targeted misbehaviors – can be more easily done if you have kept good records. You will need a system to keep track of the type of misbehavior, the frequency with which it occurs, the consequence used, and the effects. The misbehaviors should be graphed for several weeks to determine if they are decreasing with the discipline approach that is being implemented. Moreover this record-keeping will help you not only to know where your students are in the hierarchy of discipline strategies, but also to monitor how often they are experiencing the more severe types of consequences such as Time Out or loss of privileges.

For example, a teacher had been using the card-turning system for her students' impolite language and non-compliance. She turned any red or yellow cards back to green four times a day. At the end of a week she analysed her system and found that one student, Robbie, was getting at least three reds a day and showing no sign of improvement. She realized she would have to change her expectations for Robbie to work on one misbehavior at a time and to reduce the time interval for turning cards back to green so that he could be more successful. Thus she decided to change the system to give reds

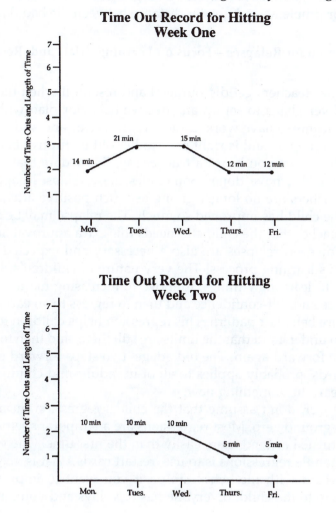

and yellows for his non-compliance and to ignore the impolite language for the time being. She also turned the cards back for Robbie six times a day. With this revised approach at the end of the week Robbie was getting some yellows and only occasionally a red. Later when his compliance problem had improved substantially, she revised the programme to include impolite language. This teacher's analysis was key to her success with her discipline plan.

The other important reason to have objective records and charts of the misbehaviors is sometimes on bad days teachers will subjectively think a behavior plan isn't working when it really is. Students on behavior plans still have bad days, but will gradually begin to have more good days. Success is a gradual downward trend in behavior problems and greater distance between the bad days.

Be Prepared for Relapses – Focus on Learning Trials and 'Restart Cards'

Sometimes teachers get discouraged and resentful when they have worked very hard to set up an effective behavior plan with a student, it seems to have worked for several weeks, and suddenly the child deteriorates and is right back to her old disruptive behaviors. How often have you heard a teacher say, 'How dare that child do that, after all I have done!' Sometimes these relapses happen because teachers are no longer giving as much positive attention because the child has improved so much. The relapse may be a signal to the teacher that the child still needs this extra approval and support. However, relapses are also a necessary and expected part of children's learning process! The very nature of children's development is to learn new things, to move to increasing maturity, independence and self-confidence and then to regress to an earlier more immature behavior pattern. This regression helps children to 'touch base', to understand that the limits are still there, and then to be able to move forward again. The old adage 'two steps forward one step backwards' probably applies to all of us, adults and children alike, when learning something new.

Moreover, don't assume that the child's regression means he is back to ground zero. Most regressions are a temporary setback that can be turned around more easily than the first time. One way you might handle regressions is to use 'restart cards', that is, to give the child a card with the behaviors on it you want to improve. You might say to the child, 'Everyone has bad days and you have been doing so well. You will get back on track again quickly. When this card is filled up with stickers for staying in your seat, we will know you are back on track.'

Remember children need many learning trials before appropriate social skills become a stable part of their interpersonal relationships. Children who are hyperactive, impulsive or learning disabled or children who have experienced family deprivation of some sort will need even more learning trials than children who are by temperament more reflective and attentive or from homes which emphasize social skills teaching. None the less, with consistent, warm and caring responses from teachers, all young children can eventually learn to be socially competent and positive contributors to their classrooms.

Involving Parents in Discipline Plans

One key to a teacher's success with a classroom discipline plan will be the degree to which the teacher has obtained parental support for the plan. At your initial school orientation, share with your parents your standard discipline hierarchy approach. As Time Out is one of the most sensitive and intrusive discipline consequences it is essential that there is a clear Time Out/Cool Off school-wide policy regarding its use which is published and explained to parents. This policy needs to explain the following:

- The purpose of Time Out (to protect students' and teachers' safety; to give time to cool down and regain control; to teach the student that aggressive behavior will certainly be stopped).
- Which behavior will result in a Time Out.
- How Time Out will be implemented safely and with respect.
- How the use of Time Out will be monitored and recorded.
- How Time Out be used on the playground or in the cafeteria.
- What backup plan is in place for the student who cannot complete an in-class Time Out.
- When parents will be informed.
- What follow-up plans have been made to teach alternative problem-solving and anger managment in addition to Time Out to stop the aggression.

It is also important at your initial school orientation to discuss your proposed methods for communicating with parents about behavior problems that may occur at school (e.g. by phone in the evening). Try to individualize your approach by letting parents specify whether they would prefer to be called at a different time or contacted in some other way such as by voice mail, a note home or e-mail. The methods you use to communicate with parents about their child's misbehavior at school should be chosen with parents' input, modified according to the family situation, ideally before problem behaviors occur. Moreover, let parents know good times when you can be reached as well.

Where possible teachers and parents should collaborate to set up behavior plans and determine meaningful incentive systems. This allows parents to reinforce their children's school successes at home. However, school behavior plans should stand on their own and not rely on parents in order to be successful. If plans depend on parents, they discriminate against the child whose parents can't be involved due to mental illness, work schedules or lack of interest. Plans which do involve parents need to be realistic about how much parents can do at home. For example, families living in a great deal of stress will find it very difficult to implement reward charts and to monitor behaviors. In these cases, teachers will need to collaborate with parents to determine how much they want to be involved. Regardless of how involved the parents can be in the behavior plan, it will important for teachers to give feedback to the parents about how the child is doing with the programme and to reinforce their efforts. A special letter or call home outlining the positive outcomes their child is making can elicit the parents' encouragement for the child's efforts at home.

How Should Teachers Let Parents Know of their Children's Behavior Problems at School? Should a Narrative Description of the Child's Problem Behaviors be Sent Home with the Child?

Often parents want to know about their child's day and want to be closely involved, but are reluctant to bother the teacher with a call; similarly teachers have limited time and may have difficulty reaching parents. When parents and teachers are unable to talk things over, teachers may have to resort to sending home impersonal notes about problems, which may foster resentment on the part of parents and misunderstandings on both sides. Particularly in the case of children who are known to be behaviorally challenging in the classroom, parents and teachers should have a workable, mutually agreed plan for how they will communicate and share information back and forth.

Do not send home daily notes to parents with descriptions of children's problem behaviors in the classroom. Many parents do not know how to interpret these notes. Some interpret them to mean they are supposed to discipline their child at home for his misbehavior at school and respond to the child by being punitive and overly critical. Thus the child receives double punishment. Not only does this reaction from parents damage the parent–child relationship but the parental discipline is so far removed from the actual problem behavior at school that it is unlikely to be effective. In fact, this discipline may create further problems because of the attention given to the child's negative behaviors. Sometimes parents respond to negative notes about their children by becoming defensive and angry and may even blame the teacher for the problem. Consequently we recommend that teachers schedule personal meetings with parents to talk about classroom problems and to collaborate and share with them their discipline plan for the misbehavior.

It is vital for teachers also to be building up a 'positive bank account' with parents by sending home 'happy grams' and other positive reports for good times and calling regularly to report something positive their child did that day. This positive base will create a trusting relationship between teacher and parents so that if it becomes necessary to discuss a behavior problem, parents will be more open and more able to collaborate with the teacher in addressing the problem.

An additional benefit of sending home happy grams or compliment notes to parents about some positive aspect of the child's behavior or attitude is that it helps the parents focus on the child's successes and focus the *child* on his or her successes, thus preparing the child to behave in similar ways the next day.

Moving Beyond Discipline

Repair and Rebuild

Children who are impulsive, oppositional, inattentive and aggressive will need constant teacher monitoring or scaffolding involving redirection, warnings, reminders and consistent follow-through with consequences. However, one of the hardest and most important things for a teacher to do when teaching a disruptive student is to move beyond the Time Out discipline to repair and rebuild the strained teacher–student and student–student relationships. This means not holding on to grudges and resentment after consequences have been implemented, welcoming students back as accepted and valued members of the class each day and continuing to teach them more effective ways of problem-solving. It means a philosophy of taking one day at a time, allowing the student a new learning opportunity or fresh start each day, and practising forgiveness. So instead of saying, 'I hope today is not going to be like yesterday, because if you are . . . ' the teacher encourages the child and predicts a successful day: 'I'm glad to see you, today is a new day and a new chance to learn something new'.

Moving to Self-Management

Initially for difficult and aggressive students, the teacher will need tight external management and consistent discipline in order to keep behavior under control. Indeed research has indicated that teacher use of incentives, differential reinforcement, Time Out and negative consequences result in decreased undesired classroom behaviors and increased positive social skills (e.g. Charlop *et al.*, 1988). However, the eventual goal is to shift away from exclusive teacher management to gradually increasing student self-management skills. This is necessary so that students can become less dependent on teachers to provide direction and incentives for their behavior. Such interventions have the potential for producing more durable and generalizeable behavior gains in situations outside the classroom (Nelson *et al.*, 1991).

Certainly one of the central features of many children with behavior problems is the absence of self-management skills. Part of the reason for this is that such children often have distorted self-perceptions and sense of reality (Webster-Stratton and Lindsay Woolley, 1999) and make maladaptive self-statements (Dush, Hirt and Schroeder, 1989). They have difficulty evaluating their own behavior, at times having an inflated sense of their performance and, at other times, being very negative about their abilities. They may misperceive others' intentions toward them as hostile when, in fact, the person might have been trying to be helpful. Although the degree of self-management expected of students will vary with the age, developmental ability and temperament of the child, teachers can begin to foster some skills of self-direction even in young pre-school children and in children with severe disabilities. Sadly, these skills are seldom taught to students, especially those with behavior problems.

Self-management interventions generally involve a variety of strategies related to changing or maintaining one's own behavior

(Shapiro and Cole, 1992). They include self-evaluation and self-reinforcement approaches. For example, teachers can invite children to reflect about how they did that day in order to get a sense of the accuracy of their self-perceptions and self-evaluation abilities. For children who have poor language skills or emotion vocabulary, a teacher might have a thermometer showing the range from calm (blue for cool) to overexcited (red hot) and ask the child to point to how active or on task he thought he was during certain classroom periods of the day. This gives the teacher an opportunity to provide students specific feedback on the accuracy of their self-perceptions or to help them remember times when they successfully calmed themselves down or stayed on task. Similar thermometers might be used for students to self-evaluate their ability to control their anger or their level of in-volvement in classroom activities. Children with behavior problems will often focus on their mistakes; however, by reviewing the positive aspects of the child's day, the teacher can help the child to gain more positive attributions.

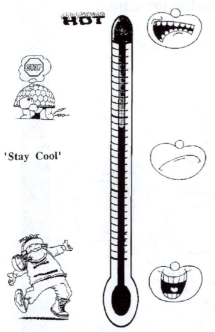

'Stay Cool'

Anger Thermometer

Another self-evaluation approach is to have children complete a form such as a self-encouragement chart (shown in Chapter 5) or Wally's balloon chart which covers certain periods in the day (e.g. reading time, Circle Time, free play, lunch and so forth). Once the desired behavior has been specified (e.g. quiet hand up, working hard, staying in seat etc.) the student marks his evaluation of his success at accomplishing the task with colours such as green for outstanding, blue for good, yellow for some blurting out, and red for loss of privilege or Time Out. As these are filled out at various time points during the day, it is ideal if the teacher can review them at the end of the day by asking, 'Let's see how you did today? What kind of day was it?' The child may respond, 'A mainly green day!' The teacher then can reflect, 'You're right, this was a great green day

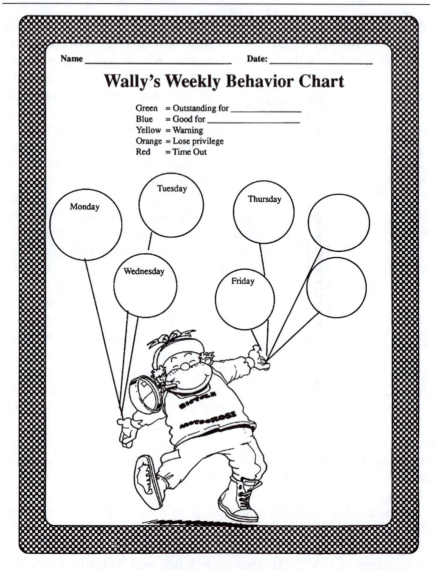

with only two yellows, maybe tomorrow you'll get one more green! Remember what do you have to do to get a green?' Through the use of the balloons and colours the child can reflect on his day at school with the teacher helping him to focus on his successes. If by any chance the child is getting more reds and yellows than greens and blues, then the time period for evaluating success needs to be shortened and the discipline plan re-evaluated.

Self-management interventions also include self-monitoring approaches such as the example in Chapter 6 in which a 'quiet hand up and blurt out sheet' was placed on students' desks for them to record whenever they did not blurt out in class. The teacher might also challenge the students that if they meet a certain criterion (e.g. ten quiet hand ups) they can can earn a chosen reward. In order to prevent disouragement in students who may not think they can meet the challenge or place a ceiling on students who are capable of exceeding the challenge the teacher might use a 'mystery challenge'. This is when the teacher writes the challenge for accomplishing the task on a piece of paper which is placed in an envelope. When the specified period is completed, the envelope is opened and the students compare their performance against the mystery criteria and earn rewards depending whether they matched or exceeded the challenge. This approach makes the self-monitoring procedures exciting and results in a high degree of student involvement. Similar programmes could be set up for self-monitoring other behaviors such as on-task or 'working' behavior or polite language in class or completion of a certain amount of work.

Teaching children self-instruction such as the internalization of self-statements is another self-management approach used to modify problem behavior (Meichenbaum, 1993). For example a child with academic difficulties who is off task a great deal of the time may be thinking negative thoughts which perpetuate the problem (e.g. 'I hate school' or 'I can never do this, it is stupid'). Teaching positive self-statements (e.g. 'I can do this eventually, I just need to keep working at it') can result in improved on task work. (See self-praise in Chapter 4 and the use of 'I can' cans in Chapter 6.) In Chapter 11 calming self-statements and scripts are described as a method to help students learn how to manage their anger. Finally, social problem-solving training which is described extensively in the next two chapters was developed to help children learn the thinking and social skills involved in making make good choices and assuming responsibility for their own behavior.

To Sum Up
- *Preparation is key* – carefully plan a hierarchy of responses to misbehaviors.
- Be prepared for testing.
- Monitor anger in order to avoid exploding suddenly; give warnings.
- Give 5-minute Time Outs with 2-minute silence at the end.
- Carefully limit the number of behaviors for which Time Out is used.

- Use Time Out consistently for selected misbehaviors.
- Don't threaten Time Outs unless you're prepared to follow through.
- Ignore child while in Time Out.
- Use non-violent approaches such as loss of privileges as a backup to Time Out.
- Follow through with completing Time Out.
- Hold children responsible for messes or destruction in Time Out.
- Support co-teachers' use of Time Out.
- Don't rely exclusively on Time Out – combine it with other discipline techniques, such as ignoring, logical consequences and problem-solving.
- Be sure you are rewarding the expected positive behaviors.
- Expect repeated learning trials.
- Use personal Time Out to relax and refuel.
- Develop discipline hierarchy for particular misbehaviors – colour card-turning system.
- Gain parental support for your discipline plan.

References

Bear, G. G. (1998) School discipline in the United States: prevention, correction and long-term social development, *School Psychology Review*, 2(1), 14–32.

Brophy, J. E. (1996) *Teaching Problem Students*, New York: Guilford.

Charlop, M. H., Burgio, L. D., Iwata, B. A. and Ivancic, M. T. (1988) Stimulus variation as a means of enhancing punishment effects, *Journal of Applied Behavior Analysis*, 21, 89–93.

Doles, D. W., Wells, K. C., Hobbs, S. A., Roberts, M. W. and Cartelli, L. M. (1976) The effects of social punishment on noncompliance: a comparison with time-out and positive practice, *Journal of Applied Behavior Analysis* (9), 471–82.

Dush, D. M., Hirt, M. L. and Schroeder, H. E. (1989) Self-statement modification in the treatment of child behavior disorders: a meta-analysis. *Psychological Bulletin*, 106, 97–106.

Forehand, R. L. and McMahon, R. J. (1981) *Helping the Noncompliant Child: A Clinician's Guide to Parent Training*, New York: Guilford.

Gardner, H. L., Forehand, R. and Roberts, M. (1976) Time-out with children: effects of an explanation and brief parent training on child and parent behaviors, *Journal of Abnormal Child Psychology*, 4, 277–88.

Martens, B. K. and Meller, P. J. (1990) The application of behavioral principles to educational settings. In T. B. Gutkin and C. R. Reynolds (eds.) *Handbook of School Psychology* (pp. 612–34), New York: Wiley.

Meichenbaum, D. (1993) Changing conceptions of cognitive behavior modification: retrospect and prospect, *Journal of Consulting and Clinical Psychology*, 61, 202–4.

Nelson, J. R., Smith, D. J., Young, R. K. and Dodd, J. (1991) A review of self-management outcome research conducted with students who exhibit behavioral disorders, *Behavioral Disorders*, 16, 169–79.

Shapiro, E. S. and Cole, C. L. (1992) Self-monitoring. In T. Ollendick and M. Hersen (eds.) *Handbook of Child and Adolescent Assessment* (pp. 124–39), New York: Pergamon Press.

Steinberg, L. (1996) *Beyond the Classroom: Why School Reform Has Failed and What Parents Need to Do*, New York: Simon and Schuster.

Webster-Stratton, C. (1997) From parent training to community building, *Families in society: The Journal of Contemporary Human Services*, March/April, 156–71, 61, 202–4.

Webster-Stratton, C. and Lindsay Woolley, D. (1999) Social competence and early-onset conduct problems: issues in assessment, *Journal of Child Clinical Psychology*, 28, 25–93.

Chapter Nine

Teaching Students to Problem-Solve

Why Is It Necessary to Teach Students to Problem-Solve?

Young children often react to their problems in ineffective ways. Some cry, have tantrums and yell, others hit, bite and become destructive, and still others gossip or lie to their parents or teachers. These responses do little to help children find satisfying solutions to their problems. In fact, they create new ones. But research shows that children use these inappropriate strategies either because they have not been taught more appropriate ways to problem-solve or because their inappropriate strategies have been reinforced inadvertently by parents' or teachers' or other children's responses.

It also has been shown that children's temperament influences their ability to learn more effective problem-solving skills. In particular, children who are hyperactive, impulsive, inattentive and aggressive are more likely to have cognitive difficulties with social problem-solving (Asarnow and Callan, 1985). Such high-risk children perceive social situations in hostile terms, generate fewer prosocial ways of solving interpersonal conflict, and anticipate fewer consequences for aggression (Dodge and Price, 1994; Rubin and Krasnor, 1986; Slaby and Guerra, 1988). They act aggressively and impulsively without stopping to think of non-aggressive solutions (Asher *et al.*, 1990) or of the other person's perspective. On the other hand, there is evidence that children who employ appropriate problem-solving strategies play more constructively, are better liked by their peers and are more co-operative at home and school (Shure, 1983). Consequently teachers have a key role in teaching children who are aggressive and impulsive to think of more prosocial solutions to their problems and to evaluate which solutions are better choices and more likely to lead to positive consequences than others. In essence these high-risk students are provided with a thinking strategy that corrects the flaws in their decision-making process and reduces their risk of developing ongoing peer relationship problems.

While teaching effective problem-solving will be particularly help-ful for high-risk students, efforts should be made to improve social skills and cognitive problem-solving of *all* students through curriculum-based lessons. Moreover, by including both high-risk or special needs students together with mainstream students in this training it will serve several purposes. First the risk of the high-risk students experiencing social rejection and negative stereotypes will be reduced. Secondly, this inclusion approach promotes classroom social cohesion, empathy among students and more co-operative learning.

Indeed it is the job of both teachers and parents to prepare today's children to be responsible citizens who are capable of thoughtful decision-making and coping with interpersonal conflict carefully and sensitively, particularly when under stress. As has been pointed out by Gardner (1993) interpersonal and intrapersonal intelligence are as vital to healthy functioning as mathematical competence. Children's successful development into adulthood and into a demo-cratic society is dependent on their ability to use critical judgement, effective decision-making skills and perspective-taking regardless of their innate ability and cultural or family background. The teach-ing of these skills early in life can serve to protect against or prevent the onset of problem behaviors such as drug abuse, pregnancy, school drop out, suicide and so forth.

What Empirical Evidence Is There for Problem-Solving Approaches?

Reviews of social skill and cognitive problem-solving instruction programmes for children have generally shown promising results (Beelmann, Pfingste and Losel, 1994; Schneider, 1992). One of the first pioneering programmes called 'I Can Problem Solve' (ICPS) was developed by Shure (1994) for children aged 3 to 11 and has been evaluated over a period of twenty-five years. Results have shown short term improvements in interpersonal as well as aca-demic behavior. Other programmes such as 'Skillstreaming' (Miller, Midgett and Wicks, 1992) and 'Social Problem Solving' (Camp and Bash, 1985) and others (e.g. Battistich *et al.*, 1989; Elias and Clabby, 1989) have also reported significantly improved social skills and co-operative strategies for resolving conflict. However, follow-up stud-ies of these and other similar programmes have revealed that the effects will be only be generalizeable across settings and long lasting if they are ongoing, integrated into the classroom environment and involve partnerships with parents. Several studies have reported that when treating highly aggressive young children with conduct problems the results indicated enhanced generalization and maintenance when training was provided to the parents as well as the children (Kazdin *et al.*, 1987; Lochman and Curry, 1986; Webster-Stratton and Hammond, 1997).

Teacher as Model

Undoubtedly, you are already teaching your students more appropriate problem-solving tactics without realizing it, especially if your students have opportunities to observe you problem-solving in the classroom. It is a rich learning experience for students to watch you resolving conflict with a student or a colleague and evaluating the outcome of your solutions. For instance, you may have a very small budget to buy all your supplies for your classroom for the year. You might share with your students the ways you are trying to solve this problem, how you are prioritizing your needs and how you are deciding what outcome is most important for your students. Your students also learn much by observing how you react to daily hassles and problems in the classroom and how you encourage on-the-spot problem-solving between students when they are experiencing conflict. You can help further this learning by thinking out loud and modelling your positive problem-solving strategies. For example, when presented with a frustrating situation such as a computer which breaks down or paint that gets spilled all over the floor, you might think out loud so your students can hear you, 'How can I solve this? I need to stop and think first. I need to stay calm. I'll take a big breath. What plan can I come up with to solve this problem?'

Teaching Problem-Solving Steps through Games, Puppets and Hypothetical Problem Situations

Clearly there are many skills involved in social decision-making; however, based on the problem-solving literature (D'Zurilla and Goldfried, 1971), researchers have suggested that for children the process of problem-solving can be divided into at least six steps and presented as the following questions:

1. What is my problem? (Define the problem and feelings involved.)
2. What is a solution? What are some more solutions? (Brainstorm solutions.)
3. What are the consequences? What happens next?
4. What is the best solution or choice? (Evaluate consequences of solutions in terms of safety, fairness and good feelings and make a good choice.)
5. Am I using my plan? (Implementation.)
6. How did I do? (Evaluating the outcome and reinforcing efforts.)

For children between the ages of 3 and 8, the second step of generating possible solutions is a key skill to learn. While evaluation and implementation are more easily done by older children, youngsters first need to consider possible solutions and to begin to understand that some solutions may have more satisfactory outcomes than others. The ability to think ahead to possible outcomes for each solution is a big developmental step and will be particularly difficult for hyperactive and impulsive children.

Methods and strategies which can be used by teachers to teach each of these problem-solving skills are highlighted next.

STEP 1: What Is my Problem? How Do I Know I Have a Problem?

1 What is my problem?

A fun way to begin problem-solving discussions with students is to ask them to pretend they are 'detectives' who are trying to solve a problem. Encourage them to put on their imaginary detective hats for these discussions. Then present your students with some hypothetical problem scenarios for them to solve.

The first step in helping children understand if they have a problem is for them to pay attention to their feelings. If they are feeling uncomfortable (sad or angry or worried) this will be an important clue that there is a problem to solve. They should be encouraged to pay attention to their 'Feelings Fingerprints' (Elias and Clabby, 1989) – the unique way their body signals them they are in distress. For some, the signal may be sweaty or clenched palms, others stomach-aches, and others a racing heart and so on. Labelling the Feelings Fingerprints involved in the situation is an important initial step for students to learn in problem-solving for it serves as a 'trigger' that problem-solving is needed. Once students have recognized and labelled their own feelings then you can help them learn how to accurately define the problem. For example, the problem may be defined as, 'I feel angry because a classmate won't share the football with me' or 'When they won't let me play with them, I feel frustrated and mad'.

Another aspect of this problem definition process also involves encouraging your students to think about the feelings of others in the situation. For example, asking, 'What do you think the boy who has the football feels?' Some students may not attend to or have difficulty reading the feeling cues or fingerprints of others in a situation or may misinterpret others' feelings, leading to inappropriate decisions. Moreover, some students may have a limited range in their ability to label emotions, that is, they only have words for emotions such as mad and glad. For such children to become effective problem-solvers it will be necessary to expand their feeling vocabulary to include other feelings such as pride, worry, calmness, stress, excitement, fear, confusion, embarrassment, disappointment and so forth. (See Chapter 11 for a discussion of this.) Once children have labels for a range of feelings they have a way to describe what they are feeling and to regulate their emotions, rather than just reacting or being overwhelmed by them.

2 What is a solution?

STEP 2: Brainstorm Solutions

After the problem has been defined, the next step is to invite your students to generate as many different solutions, options or choices as they can in order to solve the problem. This brainstorming process teaches students flexible thinking and creates an attitude that encourages them to realize that there is often more than one reasonable way to solve the problem. Avoid criticizing or ridiculing or editing any of your students' ideas, no matter how silly they may seem. Instead, encourage imaginative thinking and try to model creative solutions yourself. Be sure to praise them for their attempts to solve the problem. In particular, it is helpful to praise them for their *different* solutions (e.g. 'Good that is a different idea') because it will encourage a broader variety of solutions rather than variations of the same idea.

If students are having difficulty finding a solution you might suggest some ideas yourself or ask them to check Wally's Solution Detective Manual for other ideas. In this manual are pictures of a variety of solutions such as: walk away, wait awhile, say please, do something else fun, trade, offer to share, ask for help from parent or teacher, talk about your feelings, ignore, ask politely, calm down, admit mistake, apologize, give a compliment, and forgive yourself.

Sometimes with older school-age children you can ask them what their goals are in order to help them generate solutions. For example, 'What do you want to have happen? Picture how do you want this to end up.'

It adds to the students' enjoyment

3 What are some other solutions?

of these solution-generating discussions if you use games, puppets and stories to present the hypothetical problem situations. The following are a few games you might like to try to teach problem-solving steps 1 and 2.

The Suppose Game

The Suppose Game is a game whereby a student chooses a 'suppose card' from a folder. On this card is a picture and description of a problem situation for your students to solve. The student reads the suppose card (or has it read to him by the teacher if s/he can't read) and the class then generates possible solutions. It is easy for the teacher to make these suppose cards by using issues that are occurring every day at school. More of these problems may be found in two colourful children's books, *Wally's Detective Book for Solving Problems at School* and *Wally's Detective Book for Solving Problems at Home* (Webster-Stratton, 1998).

The Suppose Game

Here are some examples of suppose card problem situations you might try with your class. These are excerpts from the Dinosaur Curriculum – a videotape-based programme for teaching young children empathy, social skills and problem-solving (Webster-Stratton, 1991).

- Suppose a child much younger than you started hitting you. What would you do?
- Suppose a boy had been playing for a long, long time with the computer, and you wanted to play with it. What would you do?
- Suppose there was only one piece of pizza left and you and your sister both wanted it. What would you do?
- Suppose you broke your dad's favourite lamp. What would you do?

- Suppose you are constantly teased and bullied by another child at school. What would you do?
- Suppose you want to meet a new friend. What would you do?
- Suppose your teacher made you stay in for break because you called a classmate a name but she had not seen that the other child had called you a name first. What would you do?
- Suppose you ripped a brand-new pair of trousers that your father bought you for a special event. What would you do?
- Suppose you really want a cool pair of shoes which you have seen in a shop, but your mother says they are too expensive. What would you do?
- Suppose a cupcake you have been saving disappeared and you see icing on your sister's mouth. What would you do?
- Suppose another child calls you a baby for playing with dolls or says you are ugly. What would you do?
- Suppose you ask another child to play with you and he or she refuses. What would you do?
- Suppose your brother wrecks a model you've been working on for two weeks. What would you do?
- Suppose your best friend has a new friend whom you don't like. What would you do?
- Suppose there is a group of 'popular' kids, but they are kind of bossy and don't let you play what you want to play. What would you do?
- Suppose there is a group of kids who form a club but they don't invite you to join them. What would you do?
- Suppose you have trouble with reading and sometimes stutter and the other kids laugh and tease you. What would you do?
- Suppose you play chase on the playground, but it starts getting rough and there is pushing and shoving. What would you do?
- Suppose the child sitting next to you twiddles with your hair and kicks you under your desk. What would you do?
- Suppose there is a group of children playing with a skipping rope and you want to join in. What would you do?

Once the students have discussed possible solutions to a suppose card problem, you can ask them to role-play or act out their proposed solutions. For example, if the students have suggested 'ignoring' as a possible solution to the situation of the boy who won't share the football, then ask them to show you how they would do this. Choose one student to be the football player who hogs the ball and another student to be the classmate who wants to play football. Students will love participating in these 'plays' and acting them out helps students to see exactly what behaviors are involved in carrying out the solution and to practise the appropriate skills. Sometimes teachers are reluctant to do role-plays at first, but soon learn that these skills-training practice sessions are far more important to a student's actually learning and using new problem-solving behaviors than theoretical discussions which don't clearly specify the appropriate behaviors. It is ideal to do no more than two or three of these suppose cards in one teaching session so that there is time to adequately practise each one.

Use puppets to role-play problem situations
Young children love puppet shows and you can use them to engage children and bring problem-solving discussions to life. We suggest using largish, life-size puppets (preferably puppets with moving mouths) who will come to the classroom on a regular basis to ask the students for help solving particular problems. Puppets such as Wally Problem-Solver and Molly Manners can present a problem for discussion in one session and then come back the next session to tell students what happened when they tried out their ideas. Puppets can also share with the students how they coped with a difficult situation. Here are some examples of the problems which puppets like Wally and Molly can bring to students for their help solving.

Wally and Molly and their Friends Ask Students for Help Solving these Problems

Telling and listening

- Wally is afraid to bring his homework (or his behavior chart from his teacher) home because he hasn't done well.
- Wally has a fight in the school playground with other children who won't let him play with them.
- Molly and Wally fight over what channel to watch on TV and end up being sent to Time Out.

- Molly is not invited to a birthday party when most of her classmates are going.
- Wally takes his friend's football because his parents won't buy him one.
- Oscar the Ostrich hides his head in the sand and is afraid because his parents fight – he is sure they are fighting because of him.
- Tiny Turtle is afraid of an adult who gets angry at him.
- Wally tells a lie because he is afraid he will get into trouble.
- Wally is teased about the way he looks and doesn't want to go to school anymore.

Here is a sample script for how Wally would present the last problem to the students.

Sample Script for Puppets – 'Wally Gets Teased'

Wally: Today the kids at school were teasing me and calling me a monkey face!

Teacher: How did that make you feel?

Wally: I felt so mad, I called them names back!

Teacher: How did you feel about that solution?

Wally: Not so good because they called me a dummy and said I couldn't play with them.

Teacher: I wonder if there was a different solution that might have worked better? Do you want to ask these kids for their ideas?

Wally: I guess so – but I bet they never get teased.

Teacher: Oh I think all kids get teased sometimes.

Wally: Really? Well how do you kids feel when you are teased?

Teacher: (*encourages students to label their feelings*)

Teacher: Well I guess those feelings are clues there is a problem. Right? So Wally how would you state the problem?

Wally: The problem is I feel really mad because they are teasing me.

Teacher: That's right so now what can you do to solve that problem? What are some solutions? or choices of what to do? (*encourages students to generate solutions – such as ignoring, walking away, being humorous in response, taking a deep breath and calming down, explaining feelings)*

Teacher:	Wally these kids are great problem-solving detectives, look at all the solutions they came up with.
Wally:	Can we practise some of those ideas because I'm not sure I know how to do that?
Teacher:	Okay let's pick two students who will show you how to react when someone teases you. And Wally you can be the one to tease okay? *(two students volunteer)*
Wally:	Neaner, neaner, you are a monkey face!
Students:	*(role-play some of the solutions that were discussed)*
Wally:	Wow that was cool – I didn't get any reaction from either of you when I teased – it wasn't much fun. I'm going to try that next time someone teases me. I'll let you know what happens.

Next Session

Wally:	Hey you know what someone was teasing me again and saying I was stupid and couldn't even kick a ball and you know what I did?
Teacher:	Tell us Wally.
Wally:	*(Wally demonstrates)* Well I was feeling really mad and I knew I was supposed to say how I felt about the teasing but I just couldn't do it so then I took some big breaths so I could calm down. And I thought to myself, 'I'm not going to pay any attention to him, I can be stronger than him.' I walked away and found someone else to play with.
Teacher:	How did you feel about that?
Wally:	Oh it was so cool, I felt so powerful.
Teacher:	*(to students)* How do you think Wally did? Was his solution fair? Did it lead to good feelings? Was it safe?

Play Pass the Detective Hat game for practising generating solutions
Another game that can be used to present hypothetical problem situations for students to solve is the 'Pass the Detective Hat' game. This is a great game to play during Circle Time. Hypothetical problem situations and questions (such as those shown above) are written on small pieces of paper and placed in a Sherlock Holmes hat. The children sit in a circle and the hat is passed around the circle while

the music is on. When the music stops, the child who has the hat in his lap gets to choose a problem from the hat and try to answer the question. If the student can't answer the question, he can ask a friend to help him. The puppets and teachers also participate in this game by helping to read the problems for non-readers and modelling appropriate inner talk out loud. They might even add some different solutions which have not been suggested by the students. For example, the teacher or puppet might say, 'Let's see, I have a problem. I am being teased and I don't like it – what can I do? Johnny suggested I could ignore her and Anna suggested I could ask her to stop. Those are two good solutions – does anyone have any other ideas?' Here are some suggestions for the Detective Hat game for practising solutions.

The 'Detective Hat' Game for Practising Generating Solutions

- A friend comes to you and wants to know what to do when he is teased.
- What is a solution?
- How do you know when you have a problem?
- Someone took your skipping rope without asking. What are some solutions?
- You want to ride on the swing that your friend is using. (It could be book, TV show, etc.) What are some solutions?
- You are sitting next to someone who keeps bothering you by touching your hair and whispering in your ear. What are some solutions?
- The other kids are playing football and you want to join them. What are some solutions?
- You are presenting your project in front of the class and one of your friends starts making faces at you. What are some solutions?

Include some jokes in the detective hat so sometimes the student gets to ask the class a joke rather than present a problem.

STEP 3: What Are the Consequences of the Solutions? What is the Best Plan?

After generating many different solutions or possible choices, the next step is to look at what would happen if a particular solution were carried out. For instance, if a student suggested 'grabbing' or 'hitting' in order to get the football back, help him to consider the possible outcomes by asking, 'Imagine what might happen next if

you did grab the ball away'. Students will likely picture such things as losing a friend, getting into trouble with the teacher or getting into a fight. This discussion should be carried out in a non-critical way even though the solution proposed is inappropriate. If students feel criticized for their solutions they may avoid suggesting ideas in the future.

Next ask your students to imagine the possible consequences of a different solution, such as asking the friend politely for the football or offering to share. This would result in being turned down by the friend,

What happens next ? (consequences)

ignored, or perhaps being successful in getting the ball. Often, children are surprised or upset when things don't go according to their plan. Part of this can be avoided if the teacher helps students stop and predict several outcomes that might result from a particular solution. However, be sure that this does not become a burdensome or compulsive activity. Students do not need to discuss the consequences of every single solution.

STEP 4: What Is the Best Solution or Choice?

After reviewing possible outcomes of a few solutions, the next step is to help the students decide which one or two might be the best choice to try. By phrasing it as a choice it gives the students the responsibility for solving the problem.

What is the best solution?

Choosing the best solution involves students asking themselves three questions: Is the solution safe? Is it fair? Does it lead to good feelings? If the solution meets these criteria then the children are encouraged to try it out with a role-play practice session. Young children love acting and the experience of acting out the solutions not only engages everyone in the learning process but it helps everyone see the consequences of the different approaches.

Sample Script for Puppets –
'Felicity Steals Something'

Felicity: Well I came today because I have a problem that I was hoping to get some help with.

Teacher: These kids are great problem-solvers, I bet they could help.

Felicity: I did something at school this week, and well my girl friend Susie she had this soft toy and she had it in her locker. And I really wanted one like that so I just took it! She was really upset because it was her special animal.

Teacher: What happened then?

Felicity: Well the teacher asked, 'Who took Susie's animal?' and I didn't want to tell so I lied and said, 'not me'. Because I really thought I would get in big trouble if she found out it was me. I knew I shouldn't have taken that animal but I thought I would lose Susie as a friend if she found out it was me. And the teacher would send a note home and I would definitely get a spanking and be grounded.

Teacher: Well you know Wally says you're supposed to pick solutions with good consequences so do you think this was a good choice?

Students: (*brainstorm why students think her solution might not be the best one in terms of safety, fairness and good feelings*)

Felicity: I see, so I made one problem into two problems because I lied. What should I do now?

Students: (*generate solutions such as admit mistake, tell teacher and Susie, apologize, give back animal*)

Felicity: Are you disappointed in me – do you think I'm really awful because I did that?

Teacher:	Well you know, Felicity, everyone makes mistakes sometimes. How do you students feel about Felicity now?
Students:	(*tell her how they feel*)
Felicity:	Well I'm worried I won't be strong enough to admit my mistake. Can we practise doing that?
Teacher:	Sure let's have someone be the teacher, another person Susie and another person be Felicity. (*student role-plays in front of class admitting mistake to Susie and teacher and experiencing consequences*)
Felicity:	Okay let me try it now and see how I do? 'Susie I am really sorry I took your toy, here it is back. I shouldn't have taken it and I want to make it up to you. Would you like one of my toys for a while? Do you think we can still be friends?' Well, how did I do?

Pass the Detective Hat Game for Practising What to Do When a Solution Doesn't Work!

It is important for students to practise how they will respond if their solution does not result in success. For example, even though the student asked politely to play football, the other child still did not want to give up the ball and would not let him play with him. It is important for children to understand that making a good choice when attempting to solve a problem does not always guarantee success. They must learn that if their first good solution doesn't work, then they should try another good choice. Here are some other hypothetical scenarios you can discuss and role-play to help students learn how to handle the situation when their solution doesn't work.

The 'Detective Hat' Game for Practising What to Do When Solutions Don't Work

- You ask your friend politely to play a game with you and s/he says s/he doesn't like that game.
- You ask your friend who is bothering you to stop whispering (or ignore the whispers and touches) but s/he still continues. What will you do next?

- You wait patiently to get a turn with the computer but the other child is taking too long.
- Your mum is asking you to set the table and your favourite TV show is coming on. (This teaches waiting and thinking about another's perspective and feelings.)

For the problem situations listed above you can practise some of the following solutions: thinking about another's perspective and feelings; asking again politely; waiting; ignoring; walking away; doing something else fun; thinking helpful thoughts and using calming self-talk. Be sure to have the students only practise pro-social solutions not inappropriate solutions. If the consequences of an inappropriate solution are to be role-played, the puppet should be the one to demonstrate the bad choice not the students.

STEP 5: Implementation of Problem-Solving Skills

The fifth step when engaged in hypothetical problem-solving games is for the students to think of a situation where they might use the agreed upon solution. Or, if later in the day the teacher observes a similar real-life problem occurring, then s/he can help them use the solution to try solving the problem. For example, after you have been having these problem-solving discussions, one of your students comes running to you complaining that a classmate is hogging the computer, or another student comes to you in tears because she has been excluded from the hopscotch game. You can respond by following the problem-solving steps outlined above. While it may be tempting to tell students what to do, it is more effective to help them think about solutions. Problem-solving in the midst of real-life conflict is much harder than problem-solving in a hypothetical or neutral situation. Children may be so angry and upset that they cannot think clearly. You may be able to calm them through discussion, so they can come up with some solutions. Sometimes they may be so emotional that they need to go for a brief Time Out or Calm Down until they cool off. Occasionally a problem is so distressing that it is best discussed later when both you and the students have had time to calm down and gain some perspective.

Once students have learned the problem-solving steps and practised them with hypothetical problem situations they will be ready to discuss their own personal problems. Instead of the teacher bringing up hypothetical problems to discuss, s/he can begin the

Can I use the plan?

class by asking, 'does anyone have a problem today that they want help solving?' It won't take long before students are looking forward to these discussions because they know this is a time when they can share their difficulties and get some ideas for how to cope with them. Moreover, you will likely be present when some of the squabbles actually occur and can guide students through the process.

STEP 6: Evaluating Outcome

How often have you heard yourself or the parents of one of your students say, 'Joey makes the same mistakes over and over again. He doesn't seem to learn from experience or remember what happened the other times.' The reason for this is that some children lack the skill of using the past to inform the future. They do not know how to recall past experience or to see how those experiences apply to what is happening now. This is why the sixth step is so important because it helps students learn how to evaluate how successful they were in solving a problem (whether hypothetical or real life) and whether they might use it again in the future. Thus it encourages them to rethink the past event and anticipate whether this would be a good choice in future situations. You can help students evaluate the solution and its consequences by asking the same questions that they asked themselves when they were choosing a good solution:

How did I do?

1. Was it safe? Was anyone hurt?
2. Was it fair?
3. How did you feel about it and how did the other person feel?

Is your solution safe?

If the answer is negative to any of these questions then encourage your students to think about a different solution. For example, you might say, 'Okay so that was not the best choice and we wouldn't want to do that again because it led to bad feelings, what other choice could we make if this happens again?' Finally, one of the most important aspects of this process is to reinforce the students for their efforts at problem-solving. Praise them get them and get themselves to pat themselves on the back for their good thinking – regardless of the quality of the solution that was proposed.

Making Problem-Solving More Effective

The following section focuses on some of the problems teachers may encounter when they try to teach problem-solving to their students. It also includes some effective ways to be successful.

Is your solution fair?

Discover the Student's View of the Problem First

Sometimes teachers are too quick to come to a conclusion about what exactly they think is the student's problem. For instance, Juan's teacher may decide that he is having trouble sharing. It may be that from Juan's point of view, the problem is that his friend grabbed the ball away from him in the first place and wouldn't let him join in the game. Or perhaps Maria shared the crayons with her friend but then the friend refused to give them back. If the teacher makes a quick decision about the problem, s/he may focus her

**Does your solution
lead to good feelings?**

energies in the wrong direction. By misinterpreting the situation, she may lecture Juan or Maria about sharing. This can lead to the child's resistance to the problem-solving process. A child who is blamed for something he didn't do will likely become upset about unfair treatment. If the child is preoccupied with the injustice of the situation or is plotting how to retrieve the crayons or ball, he or she won't hear a word of his teacher's good ideas.

Your first task is to try to understand the problem from your student's point of view. You will usually need to ask questions like, 'What happened?' 'What do you see as the problem?' or 'Can you tell me how you feel about it?' This kind of question not only helps your student to clarify the problem in his or her own mind, but also ensures that you won't jump to the wrong conclusion about what's going on. In the previous example, Juan's teacher might say, 'Now I understand what the problem is. You shared the ball, but your friends played with it too long and wouldn't give it back. And that made you mad.' In order for children to learn anything from a problem, it is important that the solution be relevant to *their* perception of the situation. When a student believes that you understand their point of view they are more likely to be motivated to deal with the problem cooperatively.

Encourage Students to Come Up with Multiple Solutions

Sometimes teachers believe that telling their students how to solve a problem helps them learn to problem-solve. For example, two children may have trouble sharing a tricycle on the playground and the teacher responds by saying, 'You should either play together or take turns. Grabbing is not nice.' Or 'You must share. Lamar will get mad and won't be your friend if you don't share. You can't go around grabbing things. Would you like that if he did it to you?' The problem with this approach is that the teachers lecture or tell their students what to do before they have found out what the problem is from the student's viewpoint. Moreover, telling a student what to do (or what not to do) does not help them to think about their problem and how to solve it.

It is more effective to guide your students into thinking about what may have caused the problem in the first place than to tell them the solution. Invite them to come up with possible solutions. If you want to help students develop a habit of solving their own problems, they need to be encouraged to think for themselves. They should be urged to express their feelings about the situation, talk about their ideas for solving the problem and anticipate what might happen if they try a particular solution. You can offer a few solutions of your own in order to expand their repertoire of solutions once your students have suggested their own ideas.

Guided Problem-Solving

The opposite problem occurs when teachers think they are helping their students to resolve conflict by telling them to work it out for themselves. This might work if students already have good problem-solving skills but, for most young children, this approach will not work. In the case of Max and Tyler fighting over a book, it will probably result in continued arguing and Tyler, the more aggressive child, getting the book. Therefore, Tyler is reinforced for his inappropriate behavior because he got what he wanted and Max is reinforced for giving in because the fighting ceased when he backed down.

Teachers can help their students learn to work it out on their own by guiding them through the problem-solving steps. You can encourage them to talk aloud as they think and you can praise their ideas and attempts at solutions. In this way, you reinforce the development of a style of thinking that will help them to deal with all kinds of problems. Encourage them to come up with many possible solutions. Then help them to shift their focus to the consequences of each solution. The final step is to help them to evaluate which are the best ones.

**Script of Poor Teacher
Problem-Solving with Student 'It's Mine!'**

Two children are fighting over a football and each are grabbing it.

Teacher:	I've told you a million times not to grab each other's toys.
1st Child:	But it's mine.

2nd Child:	She took it. I had it first.
1st Child:	No you didn't.
Teacher:	Can't you two learn to play together? You must learn to share! (*Fighting resumes*)

Sample Script of Effective Teacher Problem-Solving with Student 'She Hit Me!'

Tina is crying and holding her arm.

Teacher:	Who hit you?
Tina:	Sarah.
Teacher:	What happened? (*teacher elicits Tina's view of problem*)
Tina:	She just hit me.
Teacher:	You mean she hit you for no reason? (*Teacher encourages Tina to think of causes*)
Tina:	Well, I hit her first.
Teacher:	Why?
Tina:	She wouldn't let me look at her book.
Teacher:	That must have made you angry. How do you think she felt when you hit her? (*teacher helps Tina think of the feelings of others*)
Tina:	Mad.
Teacher:	I guess that's why she hit you back. Do you know why she wouldn't let you look at the book? (*Teacher helps Tina to see the point of view of the other child*)
Tina:	No.
Teacher:	How can you find out?
Tina:	I could ask her.
Teacher:	That's a good idea. (*teacher encourages Tina to seek facts and discover the problem*)

Later.

Tina:	She said I never let her see my books.
Teacher:	Oh, now you know why she said no. Can you think of something you could do so she'd let you look at the book? (*teacher encourages Tina to think of solutions*)
Tina:	I could tell her I won't be her friend if she doesn't give it to me.

Teacher:	Yes, that's one idea. What would happen if you did that? (*Tina is guided to think of consequences of solution*)
Tina:	She might not play with me again or be my friend.
Teacher:	Yes, that's a possible result, do you want her to be your friend?
Tina:	Yes.
Teacher:	Can you think of something else so she would still be your friend? (*teacher encourages further solutions*)
Tina:	I could trade her one of my books.
Teacher:	That's a good idea. What might happen if you did that?

In this example, Tina's teacher helps her to think of why she was hit and define the problem. When she learns that Tina hit first, she does not lecture or offer advice, but helps her student to think about Sarah's feelings. Through problem-solving she encourages Tina to consider the problem and alternative ways to solve it.

Sample Script of Real-Life Problem-Solving with Student 'She Won't Let Me Play with Her'

Lizzie:	(*runs into classroom from break crying*) Kimmi's not going to be my best friend. I hate her! She wouldn't let me play with her.
Kimmi:	No I didn't say that, I didn't! She's a liar!
Teacher:	I can see you are both upset and feel bad. I think you both need to calm down first before we can find out what the problem is and see what we can do to fix things? (*teacher may direct children to separate seats for a few minutes or schedule a time at lunch to discuss the issue later*)
Teacher:	Remember our rules for problem-solving? (*reviews rules of no put downs, no interruptions*) Okay Lizzie you first, what do you see as the problem? (*Lizzie states problem*) How do you feel? Kimmi what do you see as the problem? (*states problem*) How do you feel? What do you think you can do to solve the problem? (*if they can't think of any ideas refer them to the problem-solving solution kit*)

If there is too much emotional arousal the children won't be able to solve the problem. So the teacher in this example reassures them and allows cool off time first. The teacher may want to use the problem-solving cue cards for the steps as they work through the problem.

Be Positive and Fun

Sometimes teachers try to be helpful by telling their students when their solutions are silly, inappropriate, or not likely to be successful. This can make them feel ridiculed and they'll probably stop generating solutions. Another type of problem occurs when teachers become obsessive about this process and force their students to come up with so many solutions and consequences that the discussion becomes confusing.

Avoid ridiculing, criticizing or making negative evaluations of your students' ideas. Instead, urge them to think of as many solutions as possible, and to let their imaginations run free. If they have a short attention span or become bored, not all the solutions have to be looked at in detail regarding the possible consequences. Instead, focus on two or three of the most promising ones.

Ask about Feelings

When some teachers problem-solve they avoid discussing feelings. They focus exclusively on the thinking style, the solution and the consequences. Yet, they forget to ask their students how they feel about the problem or how the other person in the situation may have felt. It is also important for teachers to be aware of their own feelings. Hearing your student report that she has been sent off the playground for hitting someone may provoke feelings of anger, frustration or helplessness. You need to gain control of these emotions before trying to help your student with her feelings about the situation.

Encourage your students to think about their feelings in response to a problem or to a possible outcome of a solution. Urge them to consider the other person's point of view in the situation. For instance, you might ask 'How do you think Julie felt when you did that? How did you feel when she did that?' Raise the question about how she might discover what someone else feels or thinks. 'How can you find out if she likes your idea? How can you tell if she is sad or happy?' This will help your students to be more empathetic and, because they try to understand other people's feelings and viewpoints, result in more willingness to problem-solve, compromise and co-operate. Discussing your own feelings also helps them to realize that you empathize with them.

Encourage Many Solutions

As your students come up with solutions, be careful not to criticize them because they are not good enough. Allow them to think of as many solutions as possible without comments from you as to their quality or potential effectiveness. Then you can offer a few of your own creative ideas. However, these should be offered as suggestions, not as orders. Research has shown that one difference between a well-adjusted and a poorly adjusted child is that the well-adjusted one is more likely to think of a greater number of solutions to problems. The goal, then, is to increase your students' likelihood of generating numerous ideas.

Use Open-Ended Questioning and Paraphrasing

Using open-ended questions will maximize a child's thinking about the problem. While you may be tempted to ask 'why' questions ('Why did you do that?') or multiple choice questions ('Did you hit him because you were angry or because he was making fun of you or . . .') or closed-ended questions ('Did you hit him?'), avoid these approaches because they either result in a yes or no answer or close off discussion because of feeling defensive or blamed. Instead ask 'what or how' questions such as, 'What happened?' or 'How are you feeling?' or 'What other feelings do you have?' or 'What do you think the other person feels?' These open-ended questions will be more likely to engage the child in the problem-solving process.

Paraphrasing or reflecting back to the student what they are saying also helps them feel listened to and valued for their ideas. The advantage of paraphrasing is you can rephrase some of their statements into more appropriate language. For example when the child was asked how he felt, he responded, 'He's a real dummy'. This can be paraphrased as, 'You sound really angry with him'. This will help them eventually to develop better problem-solving vocabulary.

Using Picture Cues and Solution Cards to Prompt Students

Cue cards such as Wally's six problem-solving steps shown above are useful non-verbal cues to help children remember the steps and to organize their thinking. It is helpful to show these cards frequently or post them on the walls in your classroom so that teachers can easily refer to them as an appropriate situation arises. In addition, solution cards which depict a variety of possible solutions can be put in a briefcase or file labelled 'Problem-Solving Detective Manual'. Teachers can refer students to this manual when they are having difficulty coming up with a solution to a real-life problem.

Make Solution Detective Notebooks

Teachers can strengthen students' problem-solving discussions by utilizing some of the ideas they have suggested in writing and homework exercises. For example, you could give your students a homework exercise to write about (or draw a picture of) a problem that happened and how they solved it. From these drawings and discussions you can compile a classroom solution detective manual which can viewed by parents and other students and teachers in the school.

Think about Positive and Negative Consequences

When teachers discuss the possible consequences of solutions, they occasionally focus on negative ones. For instance, a teacher and boy may be talking about outcomes of a proposed solution that hitting his friend may allow him to get the ball he wants. One obvious consequence is that the other child will cry, be unhappy, and get the hitter in trouble with his teachers. Most teachers would predict this consequence. However, many would overlook the fact that hitting *might* work to get the desired ball. It is important to be honest with students and explore both the positive and negative consequences. If hitting works in the short run, the child then needs to think about what effect such behavior might have on his friend's desire to play with him in the long run. By evaluating all of the possible outcomes, students can make a better judgement about how effective each solution is.

Model your Thinking out Loud

It is helpful for your students to observe daily problem-solving that goes on in the classroom. They can learn by watching you and your co-teacher decide who is going to pick up the supplies, write the weekly note home, or how to decide where to take a field trip. There are countless opportunities for children to observe you discussing a problem or conflict, generating solutions and then working together to evaluate what the best solution might be. It is also helpful for them to see you evaluate a solution that may not have worked out well and to hear you decide on a different strategy for the future. Research suggests that this opportunity for children to observe adults resolving conflict is critical, not only for developing their problem-solving skills, but also for reducing their stress and anxiety about unresolved issues.

Focus on Thinking and Self-Management

Often teachers believe that the objective of problem-solving is to come up with the best solution to a particular situation. While this would be nice if it happened, the real purpose for going through this process with students is to teach them a thinking strategy and a method of self-management rather than generating the 'correct' solution.

Therefore when you are problem-solving with your students, focus on *how* they are thinking rather than on specific conclusions. Your goals are to help them become comfortable thinking about conflict, develop a knowledge base for generating good solutions or choices, and understand strategies for thinking ahead to the possible consequences of different solutions. These cognitive social problem-solving skills will eventually lead to self-management when faced with real-life conflict. Try to use the problem-solving methods whenever you can throughout the day to help children find solutions to their problems. The following is an example of how a teacher used this strategy to assist a very dependent and insecure student to become more independent and confident.

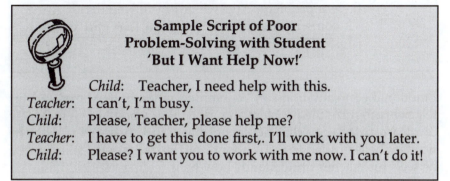

**Sample Script of Poor
Problem-Solving with Student
'But I Want Help Now!'**

Child: Teacher, I need help with this.
Teacher: I can't, I'm busy.
Child: Please, Teacher, please help me?
Teacher: I have to get this done first,. I'll work with you later.
Child: Please? I want you to work with me now. I can't do it!

Teacher: Just go work by yourself while I finish this. You have to learn how to work by yourself. You can't have everything the minute you want it.

Five minutes later.

Child: Teacher, are you finished yet?
Teacher: I'll tell you when I'm finished, don't bother me or I won't help you at all.

Sample Script of Effective Problem-Solving for Promoting Self-Management

Marty: Teacher, will you help me?
Teacher: I'm working with Anna right now. When I finish working with Anna, then I can help you.
Marty: Please teacher, please help me now.
Teacher: I can't help now as I am in the middle of something with Anna.
Marty: But I really need help! I can't do it!
Teacher: Can you think of something different to do while I finish this? (*teacher helps Marty think of alternative activity*)
Marty: No.
Teacher: You're just teasing me. What part of it can you get started?
Marty: I could draw something.
Teacher: Yes, that's one thing you could do.
Marty: Or, I could do the other part of the page and leave this section for later.
Teacher: Yeah, now you've thought of two good solutions. You are getting to be a pretty good thinker when you have a problem. And when I'm finished with Anna, I'll come over and help you with that part which is causing you difficulty.

Emotional confrontation can be avoided when both Marty and his teacher recognize the problem and each other's point of view. Marty can learn to accept what he cannot have and to wait for what he wants if he is guided to think about how his teacher is feeling and if he feels his teacher understands how he is feeling.

Make your Puppets Come Alive

As we have discussed, puppets are very helpful for teaching children problem-solving concepts. Young children are enthralled with puppets and will talk about painful or sensitive issues with them more easily than with an adult. Don't worry that you are not a trained puppeteer, the children won't notice – the important thing is to be fun and playful with the puppets. Remember that the puppets become 'real' for the children so you must give each puppet a name, an age, personality, special interests and a family situation. If you have more than one puppet you can have puppets who represent different temperaments and family situations, such as the hot-tempered or shy child or the child who is adopted and living with a single parent or grandparent and so forth. The puppets should be subject to the same classroom rules and discipline as the students. Thus use them to model earning a special privilege for successfully solving a particularly difficult problem or for handling frustration appropriately or coping with a learning difficulty and so on. In order to keep their personalities alive we even change their clothes each week!

Hold Regular Class Meetings or Circle Times

Hold regular weekly class meetings or Circle Times with your students to teach them the problem-solving steps and to discuss problems that may be identified either by the teacher or students. These meetings are more effective in a circle or semicircle format in small chairs away from desks. When starting these meetings the teacher should discuss with the students the 'ground rules' for the meeting by saying, 'Remember what our rules are for our circle meeting time?'

Classroom Meeting or Circle Time Rules

- One person speaks at a time.
- Listen and look when another is speaking.
- One problem will be discussed at a time.
- No 'put-downs' allowed when sharing opinions (about anyone, parents or other students outside the classroom).
- Keep hands and feet to yourself.
- Meetings will last no more than 30 minutes.
- Everybody's suggestions for solutions are welcomed.
- Anyone has a right to pass.

Once the ground rules have been reviewed then the teacher and students set the agenda by asking who has a problem they want to discuss. If there are several students with problems then one or two are chosen for that meeting and the others scheduled for subsequent weekly meetings. For older children (who can write) it can be helpful to have an 'agenda box' in the classroom. Students can write out their concerns or ideas for the Circle Time discussion and put them in the agenda box during the week. You can make it clear that everything won't be discussed right away, but at least they can let you know what their concerns are.

When the agenda or problem to be discussed has been settled, the students discuss their feelings about the problem and go on to to suggest possible ways to solve the problem. We encourage them to express their ideas for solving the problem as a suggestion. For example, 'Would it help if you . . . ?' Sometimes it is helpful for the person speaking or sharing a suggestion to hold a special speaking object (e.g. teddy bear such as Talking Ted or a toy microphone) and then everyone in the group knows who is speaking and who is listening. When finished sharing her ideas, the speaker passes the microphone to the next child to speak. Any child who does not want to speak may say 'Pass' and hand it on. Sometimes children who find it difficult to speak out will allow Talking Ted to speak on their behalf. During Circle Time it is important that the teacher values all opinions, summarizes what children have said, avoids interruptions or criticisms and follows the Circle Time rules just as the other students do (e.g. teacher raises quiet hand up to ask a question). It is important that students feel safe during Circle Time to say what they feel.

Occasionally the teacher may want to ask for help with a problem. Problems can be anything from playground issues, teasing and bullying, to issues such as cheating, put-downs in the classroom and noise levels. For example, one teacher of 7 to 8-year-olds was worried about put-downs in her classroom so she brought it up at the class meeting. She began by saying, 'In our class we have a politeness rule and we use language that helps people feel good about themselves and respectful to others. This means we have a "no put-down zone" in our classroom. But I have noticed some put-downs being used and I wondered if it is possible that some of you don't realize that these words are put-downs. First I would like to talk about some examples of put-downs?' The class goes on to list put-downs such as, 'you're a butthead, weirdo, nerd' or 'that's a dumb idea' or 'your mother's a dog-face' and so on. Some students may not see these as put-downs as hurtful but as something funny. The teacher continues the discussion by asking the students how they would feel if they were called these names and to discuss why someone speaks this way. Next she asks the class to brainstorm other more appropriate ways of communicating disagreement. Eventually she may suggest the idea of a 'put-up' rule. She might plan with her class that she will give a sticker whenever she notices someone giving a 'put-up' to a classmate. Finally, she will ask the students to practise or role-play with each other different ways they can give put-ups.

Invite others to Circle Time

During Circle Time not only are students and teachers encouraged to bring up problems for problem-solving but also the puppets can be invited to bring in problems. Some problems or situations are too sensitive for students to be open about. These are the issues that puppets can raise. For example, issues around bullying, stealing, being afraid of a teacher or parent, or being touched in unwanted places can be presented by Wally or Molly puppets. Lunch time and break problems can also be brought up in Circle Time. For example, the lunch time and break supervisors or bus drivers should be encouraged to come to these meetings to bring up problems regarding table manners or sportsmanship or bus behavior for the students to help solve. Finally, asking parents to join Circle Time occasionally can help promote collaboration and build strong links between home and school.

Set Up Activities to Practise Problem-Solving and Reinforce Pro-social Solutions

It is essential that teachers provide small group co-operative activities to practise the concepts discussed during Circle Time or in classroom meetings. See Chapter 10 for descriptions of these activities. The teacher's role during these activities is to coach and praise the children whenever they use appropriate problem-solving strategies.

Praise and More Praise – Issue Personal or Classroom 'Challenges'

Throughout the day, in class, on the playground and in the cafeteria you should look for students who are making good choices and effectively problem-solving and pause to praise the children's use of these strategies. For example, say, 'wow you two worked that problem out like real detectives! You are getting very good at solving problems and staying calm.' You can also issue either a personal challenge or classroom challenge to meet the goal of achieving a certain number of good solutions. For example say, 'I am going to record every time I see someone problem-solving and making good choices and when the class gets to fifty we will have a celebration'. Or, for the individual student who has particular difficulty managing conflict, you might say, 'Mathew, I am going to give you a personal challenge – when I notice you coming up with ten different good solutions you will be admitted to the detective club, level one'. You might even give Mathew a punch card with numbers on it which he can have punched whenever he is observed making good choices.

Involving Parents

Children will learn these problem-solving steps even better if parents are informed of them and can reinforce their occurrence at home. You can send home newsletters and pictures explaining the six problem-solving steps and encouraging parents to use this terminology at home whenever there is a conflict. For example, when a brother and sister are arguing parents can trigger the problem-solving process by asking, 'What is the problem?', 'What are some solutions?', 'What do you think would happen if you did that?', 'Are there any other solutions?', 'What do you think is the best choice?' (based on being fair, safe and leading to good feelings). By using the same terminology at home as is used at school it will cue children more readily into using this thinking process when they are becoming upset. Of course, if teachers can offer actual workshops for parents to train them in problem-solving strategies this will lead to even greater assurance that parents will use the process at home. Finally, give problem-solving homework assignments that ask children to discuss particular problems with their parents. For example the Dinosaur curriculum uses a student detective activities manual which includes student home activities which are to be completed in discussion with parents or guardian. For example, one such home activity is as follows: 'You and your brother seem to be fighting a lot over things like who gets sit in the front seat or who gets to watch a particular TV programme and your mother gets angry at you when

you fight. Talk to your parent about ways you can solve this problem and bring your ideas to class.' The children's books, *Wally's
Detective Book for Solving Problems at Home* and *Wally's Detective Book
for Solving Problems at School* (Webster-Stratton, 1998) are given out
to children to read with their parents at home. These books provide
a rich array of solutions to choose from when faced with a variety of
common problems.

Conclusion

Teaching these social problem-solving steps is no harder than teaching any other complex set of academic skills such as long division or
geography. First you teach the step-by-step procedures to follow
and then you provide modelling, repeated practice and reinforcement with different situations. Gradually with time and practice and
persistence these 'scripts' will become automatic for students and
with ongoing experiences they will be broadened and integrated.
Just as for teaching mathematics there is no expectation these skills
will all be mastered in one year or on one course but will require
continued instruction and infusion into classroom content through
out the student's education. Moreover, just as some students have
more difficulty with academic subjects such as reading or writing so
do some children have more difficulty with reading social cues,
understanding how to solve problems and how to express their
feelings about them. With persistent encouragement on the part of
the teacher, students will come to perceive themselves as competent
decision-makers and will be armed with the necessary skills for
meeting the challenges of adolescence and adulthood.

To Sum Up

- Use games and puppets to present hypothetical problem situa-
  tions for students to practise the problem-solving steps.
- Help students clearly define the problem and to recognize the
  feelings involved.
- For preschool children, focus on generating many solutions.
- Be positive, creative and humorous.
- For primary age students, focus on thinking through to the
  various consequences of different solutions.
- Help children anticipate what to do next when a solution doesn't
  work.

- Model effective problem-solving yourself.
- Remember it is the process of learning how to think about conflict that is critical, rather than getting the correct answers.

References

Asarnow, J. R. and Callan, J. W. (1985), Boys with peer adjustment problems: social cognitive processes, *Journal of Consulting and Clinical Psychology*, 53, 80–7.

Asher, S. R., Parkhurst, J. T., Hymel, S. and Williams, G. A. (1990), Peer rejection and loneliness in childhood. In S. R. Asher and J. D. Coie (eds.) *Peer Rejection in Childhood* (pp. 253–73), Cambridge: Cambridge University Press.

Battistich, V., Schaps, E., Watson, M., Solomon, D. and Schaps, E. (1989), Effects of an elementary school program to enhance prosocial behavior on children's cognitive social problem-solving skills and strategies, *Journal of Applied Developmental Psychology*, 10, 147–69.

Beelmann, A., Pfingste, U. and Losel, F. (1994), Effects of training social competence in children: a meta-analysis of recent evaluation studies, *Journal of Abnormal Child Psychology*, 5, 265–75.

Camp, B. W. and Bash, M. A. S. (1985), *Think Aloud: Increasing Social and Cognitive Skills – a Problem-Solving Program for Children in the Classroom*, Champaigne, IL: Research Press.

D'Zurilla, T. J. and Goldfried, M. R. (1971), Problem solving and behavior modification, *Journal of Abnormal Psychology*, 78, 107–26.

Dodge, K. A. and Price, J. M. (1994), On the relation between social information processing and socially competent behavior in early school-aged children, *Child Development*, 65, 1385–97.

Elias, M. J. and Clabby, J. F. (1989), *Social Decision Making skills: A Curriculum Guide for the Elementary Grades*, Gaithersburg, MD: Aspen.

Gardner, H. (1993), *The Multiple Intelligences: The Theory in Practice*, New York: Basic Books.

Kazdin, A. E., Esveldt, D. K., French, N. H. and Unis, A. S. (1987), Effects of parent management training and problem-solving skills training combined in the treatment of antisocial child behavior, *Journal of the American Academy of Child and Adolescent Psychiatry*, 26(3), 416–24.

Lochman, J. E. and Curry, J. F. (1986), Effects of social problem-solving training and self-instruction with aggressive boys, *Journal of Clinicial Child Psychology*, 15, 159–64.

Miller, M. G., Midgett, J. and Wicks, M. L. (1992), Student and teacher perceptions related to behavior change after skillstreaming training, *Behavioral Disorders*, 17, 291–5.

Rubin, K. H. and Krasnor, L. R. (1986), Social-cognitive and social behavioral perspectives on problem-solving. In M. Perlmutter (ed.)

Cognitive Perspectives on Children's Social and Behavioral Development. The Minnesota Symposia on Child Psychology (Vol. 18, pp. 1–68), Hillsdale, NJ: Lawrence Erlbaum Associates.

Schneider, B. H. (1992), Didactic methods for enhancing children's peer relationships: a quantitative review, *Clinical Psychology Review*, 12, 363–82.

Shure, M. (1994), *I Can Problem Solve (ICPS): An Interpersonal Cognitive Problem-Solving Program for Children*, Champaign, IL: Research Press.

Shure, M. B. (1983), Enhancing childrearing skills in lower income women. *Issues in Mental Health Nursing*, 5(1–4), 121–38.

Slaby, R. and Guerra, N. (1988), Cognitive mediators of aggression in adolescent offenders: 1. assessment, *Development Psychology*, 24, 580–8.

Webster-Stratton, C. (1998), *Wally's Detective Book for Solving Problem at Home*, and *Wally's Detective Book for Solving Problems at School*, in Incredible Years Training Series for Parents, Teachers and Children, Seth Enterprises, 1411, 8th Avenue West, Seattle, WA98119, USA.

Webster-Stratton, C. and Hammond, M. (1997), Treating children with early-onset conduct problems: a comparison of child and parent training interventions, *Journal of Consulting and Clinical Psychology*, 65(1), 93–109.

Chapter Ten

Peer Problems and Friendship Skills

Few teachers need to be convinced that friendships are important for children. Through the successful formation of friendships, children learn social skills such as co-operation, sharing and conflict management. Friendships also foster a child's sense of group belonging and begin to facilitate children's empathy skills – that is, their ability to understand another's perspective. The formation of friendships – or their absence – has an enduring impact on the child's social adjustment in later life. Research has shown that peer problems such as peer isolation or rejection are predictive of a variety of problems including depression, school drop out, and other psychiatric problems in adolescence and adulthood (Ladd and Price, 1987).

Why Do Some Children Have More Difficulties Making Friends?

For some young children, making friends is not easy. It has been found that children who have a more difficult temperament – including hyperactivity, impulsivity and inattention – have particular difficulty forming and maintaining friendships (Campbell and Ewing, 1990). Their inadequate impulse control leads to aggressive responses, poor problem-solving, lack of empathy and a failure to consider the potential consequences of their actions. These children also have significantly delayed play skills that include difficulties waiting their turn, accepting their peers' suggestions, offering an idea rather than demanding something, or collaborating in play with peers (Webster-Stratton and Lindsay Woolley, 1999). It has also been found that children with poor conversation skills are more likely to be peer-rejected (Gottman, Gonso and Rasmussen, 1975). They have difficulty knowing what to say to initiate a conversation and how to respond positively to the overtures of others. As a result, they have difficulty joining in groups (Putallaz and Gottman, 1981).

Children with social difficulties often misjudge what is expected of them in social situations: they may be impulsive or disruptive when entering a group, have trouble sharing and waiting their turns, or make inappropriate or critical remarks. Consequently, their interactions are often annoying to other children. Other children may be threatened by how easily impulsive children become emotionally upset or aggressive. These peers may respond by isolating, rejecting or making fun of them. Young impulsive children who are having these kinds of peer difficulties also report internal distress, such as loneliness and low self-esteem (Asher and Williams, 1987; Crick and Dodge, 1994). These self-perceptions contribute further to their peer difficulties by causing them to be overly sensitive to peer comments, to lack confidence in approaching other children, and eventually to withdraw from interactions and group activities. Their isolation results in fewer and fewer opportunities for social interactions and fewer chances to learn more appropriate social skills. The end result can be a bad reputation among classmates and other peers, and social isolation.

A major challenge for teachers is to prevent peer rejection and exclusion and to promote effective social skills and positive friendships for all children. Teachers are even more important than parents in this endeavour because parents are often not present to help when their children are having difficulties in large peer groups. In this chapter we discuss ways you can teach some of the specific social skills which are covered in many social skills curriculum and which research has suggested are important for children to learn in order to develop good friendships (Bierman, Miller and Stabb, 1987; Elias and Tobias, 1996; Greenberg et al., 1995; Gresham, 1995; Gresham, 1997; Grossman et al., 1997; Knoff and Batsche, 1995; Webster-Stratton and Hammond, 1997).

Teaching Children How to Initiate an Interaction and Enter a Group

One of the first social skills to teach young children is how to enter a conversation or begin an interaction with another child or group of children. Some children will be shy and afraid to initiate a conversation or join in when a group of students are already engaged in an activity. Other children have trouble because they are overly enthusiastic. They barge into a group of children engaged in play without asking or waiting for an opening. As a consequence they are frequently rejected by the group. Both types of children need to learn how to approach a group, how to wait for an opening in the conversation, and how to ask to join in. Teachers can teach these group entry skills by role-playing scenarios where a child wants to join a group of children in play. As we discussed in Chapter 9 for teaching problem-solving, we find the use of large life-size puppets (Wally and Molly) during Circle Time to be an engaging way to model and coach appropriate group entry skills. The following is an example of one role-play you might do with your students.

Sample Script for Puppets – 'Initiating Group Entry'

(three students volunteer to role-play and are asked by the teacher to start playing a board game)

Wally: *(approaches the group, pauses and watches children play the board game for a while to show interest)*

Wally: That looks like a fun game. *(say something nice and wait for a response)*

Wally: *(pauses for a while and watches them play, noting the rules of the game)* Would you mind if I played with you? *(asks permission)*

Child: Okay, we've just started.

Wally: Thanks, which piece do you want me to use? *(asks how to join in)*

Alternative version:

Wally: *(approaches the group, pauses and watches students play football for a while)*

Wally: Great goal. *(waits for response from peers)*

Wally: *(pauses for a while and watches them play)* Would you mind if I played with you?

Child: No, we're in the middle of a game.

Wally: Okay, maybe another time. When you're done, if you want another game with me, that would be fun. *(accepts decision)* *(thinks to himself)* Let's see, maybe I'll ask Freddy if he wants a game of conkers.

Change roles: Wally puppet takes on peer group member and another student demonstrates group entry skills.

This role-play emphasizes the four steps of entering a group of children: (1) watch from the sidelines and show interest; (2) continue watching and say something nice about children playing; (3) wait for a pause in game before asking to join in; and (4) ask politely to join in and accept response. Children will have their requests to join in play with others turned down about half the time. It is important to prepare them for this possibility so that it is not a crushing event and so that they can look for another group to play with.

Teaching Young Children How to Play with Each Other

While teachers need to encourage and praise all young students for using friendly play skills, they will need to give particular attention to coaching children who are impulsive, inattentive, hyperactive or socially isolated. These children are delayed in their play skills and many have not learned the principles of co-operation and balance in give-and-take relationships. They lack the skills necessary for good co-operative and reciprocal interaction. A good time to do this teaching is Circle Time or some small group time. You can start by asking your students several questions to elicit their ideas about what they think friendly behavior is. Questions such as, 'What makes a good friend?' or 'How do you play with friends?' will get children to brainstorm their ideas about how a good friend behaves. Next ask for a child to volunteer to demonstrate playing blocks or Lego with you (or one of the puppets). Before you begin playing ask the other children to notice any time one of you does something friendly. In particular, students are asked to notice the following friendly behaviors:

- sharing
- making a suggestion
- waiting
- asking for permission
- taking turns
- helping
- giving a compliment
- agreeing with each other
- asking for help
- being polite (e.g. saying please, thank you)
- giving up a turn to someone else.

Helping

Next take turns as other children practise playing with you using these skills. Once this friendly play has been modelled for the students in Circle Time, then you can pair up the students in twos or threes to practise what they have learned with unstructured and co-operative toys (such as blocks, drawing materials). It is usually best to pair up a child who is more socially competent with a child who has fewer skills. During these play periods you will need to pay particular attention to coaching and praising the socially incompetent children whenever you notice them taking turns, sharing, asking politely and waiting. Of course when teacher aides and parents are trained in these play skills they can help in the classroom so that all the small groups in the classroom will receive individual adult coaching and encouragement. You can also use socially skilled students (or trained students from older years) to be 'coaches' and ask them to notice and praise all the friendly behaviors exhibited by other other children.

Sharing

Teaching Children How to Follow Directions

Part of learning to play reciprocally with friends is not only helping, sharing and making suggestions but also being able to accept the ideas and directions of another child. Children who are non-compliant and impulsive have difficulties accepting directions from their friends as well as their parents and teachers. The teacher can help students learn the skills of listening and following directions by playing various directions games. For example, a variation of

'Simon Says', is 'Wally Says': 'Eyes here', 'Mouth closed', 'Hands in lap', 'Scratch your nose' and so forth. Another one of Wally's directions games is to provide students with cut-out dolls of Wally and Molly along with a cut-out set of clothes, jewellery, hats, shoes and clothes for each character. Ask the children to listen carefully and follow directions. Start by saying, 'Put on Wally, the cowboy hat and his soccer shirt'. You can gradually lengthen the number of items as children gain proficiency at listening and following directions. The children are praised for listening carefully and accurately following the teacher's directions. After this game has been carried out several times with the teacher giving the directions, then children can be paired up with students taking turns giving and following directions with each other.

Teaching Children How to Talk with Friends

As we noted earlier, poor conversation skills have been linked repeatedly to poor social competence and peer rejection (Ladd, 1983). On the other hand, training in conversational skills has been found to enhance unpopular children's social functioning (Bierman, 1986; Bierman, Miller and Stabb, 1987; Ladd, 1981). Through role-plays and games, teachers can practise and coach students in learning effective conversation skills such as introducing oneself, listening and waiting to talk, asking another child's feelings, taking turns in conversation, suggesting an idea, showing interest, praising someone, saying thank you, apologizing and inviting someone to play. Begin by

Praising

focusing on only one or two of these conversation skills at a time by first practising them and then praising and rewarding them whenever you observe them occurring in the classroom, cafeteria or playground.

Here are some games and activities teachers can use to practise 'friendly talk' and listening skills.

Circle Time Games and Activities for Teaching Friendly Talk

Compliment and Sharing Circle Time: It is often satisfying to end the day or the week with a compliment Circle Time. At this time the teacher asks for a volunteer (or can pull a name out of a hat) to say one nice thing about something friendly or kind a classmate has done that day. Each child is given a turn and asked to choose a different student to compliment so that everyone gets a turn. The children are encouraged to say, 'I'd like to say "well done" to . . . because . . . '. With young children it is helpful to pass a teddy bear to the person who is to receive the compliment and then that person passes the bear on to another child when they give their compliment. This is helpful particularly for children with limited language skills because they can still indicate a compliment by passing the bear to someone.

In addition having a regular sharing Circle Time can build students' sense of trust and group cohesiveness. Some examples of questions to begin this process are, 'What is the luckiest thing that ever happened to you?' or 'What is your favourite animal or food?' or 'What do you like to do on a rainy day?' Gradually over time the questions can become more personal such as asking, 'Tell us a time someone helped you this week' or 'Tell a time when you were really angry but you stopped yourself' or 'Tell us about something kind that you did'. A sharing circle activity can be used to start the afternoon or as a mode of transition.

Guided Block Building Game: Pair up students. Have each pair divide two identical sets of large wooden blocks into two piles. Put a cardboard screen between the two piles of blocks so that one child cannot see the other child's blocks. Ask one student in the pair to make a structure with the blocks. When this is completed, ask the second student to make the same thing without looking at the first child's structure. The second student will need to ask questions and receive help from the first student in order for this to happen. (A variation of this game can be with play dough.) This game helps the children learn how to ask questions, listen, take turns in conversation, suggest ideas and be helpful.

Twenty Questions Game: Guess What? Make a file of numerous pictures compiled from interesting magazines. Then ask a student to choose from the special file, one picture of a secret object. Then tell the other students they have twenty 'yes' or 'no' questions in order try to guess what the secret object is.

Clay modelling: Guess What? In this game one child makes something out of clay and the other children ask questions to guess what he is making.

Molly's Listening Game: Pair up students and ask them to talk about a topic such as, their favourite sport, a time when they were happy, something exciting, a favourite movie, or their family. Each student has 1 minute to speak while the other student listens with ears and eyes. After the speaker stops, the listener says a few words summarizing what the speaker said. Then the pair of children approach another pair and repeat what the members of the group have said.

Pass the detective hat for practising how to talk to others

Telling and listening

Put some of the following questions into a detective hat and ask for students to volunteer to pick out questions to answer and role-play (or pass the hat in a circle and stop the music to indicate a student's turn). These questions are directed at helping students practise friendly conversation skills such as: being polite when interrupting someone, asking permission of parents, asking for help, telling yourself to wait, learning how to successfully join in a group of children and thinking of someone else's point of view.

The 'Detective Hat Game' for Practising Friendly Talk

- Your parents are talking and you want to ask them if you can go over to your friend's house for the night. (Your friend is on the phone.) What will you say?

- Your teacher is talking to you after school, and your mother is waiting in the car pool line to pick you up. What will you say?
- Your mum is on the phone and you want to ask her if you can go to the football game with a friend. How can you interrupt?
- You want to sit in the front seat next to your father, but your sister got there first. What can you say?
- Some kids are playing a board game. You want to play but they are half way through the game. What can you say?
- Someone has hidden your lunch box and as a result you haven't eaten your lunch by the beginning of afternoon school. How would you explain this to your teacher?
- There are two games of football going on in the yard and the other game is getting muddled up with yours. How could you sort out the problem in a friendly way?
- The new boy in your class is hanging around the railings on his own. How could you include him in your game?

Another Idea to promote Friendship

Pass the hat which contains all the students' names. The name each student picks out is their secret friend for the day.

Use Discussions and Co-operative Learning Activities to Teach Children Friendship Skills

It is helpful for teachers to have regular discussions with their students about friendship and what it means to be a good friend. Concepts such as helping, sharing and being a good team player are key ideas for students to understand. These discussions should be held regularly (e.g. once a week), perhaps with students sitting in a circle on the floor. In these class meetings teachers can read stories about friends who face problems in their relationships. For example, a child who is uncoordinated but wants to be on his friend's football team, or the friend who is being excluded by some other kids. These stories can prompt teachers to ask questions such as, 'What would you do if you saw your friend being left out by a group of children?' Concrete examples from the classroom and playground should be used to help students think of ways they can counteract social isolation and bullying.

In addition to classroom discussions about friendships, it is also important to incorporate games and co-operative learning activities that help students practise friendly behaviors such as sharing, helping and teamwork. Carefully planned co-operative activities, where the focus is on the performance of the group, create mutual positive dependence among group members. When each member of the group is given responsibility for every other member's learning of the prescribed task, students begin to feel responsible for each other.

Teamwork

In fact, if practised frequently group projects can create cohesiveness that extends to an entire classroom. Small group co-operative learning activities also help prevent peer rejection. Below is a list of co-operative activities that encourage practice of friendly behavior. The group size for each of these activities should vary according to the age and temperament of the child and the number of adults available to supervise. The teacher should team up the more hyperactive and impulsive children with calmer and more reflective students. Students who are isolated or who tend to be victimized should be placed with positive, friendly students. Some children may require coaching in pairs before they are ready to join larger groups of children. Children with friendship difficulties will need more teacher supervision and coaching than more socially competent children. For each of the activities listed below it will be important for the teacher to circulate and reinforce the targeted friendship skills.

Games and Activities for Co-operative Learning

Blindfolded Maze Drawing: Students work in pairs and are given a maze to complete. One child is blindfolded and the other child is asked to give directions that help the blindfolded child move his pencil through the maze. For 3–5-year-old children, the teacher can make the maze on the floor with masking tape and have the friend physically lead the blindfolded child through the maze. Each child takes turn being blindfolded. This activity is designed to help children experience being helped by someone and to understand that one of the things involved in friendship is trust. A variation of this game can be to build an obstacle course of chairs, bags, tables and to guide the blindfolded person around the obstacles.

Paper Chain: Students are given strips of paper and tape. They colour their own link (or may be asked to put a secret message on the link) and then the group links the chain together. This activity is designed to teach the concepts of sharing, co-operation and teamwork.

Co-operative Art Poster: Students are divided into groups of four to six per table. The teacher instructs them to make a poster together and encourages them to share and decide together how they want their poster to look. They are given art materials (e.g. large poster board, glue, glitter, paint, scissors, stickers, magazine pictures) but each table's supplies are limited so that children are forced to negotiate. During this activity the teacher praises children for appropriate asking, sharing, discussing ideas, helping each other and waiting their turn. This activity helps children practise all the skills of co-operation.

Co-operative 'Favourite Things' Poster: Students are divided into groups of four to six per table. On each table is a variety of magazines and pictures and one poster board. Each table of students is asked to make a poster that shows their group's favourite animals and foods. In order to accomplish this task they need to ask each other questions and share their own likes and interests. This activity promotes co-operative skills, encourages self-expression and builds friendships by helping children get to know each other better.

Co-operative Tinker Toys/Lego/Clay Modelling: Students are divided into pairs for this activity and asked to plan and make something together with Tinker Toys, Bristle Blocks, Lego or clay. They are encouraged to be friendly by taking turns, complimenting each other, sharing, asking for pieces, making friendly suggestions, problem-solving and so forth. As children become more skilled, teams of three or four children will require more negotiation and sharing.

Wally's Tower: Pair the children up, give them paper, scissors, tape and a variety of old cereal boxes, toilet paper rolls and egg cartons. Ask each pair to make the tallest, strongest and most beautiful tower they can together.

Design a T-shirt with a Theme: Children discuss the theme for the T-shirt and then execute the design together.

Share a Chair: In pairs, have children devise as many ways possible to both occupy one chair with their feet off the floor.

Friendship Mobiles: Each child makes their own mobile which is hung in the classroom. This mobile is made out of long strips of a paper (4 ins by 6 ins) with holes punched in the ends and hung with yarn. On each of these mobiles is the student's name, favourite colour, favourite thing to do, a positive characteristic about the child from the teacher and two positive things other children have said about that student.

Draw a Group Body: Another co-operative activity is to have the class or small groups of children draw a group body. One child makes the hands, another the shoulders, another the ears and so on. A variation on this theme is to pair up children and have them trace each other's bodies on large drawing paper. Along side each person's body drawing the teacher writes positive comments that the children say about that person.

Use Role-Plays to Handle Typical Relationship Problems

In addition to Circle Time discussions and co-operative practice activities with students, teachers can help their students learn how to respond to typical friendship problems through guided role-plays. Again the use of puppets can make this an engaging learning process for students. The following are some examples of scenarios you might enact with your students.

Sample Script for Puppets – 'He's Teasing Me'

Teacher: Wally was teased on the playground and he wants to talk to us about how he handled it. So, I want a student to come up and tease Wally so he can show us what he did.

First Student:	Wally, you are a dummy, you look like a monkey, you can't kick the ball!
Wally:	That's so old it's got mould on it.
	or
	I fell off my dinosaur when I first heard that.
Teacher:	Wow! You just stayed so calm! You didn't let it bother you. In fact, you told a joke! Does someone else in the class want to try showing us another way for how to handle being teased. This time Wally you can be the teaser.
Second Student:	*(volunteers and comes forward)*
Wally:	Neaner, neaner, you are a dummy!
Second Student:	*(turns away and ignores and takes some deep breaths)*
Wally:	You are a dummy and your mother's a dummy too! I wonder why I can't get a response from him? I usually do. Why is he ignoring me? I can't get a response from him. He's pretty powerful. What is this breathing stuff? Well this is no fun – I guess I'll give up.
Teacher:	Wow – ignoring a teaser is a fantastic idea. How did you keep up that ignoring?
Second Student:	I just told myself I could do it!
Teacher:	Terrific, now we have two solutions to being teased. Does anyone have a different idea?
	or
	How does it feel to be called an unpleasant name? What can be done to stop the name calling?

In the above sample script, the emphasis is on staying calm, using humor to disarm the teaser and ignoring. Students may come up with other funny responses to take the fun out of teasing. Of course, it is also important to emphasize the importance of not teasing back.

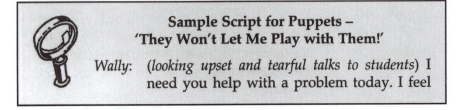

**Sample Script for Puppets –
'They Won't Let Me Play with Them!'**

Wally: *(looking upset and tearful talks to students)* I need you help with a problem today. I feel terrible. I wanted to play with some other kids on the playground and they wouldn't let me. They said I was too clumsy to play soccer. I don't know what to do. Do you have any ideas?

Teacher: Wally, that must feel terrible.

Wally: Yeah, it's rotten, I feel like no one likes me.

Teacher: (*asks students*) What should Wally do now?

Students: (brainstorm possible solutions)
- think a happy thought
- take deep breaths to calm down
- find another friend to play with
- accept their decision and remember all kids get left out sometimes
- tell them how you feel
- wait and ask them again later

Teacher: Okay let's practise some of those ideas. Who wants to try first?

The students would then go on to role-play and demonstrate how they would respond when told by other children they would not play with them.

Sample Script for Puppets – 'Handling a Put Down!'

Wally: (*looking upset and tearful talks to students*) You know sometimes I find my school work really difficult and I know it's not as neat as some people's. But today Katie came up and she said, 'You know Wally, your writing looks just like squashed flies. It's rubbish! Just look at mine. I've finished already and the teacher has given me a star.'

Teacher: Oh, how did that make you feel Wally?

Wally: It made me feel as if I wanted to give up trying and run home to my mum.

Teacher: (*asks students*) What should Wally do now?

Students: (brainstorm possible solutions or with older students you can ask them to write their ideas on cards and then randomly pick some cards and ask the student who wrote it to come up and discuss their solution)

- say to yourself, 'If I keep trying I know that my writing will get better'
- think about what you are good at – 'I'm not good at writing but I am good at painting'
- tell Katie how you feel
- recognize the put down and tell yourself that children who give put-downs aren't very happy inside
- remember some children think that being a put downer will make them popular, but it doesn't
- think about something else

Teacher: Okay let's practise some of those ideas. Who wants to try first?

Other Ideas for Scripts for Puppets Regarding Relationship Problems

- Wally knows that someone is saying mean things and lies about him behind his back.
- Molly's friend tells someone else something that Molly told her was private and not to be shared.
- Molly's friend breaks a promise.
- There is someone in your class that always wants to be first.
- There is a student in the class who is shy, has no friends and feels really lonely. Ask students to discuss ways to make new friends and to help someone who may be lonely.

Another Circle Time Activity

Have cards with compliments and put downs on them. Ask children in Circle Time to read a card out and put it in the appropriate pile (compliment or put-down pile). Ask them to explain why they think it is a compliment or put down. ('Your work is rubbish' versus 'Thank you for helping me to find my coat')

Pass the detective hat for practising how to be friendly

The Detective Hat game is again an easy way to initiate role play and practice of friendship skills. Here are some examples of questions you might put in the hat. They are designed to practise the following skills: sharing feelings; saying something friendly; helping someone else; and telling teacher.

The 'Detective Hat Game' for Practising Friendly Social Skills

- How could you help a child who won't share?
- You see your friend being left out of a game and even bullied and pushed away by some children on the playground. What should you do?
- Your friend just lost his new shoes. What can you say?
- Your dad seems angry and says he's having a bad day. What can you say?
- One of your friends is being left out by the other kids. What can you say or do?
- You notice someone crying on the playground. What can you say or do?
- Share a time you helped someone.
- One of your friends is kind of a poor loser. Whenever his team loses he throws a fit and sometimes he cries. He seems to want to win at all costs. He cheats and breaks the rules and one time he even said the other team got a foul when they didn't and then argued with the coach. He hogs the ball all the time. How can he be a good sport?
- One of your classmates never wants to try anything the other children are doing. She goes off by herself all the time and stays alone. What can you do to help?
- Your best friend wants to play with someone else. What can you say?
- You want to apologize to a friend for something you have said. What can you say?

Empathy Training

A key aspect to a child's social success is his or her ability to begin to consider the concerns, goals and feelings of others. If a child cannot take the point of view of another person, then s/he may misperceive social cues and not know how to respond. While the development of empathy takes years, and all children are self-centred and 'ego-centric' at this age, it is still possible for teachers to promote children's awareness of others' feelings and perspectives. The following game can be played to help foster empathy skills.

Apologizing

Pass the Detective Hat for Practising Thinking of Others' Feelings

This time the detective hat game is directed at helping children understand the importance of apologizing, explaining, complimenting, being friendly, being honest, having good sportsmanship, offering to help fix the situation, and resisting peer pressure and temptation. Here are the questions:

The 'Detective Hat Game' for Practising Thinking of Others' Feelings

- You've been playing chess with a friend, and after a battle lost the game. What would you do?
- You yelled at a friend when he broke your model. What should you do?
- You lost your new jacket and it is the second time you have lost it. What should you do?
- You forgot to do the chores your mum asked you to do. What should you do?
- Your friend wants you to cycle down to the shop to get some sweets, and your mother has said you are not to go beyond the front garden. What should you do?
- Your brother keeps some chocolate in his desk and you want a piece. What should you do?
- You are only allowed to watch 1 hour of TV per day. Your favourite show comes on, but you've already watched an hour of TV. Your mum asks you how much TV you've watched.
- You broke a family rule by eating an ice-cream in the living room and some of it stained the couch. Your mum seems angry and asks you if you ate an ice-cream in the living room. What should you do?
- One of your classmates is having trouble learning to read. What could you say or do?

Teaching your Students Problem-Solving/Conflict Resolution

Starting a friendship is one thing; keeping a friend is another. The key skill a child needs to keep a friend is knowing how to resolve conflict. In the absence of this skill, the most aggressive child usually gets his or her way. When this happens, everyone loses – the aggressive child may learn to abuse friendships and will experience rejection by peers for the aggression, while the passive child learns to be a victim. See Chapter 9 for a discussion of the ways teachers can help their students learn how to settle disagreements – an important aspect of keeping friends.

Teaching your Students to Use Positive Self-Talk

When children experience a peer's rejection or a disappointment, often they have underlying negative thoughts which reinforce and intensify the emotion. These thoughts are sometimes referred to as 'self-talk', although children will often express them aloud. For example, a child who tells you, 'I am the worst kid, no one likes me, I can't do anything right' is engaging in negative self-talk which s/he is sharing with you. Teachers can teach children to identify negative self-talk and to substitute positive self-talk in order to help cope with their frustrations and to control angry outbursts. For example, when a child's request to play with a friend is refused by another child, s/he can say to herself or himself, 'I can handle this. I will find another child to play with' or 'I can stay calm and try again' or 'Count to ten. Talk don't hit' or 'Stop and think first'. In this way children learn to regulate their cognitive responses, which in turn will affect their behavioral responses. Positive self-talk provides children with a means of emotional regulation with their peers.

Again using a puppet such as Wally can help to verbalize self-talk and teach students how to turn negative self-talk into more positive coping self-statements. Here is a sample scenario you might try:

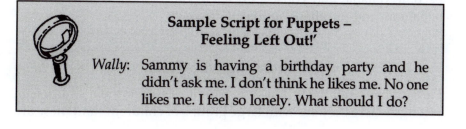

**Sample Script for Puppets –
Feeling Left Out!'**

Wally: Sammy is having a birthday party and he didn't ask me. I don't think he likes me. No one likes me. I feel so lonely. What should I do?

Students: *(generate self-talk that is more postiive)* He can only ask a few friends, it doesn't mean he doesn't like me. I'm a good friend and I can ask someone to play with me as well.

Praise and Establish Reward Programmes for Children with Social Difficulties

For students who have particular social difficulties such as shyness, anxiety or, conversely, aggression and inattention, set up an incentive programme to help strengthen particular friendship skills. Start by choosing one or two social behaviors you would like to increase such as joining in play for the shy child, or waiting and taking turns for the aggressive child. Then, practise the specific behaviors with the student so you are sure s/he understands them and list them on a chart. This chart may be placed on the child's desk or kept nearby so that it is readily accessible to the teacher. Then whenever you see the student do one of these behaviors, quietly praise him or her for remembering the behavior, and give him or her a sticker or stamp for the positive behavior. Children aged 7 and older will be less embarrassed if you call them away from the play group to praise and reward them out of earshot of others.

When praising, be sure to wait for a natural break in the interaction so that you do not disrupt the conversation and play activity. Don't just praise the identified problem child for the target behaviors; praise both children for their co-operative behavior and talk about how they are becoming good friends. For example, you might say when they are building a tower together, 'You two are co-operating and working very well together! You are being very friendly with each other and helping each other make this a cool structure.' Each day review the student's chart and the social skills you are working on. Once these first one or two social skills have become reliable and consistent, move on to some different social behaviors and put these on the chart.

Collaborating with Parents

Parents have relatively few opportunities to see their children in settings where they are with large groups of children – and these are the very settings where children need to practise these skills! Behavior in the classroom may be very different from behavior at home. While the child might be doing well when a single friend comes to visit at home, s/he may still have substantial peer problems in larger group settings. It is important for teachers to discuss with parents their children's social needs. For the child with some social difficulties, it is important to collaborate with parents to identify a few positive social skills you both want to start working on with the child. For example, a teacher may have set up a classroom chart to encourage a child for putting up a quiet hand and co-operating with peers. At the end of the day this 'friendly report card' can be sent home with the child, and the parents can add ticks earned at school to their home reward chart. For example, earning five ticks at school might equal an extra story time or a special activity at home. It also is ideal if the teacher can have an incentive programme at school. For example, each day the child earns an agreed number of ticks s/he gets to choose a special activity such as extra computer time or leading the lunch line or leading a class discussion. It is helpful if you can assign the student some special responsibilities so other classmates can see him or her in a positive light.

We have also found that for highly distractible children, it is helpful to assign a school counsellor, aide or teacher as a 'coach'. This coach would meet with the child three times a day for a brief 5-minute check-in. During this check-in the coach would review the child's behavior chart and praise any successes in interactions with peers. S/he would also review to make sure the child has his or her books ready and his or her assignments written out in his or her notebook for the rest of the morning. At lunch s/he would review expectations for lunch period or break and again, before going home, s/he would review the day's behavior as well as see that the child had his or her behavior chart, books and homework ready to take home.

Encouraging Parents to Invite Classmates Home

Parents often don't know who their children's friends are at school and which classmates play particularly well with their child. Teachers are in the best position to help parents know which classmates are positive role models and have interests and a temperament which complements their child's temperament. Encourage parents and children to invite classmates over after school or at weekends. However, in some instances (especially with hyperactive or withdrawn children) you will need to help parents understand that when friends are invited over, this play time should not be unstructured or unmonitored. Rather, help parents understand the importance of planning the visit with their child and doing some co-operative activities such as building a model with Lego, working on a craft, baking biscuits, playing football, and so forth. These activities will help children learn appropriate social skills and develop closer friendships. Parents should be cautioned to avoid letting the children spend their time watching TV as there will be very little social interaction and less chance to get to know each other. For shy or hyperactive children teachers may want to recommend to parents that their children's first play visits be relatively short and pleasant with close parental monitoring so that interactions don't get out of control and the children part having had a good time.

Encouraging Parents to Play with their Children at Home

It is helpful when teachers send home information to parents explaining the importance of parents' play with their children. Teachers can emphasize the value of parent–child play which is 'child-directed' – that is, when the parent does not give commands, intrude on the child's play, take over or criticize, but rather follows their child's lead by listening, commenting descriptively about what they doing, waiting for them to take a turn, accepting their ideas, complying with their rules and praising their play skills. Help parents understand that when they have regular play periods with their children using these child-directed play skills, they are teaching their children the friendly skills. For example, when parents model acceptance of their children's ideas and suggestions, their children learn to be more co-operative with others' ideas. Thus regular parent play with children can be very beneficial for helping children learn appropriate play skills and social skills with their peers.

How Can a Teacher Help Change a Child's Negative Reputation in the Classroom, School and Community?

As you know, children even as young as age 5 may have developed a negative self-image and may have established a reputation in the school (and perhaps the community) as the 'bully' or 'problem child'. In some instances, even before children have started school, teachers have been warned of particular students they will have who have been labelled as 'difficult'. Once school starts such reputations are often reinforced by the reactions of other students, 'You're always in trouble' or 'You're bad, the teacher doesn't like you' or 'You can't come to my birthday party because my parents say you are a troublemaker'. If a teacher doesn't control this type of comment, this child's negative reputation may expand beyond the classroom to the school and to the community of parents. It can snowball, beginning with a child's complaint to his parent that he was hit again by Robby on the playground, compounded by parental anger towards Robby and even towards his family if the parent blames them for Robby's aggression. Sometimes it even leads to parents' blaming the teacher for allowing hitting to occur at school. When parents hear that their child and other children have been bullied or hit by a particular child, they may rally other parents to complain to the principal, asserting that the child doesn't belong in that classroom. This kind of 'lynch mob' mentality is detrimental not only for Robby's future growth but for all the students' relationships in the classroom as well as for the school community. It is, in essence, a form of adult bullying of an already troubled child. If successful, it sends the message that the school community has no broad-based responsibility where everyone helps each other. It will result in a declining sense of community, fewer supports for teachers, an increasing alienation of families and children with particular difficulties and an erosion of positive relationships between the teacher and students.

What Can Schools and Teachers Do to Prevent this Ripple Effect?

Establish school policy and philosophy
Clear school policy has a vital role in preventing bullying and helping children who become involved in bullying incidents. School policies should communicate a clear message to students, parents and teachers that bullying will not be tolerated and will be handled firmly. Policies should clearly set forth the rules and specify what will happen if the rules are broken. Since victims may be afraid to bring up their experiences with bullying for fear of retaliation from the bully, the school should set up a procedure enabling students to call the school counsellor anonymously. The counsellor can encourage the child who is victimized to also talk with his or her teacher

and parents, and can involve relevant persons in providing help for the victim. If school policies have not been set up the teacher can advocate for their implementation and if they are in place teachers can help explain them to families.

Educate families so they can talk to their children about bullying
The school has an important role in educating families about the meaning of bullying – both for the bully and the victim. This educational effort can take place through the use of special workshops and through regular parent meetings. Bullying is a multifaceted problem rooted in a variety of interrelated factors such as the child's temperament, social behavior, communication skills, level of self-esteem and self-confidence, in addition to family, school and societal influences. Rather than blaming some single source such as society, the family or the child, schools can be proactive, focusing on preventing bullying regardless of the factors which may have contributed to the problem in the first place.

The school should provide comprehensive training to help prevent as well as treat the socialization difficulties that lead to bullying. This training needs to go beyond individual teachers' efforts with individual students; it should be part of an effort involving the entire school. Supportive education and training in social skills, problem solving, empathy training and esteem-building address the root causes of bullying and have long-term payoffs for the school.

It is important for schools and teachers to elicit parent support in making it clear to their children that bullying is unacceptable. Parents can be encouraged by teachers to introduce the issue with their children by talking about the problem and asking them if anyone in their class is often 'picked on' or left out. Parents can increase their children's understanding of the problem by explaining the concepts of passive participation in bullying and of 'covert' bullying (excluding the child). Parents might attempt to determine whether their child has sympathy for the victim and whether s/he would be willing to do anything to help the student. Parents should encourage their children to report bullying to teachers, explaining why 'telling' actually is not wrong but actually helps the bully (and potential victims) in the long run. Parents can strive to develop their child's empathy for the victim and involve their child in ending the victimization by inviting a 'victim' to a picnic or after school play time.

Changing the child's reputation in the classroom – promoting a sense of classroom as family

For the child who has already established a negative reputation in the classroom as a bully or troublemaker, the teacher will need to define strategies and formulate a plan for how to change this child's reputation. For example, the teacher can do this by working especially hard to develop a positive relationship with this child. The teacher may begin noticing or commenting on particular strengths this child has that refute his aggressive image, 'Robby, you are good friend – you are sharing nicely and being very gentle with that toy. Josh seems to be enjoying playing with you.' The teacher may set up formal compliment Circle Times each day where students give compliments to each other on a regular basis. The teacher may ask the other students to notice the particular times when Robby is helping and co-operating. In other words, the teacher is helping the other children know that Robby is working hard on learning a particular behavior (e.g. to ask and not grab or hit) and trains them to notice it when Robby is helpful and uses his words well – a major step in changing their perceptions of him. The teacher can then praise the children for noticing Robby's successes, so that the children become engaged and excited for Robby's successes as he learns to manage his anger more appropriately. This same strategy can also be used by the teacher for other children who are having particular difficulties such as learning to read, or to do maths or spelling. In other words, the teacher is creating a classroom environment where children learn there are individual differences in each others' cognitive, behavioral and social abilities and where they are invested in helping their friends achieve their own 'personal goals'. A sense of community is created in the classroom when children are learning to appreciate and applaud each other's accomplishments. Thus they are developing meaningful relationships with each other.

Promote friendships

The teacher can help parents know about particular friends who work well with Robby. These friends might be encouraged to invite Robby over to their houses or vice versa. It is important that students with negative reputations develop one or two good friends in the classroom, friends who are popular and socially appropriate, not friends who have similar difficulties with aggression. Teachers can help mastermind these relationships by making strategic assignments of groups for group cooperative projects or field trips and by noticing when children are being good friends with each other. For example, 'You two are working well together, Jimmy is a good friend'.

Open communication with parents

If there is a child in the classroom known to all the parents as aggressive, the teacher needs to be sure that s/he calls the parents whenever there is an incident involving their child and the aggressive child. The teacher can explain the situation to the parents before it escalates (or they hear about it from someone else) and let the parents know that s/he is carefully monitoring the child with aggressive tendencies. Teachers will need to reassure parents that their child will be safe. The teacher might also elicit the parents' support in this endeavour by telling them how they are handling the problem in the classroom through collaboration with the parents, social skills and problem-solving training and assertiveness training for all the children. The teacher's optimism and confidence in how she explains her interventions in the classroom and her belief that she will be successful are key ingredients in engendering parental support and patience. The teacher might also point out the dangers of such a child feeling ostracized by his peer group and talk about the child's unique strengths and contributions to the class. Finally, it can also be very helpful for parents of other children in the classroom to realize that in addressing the 'problem child's' behavior through strategies such as class meetings, special training, compliment circles and peer reinforcement, not only is that child being helped, but all the children are learning how to handle conflict in relationships in appropriate ways. Excluding or kicking a child out of class – and disposing of the problem – teaches children nothing about problem-solving, managing conflicts and developing relationships.

Mutual responsbility between home and school

As noted above, schools have an important responsibility for informing families about the extent and causes of the problem. The message to families can be that because of the potential seriousness of bullying, the school is going to focus on even minor cases of bullying and social isolation; moreover, the school should advise parents that this monitoring may initially result in increased contact from administrators or teachers until the problem has been resolved. Conversely, schools need to ask parents to communicate openly with them, to stay involved and to contact teachers if they suspect their own or another child of bullying.

The school should let parents know that if it is discovered that students are bullying others or being bullied, the school will contact the parents concerned and ask for their co-operation in bringing about change. They should meet together to discuss the situation with them and collaboratively arrive at a plan for solving the problem. Parents who suspect their children are bullying can help by praising their children for cooperative behavior, setting up reward systems for good behavior, applying non-violent or punitive consequences for misbehavior (e.g. loss of privileges, Time Out, work chores) and setting up rules that make it clear that they take the bullying seriously and will not tolerate the behavior. If both the school and parents are applying negative consequences, then it is less likely to reoccur. For the family who is chaotic and disorganized, teachers can help parents define a few family rules which are written down and displayed and plan a set of consequences for violations of those rules. They can encourage parents to praise their child when he or she follows the rules. Parents should be urged to spend time with their child and get to know their child's friends.

Parents who suspect that their child is being bullied should let their child's teacher know as soon as possible. They can also try to increase the self-confidence of the victimized child by helping him or her establish friendships and stand up for himself or herself assertively. Although it is understandable to want to protect a child who has been bullied, parents should avoid being overprotective, as this attitude on the part of parents can increase a child's sense of isolation from peers and thus exacerbate the problem. When parents and teachers collaborate regarding solutions without blaming each other, they can bring about significant reductions in bullying.

Normalize a child's behaviour
Another way to refute negative labels for your students is to normalize their behaviour. Remind yourself that all students throw tantrums, disobey, forget to put away their books and behave aggressively from time to time. Still another way to refute such negative labelling is to remind yourself of positive things your student has done. Think about the times he surprised you by bringing you a special drawing or cleaning up his desk. Allow yourself to recall these special positive moments, especially when you feel yourself catastrophizing.

To Sum Up
- Teach students how to enter groups, how to play, and how to talk with friends through discussions and role-plays.

- Set up co-operative learning activities to help students practise friendship skills.
- Praise and establish reward programmes for students with social difficulties.
- Collaborate with parents to promote children's social skills at home.

References

Asher, S. R. and Williams, G. A. (1987) Helping children without friends in home and school, *Children's Social Development: Information for Teachers and Parents*, Urbana, IL: ERIC, Clearing House on Elementary and Early Childhood Education.

Bierman, K. L., Miller, C. M. and Stabb, S. (1987). Improving the social behavior and peer acceptance of rejected boys: effects of social skill training with instructions and prohibitions, *Journal of Consulting and Clinical Psychology*, 55, 194–200.

Campbell, S. B. (1990) *Behaviour problems in preschool children: Clinical and developmental issues*, New York: Guilford Press.

Campbell, S. B. and Ewing, L. J. (1990). Follow-up of hard-to-manage pre-schoolers: adjustment at age 9 and predictors of continuing symptoms, *Journal of Child Psychology and Psychiatry*, 31(6), 871–89.

Crick, N. R. and Dodge, K. A. (1994) A review and reformulation of social information processing mechanisms in children's social adjustment, *Psychological Bulletin*, 115, 74–101.

Elias, M. J. and Tobias, S. E. (1996) *Social Problem Solving: Interventions in Schools*, New York: Guilford.

Greenberg, M. T., Kusche, C. A., Cook, E. T. and Quamma, J. P. (1995) Promoting emotional competence in school-aged children: The effects of the PATHS curriculum. Special issue: Emotions in developmental psychopathology, *Development and Psychopathology*, 7, 117–36.

Gresham, F. M. (1995) Social skills training. In A. Thomas and J. Grimes (eds.) *Best practices in School Psychology – III* (pp. 39–50), Bethesda, MD: National Association of School Psychologists.

Gresham, F. M. (1997) Social skills. In G. G. Bear, K. M. Minke and A. Thomas (eds.) *Children's Needs II: Development, Problems and Alternatives* (pp. 39–50), Bethesda, MD: National Association of School Psychologists.

Grossman, D. C., Neckerman, H. J., Koepsell, T. D., Liu, P., Asher, K. N., Beland, K., Frey, K. and Rivara, F. P. (1997) Effectiveness of a violence prevention curriculum among children in elementary school, *Journal of American Medical Association*, 277, 1605–11.

Knoff, H. M. and Batsche, G. M. (1995) Project ACHIEVE: Analyzing a school reform process for at-risk and underachieving students, *School Psychology Review*, 24, 579–603.

Ladd, G. W. (1981) Effectiveness of a social learning method of enhancing children's social interaction and peer acceptance, *Child Development*, 52(1), 171–8.

Ladd, G. W. (1983) Social networks of popular, average, and rejected children in school settings, *Merrill-Palmer Quarterly*, 29, 283–307.

Ladd, G. W. and Price, J. P. (1987) Predicting children's social and school adjustment following the transition from preschool to kindergarten, *Child Development*, 58, 16–25.

Putallaz, M. and Gottman, J. M. (1981) An interactional model of children's entry into peer groups, *Child Development*, 52, 986–94.

Webster-Stratton, C. and Hammond, M. (1997) Treating children with early-onset conduct problems: a comparison of child and parent training interventions, *Journal of Consulting and Clinical Psychology*, 65(1), 93–109.

Webster-Stratton, C. and Lindsay, D. W. (1999) Social competence and early-onset conduct problems: Issues in assessment, *Journal of Child Clinical Psychology*, 28, 25–93.

Chapter Eleven

Helping Students Learn to Handle their Emotions

Aggression and inadequate impulse control are perhaps the most potent obstacles to effective problem-solving and forming successful friendships in childhood. Without help, young children who are angry and aggressive are more likely to experience peer rejection (Coie, 1990) and continued social problems for years afterwards (Campbell, 1995; Pope, Bierman and Mumma, 1989). As we noted in the prior two chapters, research has found that such children have deficits in social problem-solving or conflict management skills (Asarnow and Callan, 1985; Mize and Cox, 1990). They react to interpersonal conflict situations in hostile ways without considering non-aggressive or prosocial solutions, and they anticipate fewer consequences for their aggressive solutions (Dodge *et al.*, 1986; Quiggle *et al.*, 1992; Rubin and Krasnor, 1986). In short, they have difficulty being able to regulate their negative affect in response to conflict situations.

Such children also have difficulty knowing how to 'read' social situations because they distort and/or underutilize social cues (Gouze, 1987). Furthermore, there is evidence that aggressive children are more likely to misinterpret ambiguous situations as hostile or threatening (Dodge *et al.*, 1986). This tendency to perceive hostile intent in others has been seen as one source of their aggressive behavior. Negative social experiences with parents, teachers and peers, in part the result of their lack of social competence, further exacerbate their adjustment difficulties, perpetuate their aggressive behavior problems and self-regulation difficulties (e.g. Patterson, Reid and Dishion, 1992), and reinforce their distorted perceptions and social cognitions.

As we have seen in Chapters 9 and 10, teachers can help children learn to cope more effectively with conflict situations that provoke anger (e.g. teasing, hitting, disappointment) by teaching them problem-solving strategies and communication skills, by helping them read social situations more accurately and by showing them how to use positive self-statements and other cognitive mediation stratagems. However, before students can effectively problem-solve, they need to be able to recognize and regulate their own emotional responses. Teachers can play a critical role in helping children learn to manage their anger. They do this by helping students to think differently about why an event occurred, preparing them to respond appropriately to situations that typically provoke anger and encouraging them to employ self-talk and relaxation strategies to keep themselves calm. Teachers also act as powerful models for students whenever they can remain calm and non-aggressive in response to the negative affect and aggression displayed by some students in the classroom.

What Is Emotional Regulation?

Emotions are responses to stimuli or situations that affect a person strongly. Emotional responses occur on three levels. The first – and most basic – level involves *neurophysiological and biochemical* reactions to stimuli, including all the bodily processes regulated by the autonomic nervous system: heart rate, blood flow, respiration, hormonal secretions (epinephrine, cortisol) and neural responses (EEG). For example, a person who is angry feels her heart race and her face redden. The second level of emotional response is *behavioral*, where emotions are expressed in a person's actions. This level includes facial expressions and such behaviors such as crying, sullen gazes, withdrawal from interactions with others, defiant actions and delayed responses. The third level is *cognitive* and involves language (whether spoken, written, or thought) by which a person labels her feelings as in, 'I feel angry'.

Children may differ strikingly in their emotional responses – in the frequency and range of their emotions as well as the ways they express emotion. For example, 7-year-old Billy was sobbing with tears because his football team lost their final game, while his team-mate, Dan, responded by angrily kicking the fence and hurling a football at the opposing team members. Still another team-mate, Eric, walked off the field and withdrew into himself sullenly refusing to say anything, while yet another boy yelled profanities at the coach because he thought there was a foul which invalidated the winning goal. Here we have four different emotional responses expressed by a group of similar aged boys to exactly the same situation. Children also vary widely in the subtlety of their understanding of emotions (both their own and others), in the degree of pleasure they show when they share positive emotions, and in their ability to regulate or control their negative responses to frustrating situations.

Emotional regulation refers to a person's ability to adequately control his or her emotional responses (neurophysiological and biochemical, behavioral and cognitive) to arousing situations. The term *emotional dysregulation* refers to a person whose emotional responses are chronically out of control, like the child with behavior problems whose impulsive anger and aggression are so excessive that he cannot make and maintain friendships, or the child whose withdrawal from emotionally challenging situations becomes so habitual that she cannot enter into any new activities.

How Do Children Learn Emotional Regulation?

Just like walking, talking and toilet training, the regulation of emotional responses is a developmental achievement which is not present at birth – i.e. it must be learned. The initial regulation must be provided by the environment. Picture the young infant who has a wet nappy or is hungry or is bored. She expresses her distress in the only way she can – through crying. The infant requires help from the environment to modulate her physiological state and to reduce her internal tension. The parent plays an integral role in helping the infant regulate her emotional arousal: that is, the parent tries to understand the meaning of the baby's cries and then takes the necessary action to calm her. As we all know, some babies are more easily calmed and others are more difficult. This fact suggests that there are individual differences in infants' ability to acquire self-regulation.

The transition period from infancy to toddlerhood is accompanied by maturation in the child's emotional regulatory system. During this developmental period, the burden of emotional regulation begins to shift a little from parent to child. One of the most important developmental achievements associated with the emergence of emotional regulation is the child's acquisition of language and communication skills. As children develop language skills they become increasingly able to label their emotions, their thoughts and their intentions. And as children become more able to communicate their complex needs and feelings, they can more effectively regulate their emotional responses. In part, this means letting their parents and teachers know what they need in order to be able to calm themselves.

In the transition from the preschool to the school-age years, children begin to assume greater responsibility for their own emotional functioning, so that somewhat less adult regulation is required. Nevertheless, parents and teachers do continue to have a major role in supporting children's emotional regulation. During the school age years, emotional regulation changes to a more complex and abstract process; whereas in infancy it was primarily *reflexive*, guided by physiological discomfort, now it becomes more *reflective*, guided by the child's sense of self and the environment. Instead of the angry or frustrated child hitting someone or exploding in a tantrum, now she will argue with her friend or teacher. Instead of expressing impatience by wailing, a child will be able to wait. Instead of expressing excitement by running around in circles, she will be able to talk about how excited she is. The extreme emotional responses of anger, distress, and excitement have been dampened to some extent by this age. Moreover, as children develop their own capacity for emotional regulation, the internal or subjective aspects of emotion become separate from the external expression of emotion (or affect). Thus we see the school-aged child who can be internally distressed by an event but outwardly expresses no sign of emotion. During adolescence, there is an upheaval of the child's emotional systems as hormones enter into the picture, challenging the emotional regulation which the adolescent has learned over the years. To the parents and teachers of adolescents, it may seem at times as if the teenager has regressed to the emotional regulatory stage of a 3–5-year-old!

What Determines How Quickly Children Learn Emotional Regulation?

Just as there is a wide variation in the point at which children start to walk, or talk, or learn to use the toilet, some children's neuroregulatory or self-regulatory systems develop at a slower rate than others. We know little as yet about the factors that contribute to these differences in timing. However, research does suggest that there are at least four processes underlying children's growing ability to regulate their emotions:

1. Maturation of the child's neurological inhibitory system. The growth and development of the child's nervous system provides

the necessary neurological 'hardware' required for the eventual control of emotions.

2. The child's temperament and developmental status. Some children are more vulnerable to emotional dysregulation due to learning disabilities, language delays, attention deficits, hyperactivity or other developmental delays.

3. Parental socialization and environmental support. Differences in the ways that families talk about feelings (their own and others') are related to later differences in the ways children express their feelings and their growing ability or inability to regulate their emotions and to understand the feelings of others. Children who experience chronic stress in their environment, or whose daily lives lack predictability and stability, have more difficulties with emotional regulation.

4. School and teachers' emphasis on emotional education. Differences in the ways that teachers talk to students about feelings and respond to students' expression of negative emotion in response to conflict situations at school are related to children's ability to regulate emotions.

What Can Teachers Do?

While we cannot change the first two factors described above – a child's neurological system or temperament and developmental status – it is important for teachers to understand they *can* have a major impact on students' ability to regulate their emotions through the third factor, socialization and environmental support. The following chapter explains some ways in which teachers can help their students learn emotional regulation. These strategies are based on research regarding effective anger management programmes (Larson, 1994; Lochman and Dunn, 1993; Webster-Stratton and Hammond, 1997).

Provide as Much Stability and Consistency as Possible

Teachers can support the development of emotional regulation by providing environmental stability and consistency in the classroom as well as a supportive atmosphere. For example, consistent limit-setting, clear rules and predictable routines help children know what to expect. This in turn helps them feel calmer and more secure. When children perceive their classroom as a stable, secure place, and feel that teachers genuinely care about them as individuals, they begin to develop the emotional resources necessary to deal with the less predictable world outside.

Accept Students' Emotions and Emotional Responses

It is important to remember that when children respond with emotional outbursts, these behaviors are not intentional nor are they a deliberate attempt to make teaching difficult for you. Accept the fact that it is normal for all children at times to sulk, to respond to authority by yelling or slamming something down, or to want to withdraw and be left alone. Accept the fact that some children will dysregulate or fall apart emotionally more readily than others and that this is not necessarily a sign of a 'spoiled ' or a 'neglected' or 'abused' child. Rather, it may reflect a child whose temperament is more impulsive, a child with delayed language skills who cannot express his feelings appropriately, or a child who is so hyperactive and inattentive that he has missed important social cues leading him to misinterpret and react emotionally to a relatively neutral event. While these emotional responses can be draining and distressing for teachers, your patience and acceptance are crucial factors in helping your students learn to cope with their emotional responses. By 'tuning in' and being understanding of your students' emotional states you can help them tolerate increasing amounts of emotional tension.

Express your own Feelings

One way to help children learn to express feelings and to regulate their own emotional responses is for teachers themselves to use the language of feelings with their students. For example, in the soccer example we discussed earlier, the teacher might have said something like this to the boy: 'I felt really frustrated to see your team lose after doing so well throughout the whole game. I feel sad that you lost. But the important thing is you played a really good game. You guys were doing your best and you were good team members – you all really worked together. I was proud of you.' Teachers who frequently use the language of emotions to express their own emotional states and to interpret others' (non-verbal) emotional expressions – who talk about feelings so that children learn to identify emotions accurately and become accustomed to talking about feelings – are providing their students with a powerful mechanism for emotional regulation. Their students will be less likely to resort to behavioral outbursts of negative emotions. Research has suggested that children who learn to use emotional language have more control over their nonverbal emotional expressions, which in turn enhances the regulation of emotions themselves. By using the language of feelings, teachers not only transfer a useful coping skill to their students, but also show them how they cope with particular feelings. In contrast, teachers who use language to intellectualize their emotions or to 'talk themselves out of' a particular emotion will encourage the use of an overcontrolled coping style – students will learn to 'bottle up' their emotions rather than to regulate them.

Avoid Letting It All Hang Out

It used to be faddish when treating angry children to encourage them to scream and hit pillows or punch bags. The theory was that humans were like a closed up tea kettle and needed to release the bottled up anger from their system. However, there is absolutely no evidence that encouraging verbal and physical aggression in any way reduces problems with anger control. In fact, it seems to actually encourage its expression! Thus it is never a good idea to allow children to behave aggressively, not even to toys and other objects when they are angry. Instead, you can encourage appropriate verbal expression of anger and appropriate physical release of tension such as taking a run or brisk walk or cleaning up the toy area. This is far more likely to help a child cool off.

Encourage Students to Talk about Feelings – Avoid Directives about Feelings.

The fact that children do not talk much about their emotions may be due not just to inexperience but to having experienced their parents' or teachers' disapproval of the expression of emotion or of a certain kind of emotion. For example Billy, who cried when he lost the football game, might have been told not to cry but to get mad instead. When adults give directives about emotional expression, children may find it difficult to stay in touch with their true feelings and therefore have problems regulating their emotions. Avoid statements such as, 'Don't be sad', or 'You shouldn't be angry about that'. Instead, label the child's feelings accurately and encourage the child to talk about the emotion: 'I see you are sad about that: can you tell me what happened?' As the child tells you about her experience, listen carefully without judging or giving advice. Sometimes it can be helpful to share a past experience that matches the child's. For example, 'I remember a time when I dropped the ball and it caused us to lose the game. I felt terrible.'

It is important for children to understand that, just as one child likes broccoli and another doesn't, people can have quite different feelings about the same event. It is also important for them to understand that a person may even have more than one feeling at the same time. The crucial lesson to teach students is that there is nothing wrong with any feeling; all feelings are normal and natural. Some feelings are comfortable and nice inside while others hurt, but they are all real and important. As teachers we are trying to teach children to control their behavior, not their feelings. Teachers can help give their students the message that, while it is not always okay to act on our feelings, it is always okay to talk about them.

The ability to talk about emotions not only helps children regulate their negative emotions but also gives them far greater power to express affection and concern, to ask for and receive affection, and to achieve new intimacy in their relationships with their peer group as well as their teachers.

Use Games and Activities to Promote Use of Feeling Language

Circle Time is an ideal place for discussing feelings and playing feeling games. The following are some examples of games you might play with students to encourage the development of feeling language and to help them understand the facial and auditory clues which indicate particular feelings.

Circle Time Games and Activities for Promoting Feeling Language

Feeling Spinning Wheel Game: The children sit in a circle and take turns spinning the arrow and when it lands on a face they name the feeling and tell a time when they felt that way. If the arrow lands on the blank face they can do a charade or make a face and ask the other children to guess what they are feeling. This wheel may also be used by children to point to the feeling they have during times when they cannot put a name to the feeling.

Blind Man's Feeling Detective Game: In this game the children close their eyes while one child says something in a tone of voice that may sound happy, angry, sad or worried. The children are asked to identify the feeling from the child's voice and say why they think the person may be feeling that way. Here the children are looking for clues to feelings through the sounds of voices.

Deaf Man's Feeling Detective Game: In this game the children take turns making faces (without making sounds) and the

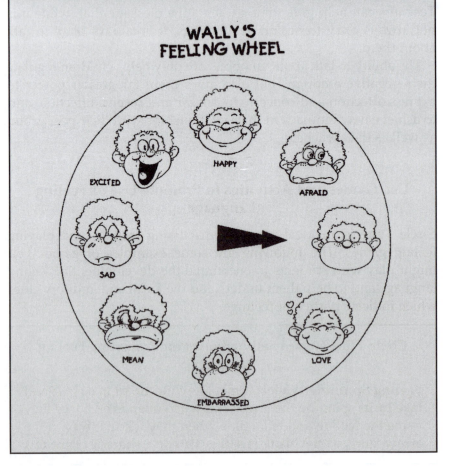

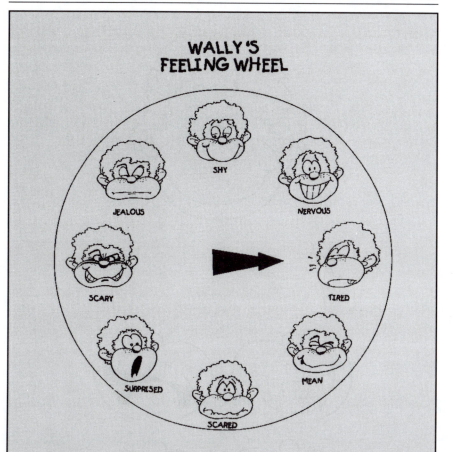

WALLY'S FEELING WHEEL

children try to guess the feeling. Another variation of this game is to show some of the feeling videotapes from the Understanding and Detecting Feelings in the Dinosaur Curriculum (Webster-Stratton, 1990) with the sound turned off and ask the children to name the feeling from the picture. Again children point out the visual clues which indicate the feeling to them.

Making Feeling Masks: In this art project and game we give the children paper plates and ask them to pick a feeling (without telling anyone) and then to draw and colour it. When their feeling masks are completed the children guess each others' feelings and tell a time when they felt that way.

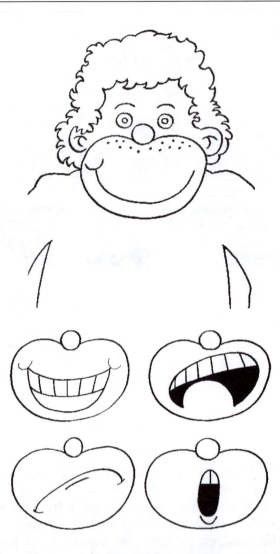

Wally's Feeling Faces Game

This game may be played individually or in pairs during Circle Time. We give each student or pair of students an enlargement of Wally's face with all the feeling face parts (eyebrows, ears, mouths, noses, etc.) We read the following story to the children and ask the children to follow the directions. You may add to this story using other parts of the face.

Wally was having a rough day

1. It all started when a boy in his class called him a monkey face. Look for the mouth that shows how Wally felt when he was called a monkey face.
2. At lunch nobody wanted him to sit at their table. Look for the mouth that shows how Wally felt to be left out.
3. When Wally finished his lunch, he walked by the table where the 12-year-olds sat and accidentally knocked over Mark's milk. The older boy said, 'Hey kid! Get over here! I want to talk to you!' Look for the mouth that shows how Wally felt when he saw the big angry boy.
4. Wally told himself to calm down. 'I need to take three deep breaths' he said. Look for the mouth that shows Wally taking a deep breath.
5. Wally told the boy that he didn't mean to spill his milk and said that he was sorry. Then he said that he'd help wipe it up. Mark thought that this was really friendly of Wally and asked Wally if he wanted to play shadow tag with him and his friends. Look for the mouth that shows how Wally felt to be included with the older children.

Another variation on this game is for the teacher to name the feeling and have the children put the appropriate expression on the face.

Use Games and Activities to Promote Understanding of the Feelings of Others

A key dimension to social success is the child's ability not only to communicate his own feelings but also to consider the concerns and feelings of others (Putallaz and Wasserman, 1990). If the child cannot take the perspective of another, s/he may also misperceive the social cues, mislabel feelings and not know how to respond appropriately. The teacher can use Circle Time to promote children's discussions of different feelings and perspectives in different situations. The games described below can be used during Circle Time to help children to think about different feelings and different reasons why people might have those feelings. These games will help children learn empathy skills.

Games and Activities for Promoting Understanding of Feelings of Others

Picture Feeling Detective: In this game you can cut out pictures of people and events from various newspapers and magazines (and laminate them). The children take turns picking a picture from the feeling bag and identifying the feeling. Ask the children questions such as:

- How do you think he or she is feeling? Is there another word for that feeling?
- What clues tell you that? (eyes, mouth, teeth, body, etc.)
- Why do you think he or she feels that way?
- What do you suppose happened to make him or her feel that way?
- What do you think will happen next? (predicting)

Wally's 'How Would You Feel If' Game: Wally asks the children to act out how they would feel in the situations listed below. Then depending on the children's level of development and ability to communicate feelings, this exercise can be taken further by asking, 'What do you think happens next?' Then ask, 'How might you feel then?' and 'How do you think the other person feels?' The ability to predict feelings and anticipate consequences is a difficult skill for young children especially if they do not yet have the words to describe feelings. If this is the case, the teacher should first focus on learning the words for communicating feelings and detecting clues to understanding the feelings of a person. The next phase will be to help the children anticipate why someone might have these feelings and what they will do next to cope with those feelings.

Wally asks how would you feel if?

- You fall off your bike and hit your head. (sad, hurt, pain)
- You don't get invited to a classmate's birthday party. (disappointment, sad)
- Your mum tells you you can have a friend overnight. (excitement)
- A student refuses to let you play on the team with the others. (anger)
- Your teacher says something nice to you. (happy)

- You lost your new football. (sad, worried)
- An adult yells at you. (fear, anxious)
- Your sister changes the channel when you have been watching a good programme. (anger)
- A student pushes you and tells you to take off. (sad, anger)
- You get to go to the seaside. (happy, excited or afraid)
- You accidentally step in dog poo. (disgusted)
- You don't know anyone in your new class. (afraid, shy)
- Your mother makes baked beans for dinner. (happy, disgusted)
- Your teacher puts your drawing on the board. (proud, embarrassed)
- You have been invited to a party. You love parties but you won't know anyone there. (excited, shy)
- Your parents are divorced. It is time to leave your dad's house. You have had a great time and wish you could stay longer. As you pack you think about your mum and brother at home and can't wait to see them. (sad and excited)

I Feel Worried When . . . : This game can be played when children are old enough to read and write and helps promote empathy and sensitivity to others. Each child is given a slip of paper with the sentence, 'I feel worried when . . .' to be completed. Then they put their anonymous response in a container placed in the centre of the circle. Then each student takes a turn drawing out a worry and trying to explain why it would be a worry. The teacher can help the children understand how people have worries about different things.

Games and Activities for Promoting Understanding of Changing Feelings

Changing Feelings: Another variation of the How You Would Feel If Game is to describe a situation and then ask the children to say, 'I used to feel _____ about (situation – see list below) and now I feel _____ about the situation.' The point of this game is to help children understand that feelings can change over time and are not permanent. It also helps students think of some of the feelings brought on by change.

- Going to school
- Eating baked beans
- Going to the doctor (dentist)
- A brother or sister
- Learning to read
- Helping with chores
- When I moved to a new city
- When my brother was born and got all the attention
- When my parents divorced
- When my aunt died
- Having a bad haircut
- Having to talk in front of class

Wally's Accident Detection Game: In this game the children practise thinking about the difference between an accident and things which are done on purpose. The teacher asks the children to discuss whether they think the following things might have been done as an accident or on purpose. Once the students have discussed the intention involved, the teacher can ask the students to practise or role play the accidental situations and help the students think about the feelings involved and how to offer an apology or repair the friendship. This game is very helpful for students who frequently have hostile attributions about anything that happens to them.

Wally's Accident Detection Game

- Not watching when you pick up your football boots, and picking up your friend's instead.
- Throwing a ball which hits another child in the chest.
- Pulling the cat's tail.
- Hiding your sister's sweets which she bought with her allowance.
- Hitting a friend because he hit you.
- Not looking when you reach to get the milk and spilling your brother's milk.
- Calling another child names.
- Sitting at your seat with your feet out and someone trips over them.
- Forgetting to wish your friend happy birthday.

Teaching Students Self-Calming and Relaxation Strategies

To control anger, children must not only learn to label their feelings but also to develop self-calming strategies. When they know they have ways to 'cool down' their anger, they gain a sense of self-control and can prevent the build up of anger that leads to tantrums and outbursts. The following relaxation and imagery exercise can be used by teachers to teach students some self-calm strategies.

Raggedy Wally and the Tin Man

We use this exercise to help children begin to recognize when they are relaxed and when they are tense. First children practise being the tin man by walking stiffly around the room, tensing up their arms and legs. Then they practise being 'raggedy Wally' by becoming limp and flopping in their arms, legs and head, just like the disjointed movements of a rag doll. The children practise making each part of their body limp until their entire body is limp. Then on a secret cue, they fall to the floor limp and relaxed.

Relaxation Imagery

Many children respond well to imagery exercises and these have been described for use in the classroom in a book by Hall (Hall, Hall and Leech, 1990). The following are two relaxation scenarios from that book which we have adapted for use with young children. Teachers ask the students to close their eyes and imagine they are sitting on a cloud relaxing or in a safe place free from worries. Once your students have had frequent practice going to these special relaxation places in their mind, you can prompt them to go there when you notice they are beginning to get angry or anxious and worried about something. Here is are two scripts you might use with your students. Be sure to read the script slowly, in a calm and relaxing tone of voice.

Learning to Relax: 'The cloud feels soft'

Close your eyes because we are going to imagine we're somewhere else. Take a slow, deep breath . . . Let it out . . . Now, one more slow, deep breath . . . Let it out slowly . . . Today we are riding on a cloud . . . The cloud feels so soft . . . Let your arms hang down so your hand sinks down in the cloud . . . Let your feet sink down, wiggle your toes a little – how about your shoulders they're sinking too . . . We're still sitting on that big puffy cloud . . . Each time I say a part of your body, sink deeper in that soft cloud . . . (Teacher names various body parts.) Now you can open your eyes. We've relaxed different ways. Last time we pretended to be Raggedy Wally and today we floated on a cloud.

Visualizing a Safe, Relaxing Place

Close your eyes . . . Take a slow, deep breath . . . Let it out . . . Take one more slow, deep breath . . . Let it out slowly and allow your body to relax . . . For a moment, I would like you to think about something that you're worried about.

Now think about a safe place you can go to where you don't need to worry about anything . . . Make a picture in your imagination of the sort of place you could go to where you would feel safe . . . What is this place like? Take a good look around . . . What sort of things do you like to have in your safe place? . . . What are the colours like? . . . What does it smell like? . . . What do the things in your safe place feel like? . . . Now, think about actually being in your safe place . . . What are you doing right now in this safe place? . . . How are you feeling? . . . You can stay in this place as long as you want . . . You can come back to this place whenever you need to . . . Try to hold onto these feelings as you gently come back to the room.

Sometimes with young children they will call out their answers in response to the questions posed above. If this happens sometimes it is better to rephrase the questions as statements.

Birthday Party

In this exercise you can ask your students to take a deep, breath and slowly blow out the candles on an imaginary birthday cake. Then, peacefully and with eyes closed, the child makes a wish and imagines a happy thought. You can use many different images for this exercise such as floating in a chocolate milkshake, or blowing up a balloon.

Keep a 'Happy Book'

Young children who are aggressive often get a lot of attention and discussion of their angry feelings. While this is worthwhile because it helps such children learn to verbalize feelings appropriately rather than acting them out in hurtful ways, it can sometimes result in an overemphasis on the anger emotion. Indeed, many of these children often only recognize their angry emotion and sometimes confuse this emotion with other feelings such as excitement, being anxious, worried, sad or happy. It is important to help children learn emotions and language for expressing a wide range of feelings. In particular for sad and angry students we find it helpful to focus on times when they are pleased, happy, excited, calm and proud. A teacher might want to start a Happy Book which includes examples of times when students were happy and celebrated special moments and feelings.

Model Emotional Regulation – Stay Calm

How do you handle your own emotions? Do you fly off the handle easily? or withdraw in sullen protest? Remember that along with emotional tension or overstimulation, another factor contributing to children's outbursts is modelling – i.e. exposure to adults who themselves display outbursts of anger or frustration. As they try to manage their everyday frustrations, your students are likely to imitate your example. You can help your students by remaining calm and appropriately verbalizing your emotions and your strategies for coping. For example, if you are getting frustrated with your students' lack of attention when you are trying hard to give an instruction for an assignment, instead of exploding, you might say out loud, 'I'd better stop and calm down and relax a little before I continue. I'm getting frustrated because people aren't listening and I don't want to make things worse. Maybe if I get away from it for a while I'll figure out what it is I need to do.' Or, 'I'll be ready to listen once I calm down. I need a break, then I'll be ready to deal with this.' As always, it is important to model the kind of behavior you expect your students to exhibit. If you want your students to manage their emotions, it is important that they see you doing the same and that they see how you do it.

Of course, teachers are human and do get angry, make mistakes and lose their patience with students from time to time. Apologizing to students when this happens does not diminish your authority but rather enhances it. It helps students to realize that everyone makes mistakes and can learn from the experience. One teacher explained to her class her problem with getting cross at times, 'I sometimes feel irritable and naggy and I'd like you to help me during that time.

So I am going to put on this hat whenever I feel that way and I wonder if you can try to be extra quiet during that time.' This teacher's approach of asking for help from her students can really foster team spirit in the class.

It is particularly crucial to stay calm yourself when your students' emotional responses are escalating. Sometimes when a child is frustrated or shows increasing tension and anger about something, a teacher responds with additional anxiety or frustration. Instead, the teacher should try to offer calm and soothing words of advice, perhaps even a stroke on his arm or back. Such support often can help children calm themselves enough to able to state how they are feeling.

Teach Children Positive Self-Talk about the Event

When children experience a negative emotion such as anger, frustration, fear or discouragement, often there are underlying thoughts which accompany the emotion and which reinforce or intensify it and may even be causing it. These thoughts are sometimes referred to as 'self-talk', although children will sometimes express them aloud. For example, a child who is feeling discouraged may say to you or to himself, 'I'm just a failure', 'I can't do anything right', 'I might as well give up', 'You don't like me', 'You're just trying to make me fail', or 'No one ever helps me' and so on.

In the football example, Billy and Eric may have been reacting differently because they are telling themselves different things about the incident. If we asked Billy why he cried, he might have said, 'My dad will be so disappointed with me that we lost the game. I am such a bad player.' If we asked Dan why he got angry, he might have said, 'It was not fair, the other team was cheating'. While Billy responds with negative self-talk, and Dan by blaming the other players, in both cases they were caught up in negative behavioral responses and negative emotions that might have been averted if they had said something different to themselves such as, 'I did my best', or 'I can do it, it just takes practice, everyone loses sometimes'.

Research indicates that children whose 'self-talk' is negative get angry more easily than children whose self-talk is positive. Children can be taught to identify negative self-talk and to substitute positive self-talk. Teach your students how to counterbalance their inevitable frustrations and insults by saying quietly to themselves thoughts which calm them down, thoughts which help them control themselves, thoughts which put the situation in perspective. For example, when a child is teased by another child, the teacher can encourage her to stay calm by thinking to herself, 'I can handle it, I will just ignore him. It is not worth getting upset about. I can stay calm, I am strong.' In the football illustration above, the teacher might prompt the child to begin thinking this way by saying, 'Tell yourself, "I played the game well, my dad will be proud of that" or, "We played a great game. Someone has to lose. We are good sports" '. In this way children learn to regulate their cognitive responses, which in turn will affect their behavioral and physiological responses.

Examples of positive self-talk:

- 'Take three breaths.'
- 'Think happy.'
- 'I'm not going to let it get to me.'
- 'I am not going to blow my cool.'
- 'Everyone gets teased at times.'
- 'I can handle this.'
- 'I can calm down.'
- 'I have other friends who like me.'
- 'He didn't do it on purpose, it was an accident.'
- 'Everyone makes mistakes. No one is that perfect. I'll do better next time.'
- 'With more practice, I'll get it.'
- 'She's just in a bad mood today. She'll be better later.'
- 'I'll calm down and use my brave talk.'
- 'My friends still like me even if I make mistakes.'
- 'I'll feel happier in a little while.'
- 'Just stay calm.'
- 'It's no big deal.'
- 'Take a deep breath.'

Teach Students the 'Turtle Technique' and Practise Frequently

Teaching students to use positive self-talk and problem-solving strategies provides them with a means of emotional regulation on the cognitive level. However, it is sometimes necessary to help children deal with the neurophysiological/biochemical aspects of emotional arousal. For example, some children – or all children in some situations – may become so agitated with a racing heart and rapid

1

2 Think STOP

3 Take a slow breath

4 Withdrawing into shell

5

breathing that they have no control over their self-talk and cannot do the necessary problem-solving; their physiological arousal produces cognitive disorganization. While teaching your students positive self-talk will alleviate some of this overarousal, the student may need additional suggestions for how to calm down first. Researchers have found that the 'turtle technique' is an effective way for children to calm down and a good first step before engaging in problem-solving.

When teaching this to your students, ask them to imagine they have a shell, like a turtle, where they can retreat when they are getting angry. Then ask them to go into their imaginary shells, take three deep quiet breaths, and say to themselves, 'Stop, take a deep breath, Calm down, and Think'. As your students are taking these slow deep breaths, ask them to focus on their breathing and to push the air into their arms and legs so they can relax their muscles. Sometimes we ask children to picture a particularly relaxing scene while they are in their shell. As the students continue this slow breathing, coach them to say to themselves, 'I can calm down. I can do it. I can control it. I can stay out of fights.' Encourage your students to stay in their shells until they feel calm enough to come out and try again. Some children will need quite a bit more time than others to get their physiological reaction under control. When they come out, praise them and give them feedback for their efforts.

It is important that you teach and practise this calming self-talk script with your students frequently because eventually you want the actual words, 'stop, take a deep breath, calm down, and think' to trigger a calming response and internal language within the child when faced with a real-life conflictual situation. You might also want to read the book, *Wally Learns a Lesson from Tiny Turtle* to your students or show the Tiny Turtle tape from the Dinosuar curriculum to enhance this learning (Webster-Stratton, 1990).

In addition to the teaching and role playing, model this 'turtle technique' yourself for your students. For example, you may find yourself getting irritated because your students are taking so long to settle in their desks after break. You could say, 'I'm getting frustrated because students are taking so long to settle down and listen to me, I had better go into my shell for a while and calm down. Guess I had better use my turtle power and take some deep breaths . . . I had better say to myself, "Stop, take a deep breath and calm down and think". Well, I feel better. I had better think of another plan. Maybe I will give stickers to those who are sitting in their seats already.'

As you can see, just as you use the teaching principles of modelling, practice, role-play and feedback for teaching your students academic skills, so you do for teaching them social skills.

Help Children Recognize Body Cues that Signal the Build Up of Tension

The first 'early warning' stage of anger or negative emotion is familiar to every teacher or parent. The child grumbles under his breath, looks grouchy, sulks around the classroom. In the second stage the child becomes increasingly tense, restless and moody; no matter what you suggest, nothing seems to satisfy or interest him. An explosive outburst may occur at the slightest provocation. The child may shout, swear or even break something. He usually resists the teacher's efforts at control at this outburst stage and may increase his opposition to anything the teacher says. In the third stage, after the tantrum subsides, depression replaces aggression; this is the 'leave me alone' stage. The child is sad or placid and does not want to interact with his teachers or peer group. In the fourth stage the child is ready to resume normal activities and may act as if nothing had happened.

The point for teachers to intervene with suggestions of 'turtle technique' or prompting the calming self-talk script or relaxation methods discussed earlier is in the first stage. The second or third stages are the least teachable moments. Often in the first stage children are not aware of their physiological signs of distress nor are they even aware they are becoming angry or frustrated. Consequently, they will not communicate these feelings until they emerge in a full-blown tantrum. Therefore it is helpful in this early warning stage to help children become more self-aware of these early physiological signals of anger or distress and to encourage them to talk about feelings and to express their frustrations in socially acceptable ways. You might say, 'I can tell by your muttering that something seems to be bothering you, can I help in any way?' If your student has difficulty expressing herself, you might try to put into words what you suspect the child is thinking and feeling. Or, you might also ask the child to point to an anger or relaxation thermometer to indicate how he or she is feeling (see below). Teachers' understanding and concern at this stage can go a long way toward reducing the build up of negative and angry feelings. Once the child learns to recognize the early physiological signs of distress, she can be signalled to use calming procedures such as deep breathing, the 'turtle technique' and calming self-talk and relaxation exercise to prevent further escalation.

Another possible time to intervene is in the fourth stage, after the incident is over. At this point, the teacher can lead the child through problem-solving. Discussing the event helps promote better understanding in the child of what the triggers are that set him off (e.g. teasing), why it happened, and how he might handle it differently next time. The discussion should include how you and the child each felt about the episode, the causes and early warning signals, alternative ways to solve the problem in the future. Furthermore, once the child and teacher understand what triggered the child's loss of control, they can begin to role-play and practise how to handle these stressful situations.

Using the puppets can be a very effective way of helping children learn to recognize the early signals of escalating anger and arousal. Here is an example of a possible script:

Sample Script for Puppets – 'Recognizing Early Signals of Anger'

Wally: I kind of had a problem at school today. It was break time, you know, and I was out by myself on the playground and I was building some Star Wars stuff out of sand. I was making a big destroyer and a falcon and stuff. And when I was out there by myself I saw Tony, Dave and Ian, they're three cool popular boys, and they were walking towards me and I was getting all excited because I knew they had brought their Star Wars toys and I thought maybe they wanted to come play with me. I was all excited, and when they got over, they started teasing me. They said, 'Look at Wally, he has nobody to play with him. Look at his dumb Star Wars stuff he made. Our toys are much cooler.' Oh . . . gosh, I felt my hands ball up in fists and my face get red and I felt like exploding. Then I remembered these feelings in my body were signals that I was getting angry and that I had to stop, think and calm down. Have any of you ever noticed how other people signal when they are getting angry? You know like your parents or teachers?

Students: (*Students discuss what they notice when their parents or teachers or friends get angry*)

Wally: You know I can always tell when my teacher is angry because his jaw clenches and twitches. What does your body do when you get angry? Does anyone find their fists get tight like mine do? What does your body do when you get angry?

Students: (*Students discuss their own body reactions and what they notice in each other*)

Wally: Wow you all have body signals that tell you when you are angry. So what are you going to do next time you feel this happening?

(*Brainstorm solution such as going in turtle shell and saying stop, calm down, think; or taking deep breath, or counting backwards, or thinking of happy place*)

Use Time Out for Inappropriate Emotional Angry Outbursts

Research has shown that Time Out is an effective method for discouraging children's inappropriate behavior and for helping a child calm down. When a child who has hit another child or has been destructive is sent to a Time Out spot, he is deprived of adult attention for the aggressive behaviors. Children hunger for attention – even negative attention is preferable to none at all, and will reinforce the behavior. Thus yelling at the child for his misbehavior or giving in to the child's emotional outbursts actually increases the likelihood they will continue in the future. However, if there is no payoff for the misbehavior and if the teacher withdraws her attention, the aggressive behaviors will subside – especially if you are teaching alternative responses which you reward with your approval.

When sending a child to Time Out for hurting someone be sure you are matter of fact when enforcing the rule (show no sympathy or anger). For example, you might say, 'I am sorry Josh, you have made bad choice because your solution was unfair and unsafe so you need to go to Time Out'. (See Chapter 8 for more information on enforcing Time Out.)

Appropriate Expression of Negative Feelings

As mentioned earlier, children need to know that all feelings are okay – anger, anxiety, sadness and other negative feelings are unavoidable and they are normal – but that there are different ways of expressing those feelings, and that they have a choice in how they express them. Children should be taught to put their negative feelings into words in ways that are assertive but not hostile. Teachers can help them learn the difference between sticking up for their rights and attempting to hurt someone else, and can praise them when they express difficult emotions in appropriate ways.

Identify Typical Situations which Trigger Emotional Explosions and Use Them as Springboards to Teach Problem-Solving and Anger Management

Once children have learned to recognize some of the physiological cues in their body that signal their anger is increasing, next they need to learn to use anger reducing skills such as the turtle technique or deep breathing or relaxing imagery. It is helpful for children to practise responding to hypothetical situations which normally trigger their angry responses. This will help them learn to control their anger in the future. Once they learn to anticipate such situations and have some strategies for dealing with them, they can take them in their stride instead of responding impulsively. It is important when doing these practice role plays that an attempt is made to simulate the intensity of feelings that occurs when the situation actually occurs in real life. Through the use of puppets situations can be presented which have actually occurred to many of the children. For example, fights with a sibling over who sits in the front seat of the car, being teased and called names by peers, being yelled at by a teacher or parent, being left out, being bullied and being prevented from doing or having something you want.

Pass the Detective Hat for Practising Anger Control

The Detective Hat game is fun and an easy way to initiate role-play and practice of anger control skills with your students. The questions listed below are designed to practise the following responses: calming self-talk ('Cool down. Take it easy. I can do it. Use my brave talk. If I fight I could get into a lot of trouble. I'm stronger than him; I won't fight'), deep breathing, positive imagery (think of your happy or safe place) thinking about the consequences of fighting or arguing, using your brave talk about your feelings, staying out of a battle and accepting consequences. Some suggestions for questions include the following:

The 'Detective Hat Game' for Practising Anger Control

- What can you think about when you are in your shell?
- Wally's face looks angry – how can you tell if he really is angry?
- Why is it important not to fight?
- A friend makes fun of what you wear to school and then says you are stupid and fat. What can you do to control your anger?

- A kid won't get off the swing and you have already waited 10 minutes and are getting angry. What can you do to stay calm?
- Where are some places you can go to calm down?
- What are some nice thoughts which might help you calm down?
- What usually happens after Time Out?
- Your mother asked you to clean up the living room and your friend won't help even though you both made the mess.
- A classmate bumps into you and you trip and hurt yourself. (He doesn't say he is sorry.) What do you think to yourself?
- You're playing at a friend's house and s/he doesn't want to do anything you want to do. What can you do?
- A classmate accuses you of cheating on a board game. What can you do to stay calm?
- A classmate teases you because you aren't able to read. How do you know if you are angry?
- A kid grabs your ball away from you. What can you do?
- Your parent tells you, 'You're always in trouble, you never help, or share with your sister and you don't try'. What can you do to handle your anger?
- Some kids are playing tag but they won't let you play with them. You think they hate you. What can you do about these thoughts?
- Your dad says he won't take you to the football game because you fought with your sister.
- You lost the privilege of going on a field trip because of your behavior. What can you do to deal with your disappointment?
- You are playing football and are constantly being beaten by the other kids.
- You are having a bad day, what can you do to feel better?

Fairness Game

In this game children are given situations and asked to think about the solutions and whether or not it is fair and how each person feels about the situation. This game helps children evaluate their solutions in terms of fairness and feelings.

Molly Says That's Not Fair – Is It Fair or Not?

- One person is watching TV and another comes in the room and changes the channel. Is that fair? Why?
- There is one piece of pizza left and two children. One child takes the piece of pizza. Is that fair? Why?
- A brother and sister are going to camp and there is only one camera. The girl insists she should have the camera. Is that fair? Why?
- You want to read a book, but someone else is reading it and won't give it to you. Is that fair? Why?
- One student refuses to do what the teacher asks him or her to do, so loses break privileges. Is that fair? Why?

Use Anger Thermometer to Self-Monitor

For students who have identified problems with anger outbursts, you might want to use an anger thermometer to teach them self-control and to monitor their improvements. You can use the thermometer we have pictured here or make one together with your student. Children often enjoy decorating the thermometer with pictures. You might want to add numbers to your thermometer from one to ten with 'one' indicating very calm or cool and 'ten' indicating very hot. Then take a recent conflict and together with the student retrace the steps that led to the angry explosion. Write down the student's actions, thoughts and words that indicated an escalating anger pattern (e.g. demanding, thinking 'he always teases me or, they never let me', yelling, slamming doors, kicking etc.). Next discuss with the student the thoughts, words and actions that the student could use to reduce their anger (e.g. blow out candles on cake, imagine happy place, think 'stay cool', practise relaxing and tensing muscles, etc.). As you retrace the conflict situation, see if you can get the student to point

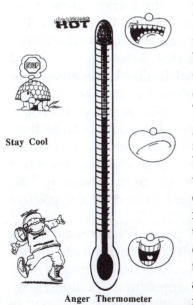

Anger Thermometer

to the place where they first were aware they were getting angry. Mark this as *Danger Point* on the thermometer.

Once you and your student have discussed the situation and established a danger point, then ask your student to give it a name. For example: cool it, chill, code red and so forth. This code word will then be your secret word to be used with that child to signal each other that anger or tension has reached the threshold. When this code word is used by either the teacher or student it triggers the use of any of the agreed cool-down responses which have been listed or pictured on the thermometer.

This thermometer can be revised and expanded over time when other explosions occur. After several weeks of using it, the teacher can review with the student their progress in terms of reduction in the use of the code word and angry outbursts. You might want to define a target number to define the student's success each week (under four outbursts in a week). When you reach your goal, celebrate.

Praise Children's Efforts to Regulate their Emotions

Be sure to praise students for respecting the secret codeword or signal and for handling their frustration without losing control of their anger. 'I am really pleased that you worked so hard even though you were losing.' Research has shown that aggressive and impulsive children receive more critical feedback, negative commands and less praise than other children – even when they are behaving appropriately. In essence, they train their teachers not to praise or reinforce them for their positive behaviors because their emotional responses are so exhausting to deal with. However, they need positive feedback even more than other children, for when they are praised, they are likely not to notice or process it. This means you will have to work extra hard to find all the positive behaviors you can to reinforce.

It is particularly important to try to praise behaviors involving self-control and persistence with difficult tasks, appropriate expression of feelings (be they positive or negative) and control of their emotional outbursts in frustrating or disappointing situations. Reinforce any calm, purposeful activities following a disappointment or frustrating event. For instance, you might say, 'That was great. You calmed yourself down, you made a good choice', or 'That was cool. You were patient and kept trying even though you were getting frustrated with that difficult maths assignment'. You can also teach students to reinforce themselves. Teach them to praise themselves out loud through positive self-talk such as, 'I did a good job', or 'I stayed really calm, I am strong inside me. I was patient with myself and it paid off in the end. I made a good choice.'

Through your praise, you will help your student change his or her self-image to that of a person who is able to handle emotions. It's not necessary to wait until a student has become fully capable of emotional regulation. By using the 'language of becoming' to express your confidence in your student's future success at this aspect of development – 'You are becoming a person who can really control your anger well. You are very strong inside' – you can help make it a reality.

Work Collaboratively with Parents

Naturally you will have even more success in helping students regulate their emotions if their parents are also using feeling language and the turtle anger management script with their children. First you can begin by sending home a weekly letter explaining how some children mislabel feelings and why it is important for parents to accurately label their children's feelings. For example, you might ask parents to notice times when their children appear excited, happy, worried, angry, calm, frustrated and sad, and label those feelings. Suggest to parents that they play the 'guess the feeling' or 'why because' game. This is where the parent says, 'I'm happy' and asks the child to guess why. Then the parent can reverse roles with the child. It is important that parents be encouraged to talk about happy, satisfied, relaxed and pleasant feelings and not only angry, sad or frustrated feelings. It is also important that children know that they are not to blame for their parents' feelings. One home work assignment might be for children and parents each to share a time they were happy and then bring this to the circle discussion the next day.

It is also important for parents and teachers to understand Tiny Turtle's script, 'stop, take a deep breath, calm down and think'. Then whenever a parent or teacher notices a child starting to get angry and out of control, they can cue their child's de-escalation responses. Encourage parents to stay with the exact script words for it will be more effective in helping the child to become calm. When teachers and parents work together to support the use of these anger management strategies, children will have the necessary environmental support to learn to regulate their emotions.

To Sum Up

- Use feeling talk with your students and encourage them to talk about feelings.
- Acknowledge individual differences in students' ability to regulate emotions.
- Use games and activities to teach the language of feelings and to promote understanding of differences in others' feelings.
- Use Time Out for destructive behavior.
- Teach children positive self-talk strategies.
- Teach the 'turtle technique' for managing anger.
- Practise anger management responses to hypothetical conflict situations.
- Elicit the support of parents in managing anger and teaching children to express their feelings.

References

Asarnow, J. R. and Callan, J. W. (1985) Boys with peer adjustment problems: social cognitive processes, *Journal of Consulting and Clinical Psychology*, 53, 80–7.

Campbell, S. (1995) Behavior problems in preschool children: a review of recent research. *Journal of Child Psychology and Psychiatry and Allied Disciplines*, 36(1), 113–49.

Coie, J. D. (1990) Toward a theory of peer rejection. In S. R. Asher and J. D. Coie (eds.) *Peer Rejection in Childhood* (pp. 365–98), Cambridge: Cambridge University Press.

Dodge, K. A., Pettit, G. S., McClaskey, C. L. and Brown, M. M. (1986) Social competence in children, *Monographs of the Society for Research in Child Development*, 51 (Serial No. 213).

Gouze, K. R. (1987) Attention and social problem solving as correlates of aggression in preschool males, *Journal of Abnormal Child Psychology*, 15, 181–97.

Hall, E., Hall, C. and Leech, A. (1990) *Scripted Fantasy in the Classroom*, London: Nichols.

Larson, J. (1994) Violence prevention in the schools: a review of selected programs and procedures, *School Psychology Review*, 23, 151–64.

Lochman, J. E. and Dunn, S. E. (1993) An intervention and consultation model from a social cognitive perspective: a description of the anger coping program, *School Psychology Review*, 22, 458–71.

Mize, J. and Cox, R. A. (1990) Social knowledge and social competence: number and quality of strategies as predictors of peer behavior, *Journal of Genetics Psychology*, 151(1), 117–27.

Patterson, G., Reid, J. and Dishion, T. (1992) *Antisocial Boys: A Social Interactional Approach*, (vol. 4), Eugene, OR: Castalia.

Pope, A. W., Bierman, K. L. and Mumma, G. H. (1989) Relations between hyperactive and aggressive behavior and peer relations at three elementary grade levels, *Journal of Abnormal Child Psychology*, 17(3), 253–67.

Putallaz, M. and Wasserman, A. (1990) Children's entry behavior, in S. R. Asher and J. D. Coie (eds.), *Peer Rejection in Childhood* (pp. 60–89), Cambridge: Cambridge University Press.

Quiggle, N., Garber, J., Panak, W. and Dodge, K. A. (1992) Social-information processing in aggressive and depressed children, *Child Development*, 63, 1305–20.

Rubin, K. H. and Krasnor, L. R. (1986) Social-cognitive and social behavioral perspectives on problem-solving. In M. Perlmutter (ed.) *Cognitive Perspectives on Children's Social and Behavioral Development. The Minnesota Symposia on Child Psychology* (vol. 18, pp. 1–68), Hillsdale, NJ: Lawrence Erlbaum Associates.

Webster-Stratton, C. (1990) *Dina Dinosaur's Social Skills and Problem-Solving Curriculum*, Seattle, WA: 1411 8th Avenue West.

Webster-Stratton, C. and Hammond, M. (1997) Treating children with early-onset conduct problems: a comparison of child and parent training interventions, *Journal of Consulting and Clinical Psychology*, 65(1), 93–109.

Conclusion

Taking Charge

Violence and aggression in young children is escalating around the world. As the intensity increases, the age of the offender decreases. Families and educators struggle to maintain hope in the face of grim forecasts by news reporters and statisticians. But instead of getting caught up in feeling powerless, teachers and parents can 'take charge' by supporting one another and creating an emotional and social teaching approach that will both prevent and reduce aggression in young children as well as build their social competence. Starting early is the key to helping 'immunize' children against bullying, peer rejection, and violence.

There is no one way to begin this process. Each early childhood program and school will have its own resources. Each teacher will have his or her own unique situation. But as you take responsibility for your part in this effort, you will find you will connect with other teachers, parents and social service providers interested in this endeavor and will begin to create a strong network of support for your creative initiatives. By taking action and using some of the suggestions in this book combined with your own practical wisdom, you can make a positive difference in the lives of children and families.

Index